Miss Marks
and
Miss Woolley

Other books by Anna Mary Wells:

*Dear Preceptor: The Life and Times
of Thomas Wentworth Higginson*

ENTERTAINMENTS

*A Talent for Murder
Murderer's Choice
Sin of Angels
Fear of Death
The Night of May Third*

Miss Marks
and
Miss Woolley

by

ANNA MARY WELLS

Illustrated with photographs

Houghton Mifflin Company
Boston 1978

Library of Congress Cataloging in Publication Data
Wells, Anna Mary.
Miss Marks and Miss Woolley.

Bibliography: p.
1. Woolley, Mary Emma, 1863–1947.   2. Mount Holyoke
College.   3. Marks, Jeannette Augustus, 1875–1964.
4. Wellesley College.   5. Lesbians — United States
Biography.   I. Title.
LD7092.7 1901.W44   378.1'12'0974423   78-1391
ISBN 0-395-25724-7

Printed in the United States of America
M 10 9 8 7 6 5 4 3 2 1

To Dr. Frank Pignataro,
wise counselor and faithful friend

". . . when we set our hand
To this great work, we purposed with ourself
Never to wed. You likewise will do well,
Ladies, in entering here, to cast and fling
The tricks, which make us toys of men, that so,
Some future time, if so indeed you will,
You may with those self-styled our lords ally
Your fortunes, justlier balanced, scale with scale."

— *The Princess,*
Alfred Tennyson

Foreword

MORE THAN FOUR YEARS ago I undertook to write a
biography of Mary Emma Woolley, president of
Mount Holyoke College from 1901 to 1937 and pioneer in
the higher education of American women. The only existing one, written by her friend Jeannette Marks and published in 1955, was generally regarded as inadequate. It was
the casual remark of a friend who had leafed through it —
"You ought to write one yourself" — that sparked the idea
for me.

My Mount Holyoke friends and the officials of the college
accepted the project with enthusiasm, tempered by a certain
caution among some of the alumnae.

"What will you do about 1937?"

In that year, at the time of her retirement, Miss Woolley
objected strenuously and openly to the sex of her successor,
Professor Roswell Gray Ham of Yale University. Her protest, though it failed of its purpose, received nationwide
publicity. Many alumnae supported her, but many others
felt that her conduct was undignified and uncharacteristic.
Most even of those who had supported her were disappointed when she refused to be reconciled after the active
controversy was settled. She never returned to Mount Holyoke during the remaining ten years of her life, never con-

sented to meet President Ham, and almost never accepted any of the honors the college continued to offer her.

The problem this presented to a biographer did not at first seem to me a serious one. After all, 1937 had come at the end of a long, full, and illustrious career; it should be possible to slide gracefully over it at the end of my book.

The change in my thinking about it was slow and painful. In the end I came to believe that 1937 was the logical conclusion of a career by no means so triumphant and untroubled as it sometimes appeared and that Jeannette Marks' failure as a biographer was due primarily to a failure to recognize or acknowledge her own part in the events she recorded. It might even be possible to go so far as to say that Mary Woolley's friendship with Jeannette Marks was the major cause of the trustees' reluctance to elect another woman to the presidency of Mount Holyoke.

Since my own college days in the twenties I had known that there was gossip about Miss Woolley and Miss Marks, who was at that time chairman of the Department of English Literature, but I had never taken it seriously or indeed thought much about it. It did not occur to me until my work was well advanced that the relationship would present another problem.

The libraries of both Wellesley and Mount Holyoke contain a number of papers relevant to my subject. Miss Marks was a student and Miss Woolley a professor of Biblical history at Wellesley when they met in 1895. Almost all of Miss Woolley's official papers are now at Mount Holyoke; several successive manuscripts of Miss Marks' biography and a good deal of correspondence about it at Wellesley. In addition Mount Holyoke had, at the time my work started, a mass of unsorted papers belonging to Miss Marks and a very large unopened wooden box listed as Mary E. Woolley papers, as to which no one was accurately informed. Both colleges offered me access to these papers and generous assistance. The Mary E. Woolley papers, when that box was opened, radically altered both my plan and the feeling of the college authorities about it.

The box was filled with neat brown paper packages labeled with initials and dates — MEW to JM 1900, JM to MEW 1922, and so on. It was difficult to know where to begin, but I started with MEW to JM 1901, Miss Woolley's first year at Mount Holyoke. The letters in the packages were in their original envelopes, addressed in Miss Woolley's now-familiar hand or Miss Marks' difficult scrawl, stamped and postmarked. The first few that I read were ardent love letters expressed in terms that both shocked and embarrassed me.

My immediate impulse was to abandon my plans for the book. It seemed to me impossible to ignore or suppress the content of the letters, impertinent to continue to read them, and quite unthinkable to publish them. I came very slowly to realize how deeply my own prejudices were involved in any such decision. I had supposed myself to be open-minded and tolerant about sexual deviation, but it now appeared that I was not so at all when it occurred in women I admired and respected. I was aware and ashamed of a certain amount of prurient curiosity in my ambivalent desire to continue reading, but I became aware also that my discovery was altering my concept of the characters and careers of both women.

My personal contact with Miss Woolley had been limited and remote, but I had known Miss Marks as teacher, dramatic coach, even as personal friend. I was never quite able to bridge the enormous gap created by our differences in age and position in life, and Miss Marks was so unpopular at Mount Holyoke that to like her was an eccentricity I felt it necessary to conceal.

Now, however, as I browsed through her papers, I found her coming to life in my memory much more fully than Miss Woolley did. I found also in my work in other libraries that although Miss Woolley had practically disappeared from card catalogues as either subject or author, several of Miss Marks' books had been reprinted after their copyrights had expired, and those still in print were still being read and responded to. I toyed with the idea of abandoning Miss

Woolley and writing a book about Miss Marks. I reread her books with that in mind, but they did not seem to me to support a claim that she was an author unduly neglected, and her career was so intimately connected with that of Miss Woolley that it would be impossible to write about either of them alone.

The idea of writing a book about both seemed to me at first a most satisfactory solution of my problem, but the reaction of my Mount Holyoke friends was as strongly negative as it had been positive toward the first plan. Indeed it came eventually to seem to me that this reaction was an important part of the story of the two lives. So far as knowledge of the relationship went, the comments of those who remembered Miss Marks and Miss Woolley ranged all the way from "Of course, everybody knew that" to "I never dreamed of such a thing." What seemed to me odd was that it was the former group that most objected to my plan. It was as if I had not stumbled upon a discovery embarrassing to all but proposed to violate a tacit agreement among loyal Mount Holyoke alumnae to keep our shameful secret to ourselves.

I use the word "shameful" advisedly. If I found myself less tolerant of sexual deviance than I had supposed, I was still a great deal more so than most of my contemporaries. I was myself careful to avoid the use of the words "lesbian" or "homosexual," since both seem to me imprecise as well as pejorative. (There is substantial doubt that Sappho herself was Lesbian in any sense except that she lived on the island of Lesbos.) In spite of my verbal caution the words were promptly applied by others to my subjects.

It seemed to me impertinent in the original as well as the derived meaning of the word to attempt to discover exactly how far the two women had permitted themselves physical expression of their affection. My own opinion, for what it is worth, is that the relationship began in the childlike ignorance of sexual matters in which many young women of their generation were kept before marriage, and that when they became more sophisticated they voluntarily renounced all physical contact. The emotional relationship, once established, continued for the rest of their lives, altering with the years but steadily deepening until death parted them. It strongly affected both careers. It seems to have satisfied all of Mary Woolley's emotional needs, freeing her for the fullest possible use of her remarkable abilities. For Jeannette Marks it was less adequate. Whatever the reasons may have been, she never realized her full potential as a creative artist; her conduct was often erratic and self-defeating, and her life was not happy.

Her extreme unpopularity at Mount Holyoke was due largely to her association with Miss Woolley. True, she made it easy for people to dislike her; she was arrogant, demanding, and conceited, and yet in her own way she made substantial contributions to the college, few of which have ever been recognized. She founded the Laboratory Theatre; she introduced the custom of bringing distinguished poets and playwrights to the college to confer with small groups of interested students rather than to deliver formal lectures; she pioneered on the campus in work for women's suffrage and the Equal Rights Amendment. Yet her name is not associated with any building, scholarship, or prize. It is still possible to collect anecdotes about her eccentricities at the college, but her accomplishments are forgotten or neglected.

The tacit agreement to keep the secret within the college carried with it a tacit acceptance of the view that Miss Woolley was a great and admirable woman whose affection for Miss Marks was her only serious fault. This in turn meant that Miss Marks must take the blame for everything bad in the association. But in actual fact the conspiracy of silence was not working. At the very beginning of my research I was housed at one time in a college dormitory and took my meals with students. I asked a freshman what sort of concept she had of Miss Woolley, and she replied that her only impression was that there was something "vaguely scandalous."

Vaguely scandalous about *Miss Woolley*! I thought. It's high time for someone to write a book to set the record straight.

The book I have written does not set it straight in the way I then proposed, but it is almost certain that a new generation will see the facts in a new light. Its judgment will probably be akin to Browning's in "The Statue and the Bust."

> And the sin I impute to each frustrate ghost
> Is — the unlit lamp and the ungirt loin.

I cannot hope to justify the lovers' self-denial to the young any more than to justify their love to the old, but I have told their story to the best of my ability and perforce in the light of current social opinion.

Revisionist historians today remind us that it is very difficult to understand the past from the viewpoint of the present. The choices Mary Woolley and Jeannette Marks made in going to college at all, in working at careers of their own rather than finding husbands to work for them, in maintaining a home together in the face of bitter criticism, are very different from the choices young women today must make. The much wider range of options now available is due in large part to the pioneer work of women like Miss Woolley and Miss Marks.

The professional women of their generation sublimated their sexual drive in the sense in which Freud originally used the word, a sense now largely lost. They abjured sex, but they maintained femininity while doing outstanding intellectual work in a variety of fields. Miss Woolley said in her inaugural address that the sacrifice of gracious womanhood was too high a price to pay for education. Miss Marks found the phrase particularly irritating; for her the sacrifice of gracious womanhood was no loss at all but a step forward into greater freedom. Both exemplified their views in their lives, and Mount Holyoke faculty and alumnae have generally agreed with Miss Woolley and admired the way in which her practice followed her theory.

The question of what to do about the letters I had seen was not easily resolved. They had been in Miss Marks' possession up to the time of her death, but whether they went to the college by her request or as the gift of her heir was uncertain. Almost forgotten in the president's office was a packet from Miss Marks not to be opened until 1999. It seemed a reasonable deduction that it contained an account of her motives in preserving the letters and having them sent to the college — if, indeed, it was by her wish that they were sent. President David Truman decided that the letters also should be closed to further research until the time specified. This decision has since been modified; the letters are now available to qualified scholars — not to research assistants or associates — on application to the librarian.

It is at least arguable that Miss Marks intended that a book such as this one should not be published while anyone who remembered her or Miss Woolley was still alive. But if I were to write it, it had to be written now. It is also, of course, entirely possible that the packet to be opened in 1999 has nothing whatever to do with the subject or will disprove all the conclusions I have reached. Either way, it is most unlikely that I will ever know.

Even before the letters were opened to anyone else, I was permitted to use the notes I had made. This means that my verbatim quotations were copied from the originals but could not be rechecked for accuracy. In Miss Marks' handwritten letters in particular it was often difficult to decide among alternative readings of a given word. It was a great relief to me that in her later years she turned to the typewriter for her personal correspondence.

My original intention in making verbatim copies from some of the letters was not to quote them but to record accurately for my own consideration what they said. That the language of personal letters must be interpreted in the context of the social custom of the period in which they were written is obvious. Carroll Smith-Rosenberg made this point in a very useful article in the first number of

Signs: A Journal of Women in Society, discussing affectionate letters between women in nineteenth-century America. I found eventually that my own uncertainty as to what meaning should be derived made paraphrase impossible in some cases, and I am the more grateful to the college for allowing me to use quotations.

I should like here to acknowledge the assistance of many Mount Holyoke faculty and staff members, alumnae and students, but in view of the strong division of opinion there I hesitate to use names. Suffice it to say that I am grateful to all those who have helped me so generously, and not least to those who spoke frankly and openly of their objections. I do want, however, to name the librarians both at Mount Holyoke and Wellesley whose patient assistance has been particularly useful: Anne Edmonds, Elaine Trehub, and Linda Wendry at Mount Holyoke; Eleanor Nicholes and Wilma Slaight at Wellesley, and Hannah French, Mount Holyoke alumna and Wellesley librarian emeritus. Elizabeth Green, professor of English emeritus and compiler and editor of Mount Holyoke's oral college history has been consistently helpful. Professor Eloise Goreau of Rider College, who first suggested the subject to me and then faithfully supported my work through all its vicissitudes, was of great practical assistance. I am grateful also to Mrs. Elizabeth Cross, who provided devoted professional care to Miss Marks during the last years of her life and inherited her beloved house, Fleur de Lys. Mrs. Cross graciously permitted me to inspect it at leisure in 1975, an experience which contributed largely to my chapter on the old age of Miss Marks and Miss Woolley.

I am optimistic enough to hope that the book I have written may serve the college as usefully as the one many alumnae hoped I might write and that, if immortality should prove to be something more than a wishful fantasy, Miss Marks and Miss Woolley will before too long tell me it's quite all right with them.

Contents

Illustrations

(following page 124)

Miss Marks
and
Miss Woolley

I

Beginnings

IN 1847 Alfred Tennyson published a long poem called *The Princess*, a medley, as he himself described it, and a very curious one. Its tone is alternately romantic, satiric, mystical, and mock-heroic. Its theme is the higher education of women, or perhaps more accurately though more vaguely "the woman question," as it was then called. Its story is preposterous, no doubt intentionally, since it is presented as the spontaneous invention of seven male undergraduates to amuse a young lady sister of one of them during a holiday afternoon.

To summarize it as briefly as possible: a princess named Ida, who has been affianced in her infancy to a neighboring prince, persuades her father, when she comes to maturity, to break his promise and allow her to retire to one of his summer palaces with a company of women, there to set up a college for the instruction of younger members of their own sex. Men are forbidden to enter it on pain of death. The disappointed prince and two of his friends disguise themselves as women and enter the college; they are at once detected by Psyche, a young professor who is sister to one of the three and therefore reluctant to denounce them publicly. They continue the masquerade for a brief period, attend classes, accompany Ida and some of the students on a geological expedition, and are betrayed by the imprudence and impudence of one of the three, who gets drunk and sings a ribald song in his natural male voice. The princess in a rage flings herself onto her horse and rides off so impetuously that she falls from a bridge and is rescued from drowning by her affianced prince. Far from feeling gratitude, she is more bitterly angry than before. On her return to the college she learns that her own father has been captured by her fiancé's and is being held hostage. The prince escapes to his father's camp unharmed, and the two fathers are reconciled, but Princess Ida's brother insists on fighting for her. Fifty picked young men on each side hold a tournament, which Ida watches from the walls and in which the prince is wounded, it seems fatally. Ida, with the help of her students and faculty, then takes all the wounded into the college, which is turned into a temporary hospital. In the process of nursing her prince back to health her heart is softened; he promises to help her advance the cause of women, and she agrees to the promised marriage. The young people, narrators and hearers alike, then go home from their picnic "well pleased."

The poem was not well reviewed and has never been considered one of Tennyson's best, but it had an immediate and continuing popular success, particularly on this side of the Atlantic. It was sufficiently well known for Gilbert and Sullivan to parody it in *Princess Ida* with comfortable certainty that the source would be recognized. In America it was required reading in many school and college literature courses up to the 1920s. Even more curiously, many of the women's colleges founded during the latter half of the nineteenth century boasted of being like the one in *The Princess*.

Speaking through his various characters and through his young undergraduate narrators, Tennyson was able to express violently conflicting views as to the nature of woman and the practicability of her aspirations. In the conclusion he would seem to have committed himself to Hitler's view that *Kinder, Küchen,* and *Kirche* were women's work, but he left himself plenty of outs, and brief passages may be quoted in support of any imaginable position. However, reading the whole poem for the first time, any woman is likely to be struck by his almost superstitious fear of the power of femininity. Ida's two chief assistants are widows, each with a girl child. Victorian critics had a good deal of fun over the idea of Psyche lecturing on the structure of the universe with her baby beside her in its cot; one of them referred to her as "a lactiferous doctor of philosophy." The combined intelligence of these women scares the young men even more than the physical force of the Amazonian bodyguard.

Although the very existence of the poem makes clear that the idea of higher education for women was in the air in 1847, its realization was still in the future. In America Oberlin College admitted women, and Mount Holyoke Female Seminary was in a flourishing state, but with no idea of claiming comparability to a college. Emily Dickinson was a student there in 1847–48; Squire Dickinson sent his son to Amherst, the local college, and to Harvard Law School; his daughters had a year each of finishing at highly regarded seminaries. Emily's was at Mount Holyoke and Lavinia's at Ipswich Seminary. One of Emily's letters to Austin during the year suggests a view of Mary Lyon, head of Mount Holyoke, that might have come straight out of *The Princess*.

Has the Mexican War terminated yet and how? Are we beat? Do you know of any nation about to besiege South Hadley? If so, do inform me of it, for I would be glad of a chance to escape, if we are to be stormed. I suppose Miss Lyon would furnish us all with daggers and order us to fight for our lives, in case such perils ever should befall us.

But Mary Lyon was no Ida. For all her independence of spirit, she had been a poor girl who had had to fight for her own education, and in establishing her seminary she was heavily dependent on the good will of rich male trustees who must not be offended by any excessive ambitions for herself or her sex.

The women's colleges were still to come — Vassar in 1865, Smith and Wellesley in 1875, "Harvard Annex" in 1879, Bryn Mawr and Goucher in 1885, Barnard in '89, Pembroke, Randolph-Macon, and Radcliffe in the nineties.

O I wish
That I were some great Princess, I would build
Far off from men a college like a man's
And I would teach them all that men are taught;
We are twice as quick.

Thus speaks young Lilia in *The Princess.* It does not occur to her to suggest that women might go to college along with men; she is sophisticated enough to understand that the British universities are places where the future rulers of the Empire meet and mingle with its future poets, historians, and company directors; to admit women would change the character of the institution quite as much as to admit laborers or colonials. The young men in the elaborate tale with which they answer her suggest a point she has overlooked: the business of college is not merely teaching and learning; a college for women must necessarily change the whole lives of the women who enter it — their emotions, their sexual and maternal feelings, their physical strength, their daily activities. They even hint, with Tennysonian delicacy, at lesbianism.

Now could you share your thought; now should men see
Two women faster welded in one love
Than pairs of wedlock.

Twelve years later Thomas Wentworth Higginson contributed to the *Atlantic Monthly,* then known throughout America as "the new magazine," an essay called "Ought Women to Learn the Alphabet?" With rather heavy-handed sprightliness and enormous erudition he considered the current status of women in law, in literature and the arts, and in education. The essay made a greater impression than he or the editors might reasonably have expected; it was quoted and cited for at least fifty years. Higginson was always on the side of women, but the major point he made in this essay was one that seems to have touched on the deepest fears of men: if women had equal opportunities for education they would invade all professions and businesses. Here, as in *The Princess*, education was equated with power, and it was clearly a power that men feared.

The proponents of higher education for women were much less noisy than those who fought for legal rights and the ballot; just as bright girls had for centuries picked up instruction intended for their brothers, so in the latter half of the nineteenth century they slipped quietly into annexes to colleges for men, changed their seminaries into colleges, and profited by the eccentric charities of men.

The last-ditch battle of the males came, of all sources, from the field of medicine. It was one of the first to be invaded by women, but the counterattack was not directed to women physicians alone. During the seventies and eighties, as the first women's colleges and coeducational colleges were becoming established, a series of magazine articles and books offered dire predictions as to the effect of higher education on the health of young women and particularly on their ability to bear healthy children. The assumption that childbearing and rearing was a woman's major function in life was implicit and unquestioned. Dr. Edward Hammond Clarke in 1873 published perhaps the most effective and terrifying of these works under the somewhat misleading title: *Sex in Education: or A Fair Chance for the Girls.* He predicted for girls who went to college "neuralgia, uterine disease, hysteria, and other derangements of the nervous sytem." Leukorrhoea, amenorrhoea, dysmenorrhoea, chronic and acute ovaritis, and prolapsus uteri were all connected in his presentation with attendance at college or seminary, though he qualified the assertion by observing that there were also other causes for some of these ailments. He was particularly skillful at using case histories.

I have seen females [who] ... graduated from school or college excellent scholars but with undeveloped ovaries. Later they married and were sterile.
    The system never does two things well at the same time ... The muscles and the brain cannot functionate in their best way at the same moment ... Nature has reserved the catamenial week for the process of ovulation and for the development and perfectation of the reproductive system. The brain cannot take more than its share without injury to other organs. Fortunate is the girls' school or college which does not furnish abundant examples of these sad cases.
    It is not asserted here that improper methods of study and a disregard of the reproductive system and its functions during the educational life of girls are the sole causes of female diseases; neither is it asserted that all the female graduates of our schools and colleges are pathological specimens ... But it is asserted that the number of these graduates who have been permanently disabled to a greater or less degree by these causes is so great as to excite the gravest alarm.

After this disclaimer Dr. Clarke proceeds with his case histories. In the first of them:

Miss A., a healthy, bright, intelligent girl entered a female school ... in the state of New York at the age of fifteen. She was then sufficiently well developed and had a good color; all the functions appeared to act normally, and the catamenia were fairly established. She soon found ... that for a few days during every fourth week the effort of reciting produced an extraordinary physical result. The attendant anxiety and excitement relaxed the sluices of the system that were already physiologically open, and determined a hemorrhage as the concomitant of a recitation.

(Dr. Clarke alternates blunt clinical description with extraordinary Victorian circumlocution.) By the end of her second year she was pale and had developed St. Vitus' dance; her father took her out of school for a year and sent her to Europe, but on her return to school "the old menorrhagic trouble" returned "with the addition of occasional faintings to emphasize nature's warnings." Nevertheless she continued until graduation, had another trip to Europe, Egypt, and Asia, married at twenty-two, and consulted Dr. Clarke about "prolonged dyspepsia, neuralgia, and dysmenorrhoea, which had replaced menorrhagia." At the time the book was written she had been unable to conceive a child.

Miss D. was an even worse case. She entered Vassar College at the age of fourteen, developed "the catamenial function" the next year, began fainting in gymnasium classes, developed dysmenorrhoea and then amenorrhoea, and was eventually found by Dr. Clarke to have an undeveloped uterus and infantile breasts, "where the milliner had supplied the organs nature should have grown."

Things get worse as he proceeds through the alphabet. Miss E. was the daughter of a famous scholar and a highly accomplished mother. She went through school and college in seemingly excellent health, but shortly afterward "the catamenial function began to show symptoms of failure of power . . . Soon . . . the function ceased altogether and . . . has shown no more signs of activity than an amputated arm." Next "her head began to trouble her. First there was headache, then a frequent congested condition . . . and, by and by, vagaries and forebodings and despondent feelings. Coincident with this mental state her skin became rough and coarse, and an inveterate acne covered her face . . . I was finally obliged to consign her to an asylum."

A college education, it would appear, was second only to masturbation as a cause of insanity.

There follow even more unpleasant comparisons of college-educated women to such sexless creatures as termites and eunuchs. "Clinical illustrations of this type of arrested growth might be given, but my pen refuses the ungracious task."

Lest any optimistic young lady continue to think of the

case histories as isolated instances, Dr. Clarke continues on the subject of Miss F.

> *. . . The principal of any seminary or head of any college judging by her looks alone would not have hesitated to call her rosy and strong . . .*
>
> *A class of girls might and often do graduate from our schools, higher seminaries, and colleges, that appear to be well and strong at the time of their graduation, but whose development has already been checked, and whose health is on the verge of giving way . . . on graduation day they are pointed out by their instructors to admiring committees as rosy specimens of both physical and intellectual education. A closer inspection by competent experts would reveal the secret weakness which the labor of life that they are about to enter upon too late discloses.*

How many girls or their parents were frightened away from a college education by these horror stories it would be impossible to learn, but colleges for women and coeducational colleges proliferated steadily nevertheless. M. Carey Thomas of Bryn Mawr mentions that Dr. Clarke's book, which went through twelve editions in its first weeks, haunted the dreams of young college women in her generation. Louisa May Alcott mentions the fear in *Jo's Boys*. One of the girl students in the rather improbable college the Lawrences have endowed on the grounds of Plumfield says: "The minute we begin to study people tell us we can't bear it, and warn us to be very careful . . . my people predict nervous exhaustion and an early death."

The number of girls kept away from college is probably less important than the effect on the self-image of women who persevered in spite of these warnings. The idea that a woman must choose either marriage or a career persisted well into the twentieth century. In *This Freedom* by A. S. M. Hutchinson, a best seller in 1922, all three promising children of a woman who keeps her job while they are growing up are destroyed. She is left with a female grandchild whom she tutors personally, presumably as a form of

penance, and presumably unaware of the dangers of allowing a girl child to learn the alphabet.

The women who chose to cultivate their intelligence and
their intellectual skills in the late nineteenth century did
so in the belief that they were sacrificing their femininity.
The society of women thus formed found a variety of substitutes for normal sex, if such a thing exists. In their larger
society it certainly did; heterosexual relations within the
framework of marriage for the purpose of procreation provided the only safe and respectable life for a woman. That
it was not always safe and not altogether respectable, sati-
rists like Shaw and Ibsen were pointing out toward the end
of the century, but for the ordinary middle-class girl their
lessons were without much effect. A woman who did not
marry a good provider and bear and rear his children was a
social outcast in one direction or another. She might be a
prostitute (and of the real lives of such creatures the shel-
tered respectable woman knew very little, Victorian novelists not serving her well in this area) or a Mormon or a
college professor.

In the women's colleges of the late nineteenth and early
twentieth century twosomes were an established institution in the faculty. Little or no question was raised as to
the sexual nature of such pairings. Women were not supposed to have sexual feelings either normal or abnormal;
they suffered sexual intercourse with their husbands for the
sake of the race or out of love and compassion for the man
(filthy creature!) or because they believed it to be their
religious duty. There are many well-authenticated stories
of brides who approached the wedding night with no idea
of what it entailed. This being the case, it seems reasonable
to suppose that comparatively few of the women who es-
caped the demands of heterosexual intercourse sought or
discovered a substitute in homosexual.

The twosomes nevertheless provided many of the social
benefits of marriage: sympathy, companionship, economy
(two women could live as cheaply as one just as well as a
man and a woman, and with no danger of an increasing

family), moral and physical support in times of illness or grief. Any attempt to define them calls into question the definition of homosexuality, which can mean anything from a pleasant vice to a lifetime commitment.

These problems lay in wait for Mary Woolley during her early maturity; at her birth nothing could have been further from the thoughts of the loving relatives who welcomed her.

She was born July 13, 1863, the first child of Joseph Judah and Mary Augusta Ferris Woolley. Although her father was already established in a pastorate in Meriden, Connecticut, the child was born at the home of her maternal grandparents in South Norwalk. Mary Augusta was always something of a mama's girl, returning to her parents' home during her pregnancies, illnesses, or family troubles of any kind for as long as her mother lived. Mr. Ferris was a hat manufacturer prosperous enough to maintain a large and hospitable house, and Mary Emma Woolley always thought of it as her childhood home.

Mary Augusta had been a schoolteacher for a year or two before her marriage, but she had no career ambitions that she was not happy to sacrifice when J. J. Woolley proposed. They were married on December 11, 1861, immediately before the young bridegroom left for military service in Annapolis. He served for six months as a chaplain in the Eighth Connecticut Volunteers before he was invalided home. His duties included visiting sick soldiers in the hospital, lecturing, teaching Sunday school, conducting prayer meetings, preaching, and distributing the mail. This somewhat prosaic military service entitled him afterward to ride at the head of the veterans in the annual Memorial Day parade and to use the title of chaplain in his civilian ministry. His daughter's stories about him invariably stressed the dangers of his army experience and his own physical courage; she liked to watch him on a cavorting horse in the parades. The illness that released him from the army was not serious enough to keep him from accepting the pastorate in Meriden, where he assumed his duties in July 1862.

Presumably Mary Woolley's parents were somewhat disappointed that she was not a boy; it is traditional in American families to hope that the first child will be a son and heir. If there was any disappointment, her brother Erving's arrival three years later saved her from its worst effects as she was forming her notion of self and sex.

In 1939, when she was seventy-six years old, Mary Emma Woolley undertook to write an autobiography. Although childhood memories are supposed to be a pleasure readily accessible to the old, she made heavy work of it. She dropped it no less than five times, but until 1943 she resolutely took it up again each year. These were not successive false starts; in each case she picked up where she had left off, carefully noting on the covering folder the date on which work was resumed. In spite of her resolution, the section on her childhood and youth remains labored and dull, in sharp contrast to the completed chapter on her service at the Disarmament Conference in Geneva in 1932.

The assertion that her childhood was very happy was reiterated in general terms with little or no supporting detail. To a generation raised on Freud this is in itself suspect; the blocked-out memories must have been unhappy or they wouldn't have been blocked out. Q.E.D. It is also noteworthy that the manuscript autobiography contains no record of adolescent *Sturm und Drang*. Almost all of the women of her generation who became notable in their adult life confessed to a bitter childish unhappiness over their sex. There is nothing of the kind in Mary Woolley's autobiography; in fact there is no mention of sex at all. According to her repeated assertions she loved both her parents, but her vivid memories are of her father on his prancing horse. Her mother remains a shadowy figure in the background, much less distinct than Grandma Ferris.

As soon as that lady thought her daughter able to travel, Mary Augusta returned with the baby to Meriden and the manifold duties of a pastor's wife. This was when the child was about a month old, and Grandma Ferris feared that the return had been too soon. "Your friends here . . . think you ought to have remained at home till your health was more established. I hope no harm will come to you from going."

Meriden was still semirural, and in addition to his pastoral duties young Chaplain Woolley took care of his horses, his cow, his pig, and his chickens. Mother and baby May made frequent lengthy visits to South Norwalk. The child's earliest recorded memory of these years is, she admits, a family story she heard so many times that she could not in her adult life be sure whether or not she really remembered it.

When she was about three years old she set out one Sunday afternoon to walk to Norwalk, some fifty miles to the south. Her father pursued her on horseback, presumably guessing the direction she must have taken, and when he overtook her she said, "May is goin' to Grandma's." He scooped her up and took her home riding in front of him on the saddle, a position she remembered with delight. When they reached home she found her pregnant mother walking up and down in the front yard wringing her hands.

A few months later Erving Yale Woolley was born. If May envied her brother as a child she outgrew it and never remembered it; their affection in later years was close and tender to the end of his life. In her autobiography there is no mention of him as a child.

The war was over now, and New England, having appeased its conscience over the sinfulness of slavery, was ready to settle down to the business of getting rich. The reformers who had been drawn together by the cause of abolition turned their attention to health, religion, and politics, and a very substantial number of them to the question of women's rights. In 1865 a wealthy and childless brewer in Poughkeepsie, New York, devoted his fortune to establishing a college for women.

None of this seems to have had very much effect on the Woolley household. Young Mr. Woolley was sympathetic with the reformers. His theology was optimistic and kindly in contrast to the narrow evangelicalism of the earlier part of the century. He was, his daughter later said, genuinely democratic, liking and accepting all kinds of people; he wanted to ameliorate the poverty in which the working class of New England existed, but he had no social ideals revolutionary enough to offend his manufacturer father-in-law. His position in society was secure; when little May saw him on Sundays standing in the pulpit in his good black suit with all their friends and neighbors listening respectfully to him, she imbibed without conscious thought the idea that he was a man apart, someone quite special in the great world as well as in her small one.

Formal education began for her in a small school kept in the basement of her father's church and at her father's suggestion, by a Mrs. Fanny Augur. Apparently the Meriden church did not provide a manse, for May rode to school on horseback perched in front of her father as she had returned from her attempt to run away to Grandma's. The school had fewer than ten children enrolled, so that Mrs. Augur had no difficulty in finding time for personal attention to each one. To the end of her long life Mary Woolley remembered the humiliation she felt at misspelling the word "bowl" when she was five years old. Whether this is a commentary on her own drive for achievement or on Mrs. Augur's pedagogical methods the reader must decide, since no other record of that period in Mary Woolley's education survives.

In 1868 Louisa May Alcott published *Little Women*, that charming celebration of feminine adolescence under the surface of which the passions of frustrated women seethe and boil. In 1869 John Stuart Mill published *The Subjection of Women*. In 1870 several state universities opened their doors to qualified women, and preliminary moves were made toward the establishment of two Massachusetts colleges for women. Henry Durant, whose only son had died tragically in childhood, turned over his estate and devoted most of his capital to the founding of Wellesley, and Sophia Smith of Hatfield left $365,000 to establish Smith. Both schools started as seminaries on the pattern of Mount Holyoke, of which Mr. Durant was a trustee. The intention was that both should become colleges as soon as they could be properly chartered. In the same year President Charles W. Eliot of Harvard expressed amusement at the idea of women as professors. He had "come to the conclusion that a mixed education was not possible in settled countries or in England."

The household in Meriden must have been aware of at least some of these events. Mary Woolley probably read *Little Women* as soon as she could read easily; most New England girls of her generation and social class did. Her father probably read Mill, but it is unlikely that she did; novels were for girls. President Eliot's views and Miss Smith's and Mr. Durant's beneficences were doubtless featured in the journals the Woolleys read. But for all of this we must guess; the autobiography tells us nothing except a few incidents of the idyllic life in Meriden, and the birthday, Thanksgiving, and special visits to Grandma's in South Norwalk.

In 1871 J. J. Woolley received a call to the Congregational Church in Pawtucket, Rhode Island, an event which drastically altered the lives of the whole family. Pawtucket was a city, and many of the parishioners of the Congregational Church there were men of substantial wealth. It was an opportunity that a young minister could not reject.

There was, however, one fairly serious drawback. The Reverend Mr. Constantine Blodgett, D.D., who had served the parish for thirty-five years, was still occupying the manse with the title of "retired pastor." J. J. Woolley apparently thought that this would be a temporary arrangement, for he established his family in a hotel. This designation at the time meant a large boardinghouse; the term "American plan" still commemorates this living arrangement. A surprisingly large number of mothers of families preferred it to the arduous work of running their own homes with no labor-saving devices and only ignorant and untrained servants. It cannot have been a very comfortable existence for a family with children of eight and five, but for the Woolleys it lasted three years.

II

The Education of Mary Woolley

THE WOOLLEY CHILDREN settled happily into life at the Pawtucket Hotel. There were four other children among the boarders; Mr. and Mrs. Jilson, the proprietors, were friendly and the bachelor boarders indulgent. The hotel was close to the church, where social activities for children were numerous, and the elderly parishioners took a kindly interest in the children of the new pastor. They regarded him with somewhat more cautious approval; he went upstairs three steps at a time, which some felt to be undignified in a minister, and he did not seem to be as fully aware as he should be of the social distinction of the wealthier members of the church. He visited without hesitation in the Water Street slums, and he encouraged the immigrant mill workers to attend his church, which was the only opportunity their lives afforded for an appearance of social equality with the mill owners.

May was entered in another small school kept by another brave and indigent lady: Miss Bliss' opposite St. Paul's Episcopal Church. There she formed some friendships that endured for the rest of her life but evidently learned little. Hotel life left Mrs. Woolley free to indulge her penchant for going home to mother, and the children of course went along, school attendance not being a matter of great importance. A little sister, Grace, was born in South Norwalk in 1873, when May was ten. She was sickly from birth and died after a little more than a year, much of which time was spent at Grandma's. Mrs. Woolley suffered from a depression that endured until the birth of her last child in 1878.

May meanwhile moved from Miss Bliss' to a somewhat larger private school held in a room above the store of her father's senior deacon. The preacher, of course, must trade with his parishioners; when several of them were engaged in the same business the matter sometimes became delicate. The education of his daughter was not merely a matter of meeting this obligation but also a disguised charity. Mrs. Lord, who conducted this new school, was a widow with two small children to support. As such her choices were very few: she could teach or she could become a dependent in the home of a prosperous relative. A little lower in the social scale she might have elected to nurse or to keep a boardinghouse; still lower she could have been a cook, a washerwoman, or a mill hand. Teaching, while perhaps harder and less rewarded work than some of the other options, maintained her status and provided for the education of her own children.

After three years J. J. Woolley apparently gave up the hope that the Reverend Mr. Blodgett would move away or die and leave the parsonage to him. He bought a house of his own on Summit Avenue and prepared to move his family into it in 1875.

In January of that year May wrote a letter to her grandfather which affords a tantalizing glimpse of the child and the society in which she was growing up. Written on the evening of New Year's Day, it inquires:

. . . Did you make calls this afternoon? Did Aunt Emma receive calls this afternoon? I did. Here is a list of the gentlemen who called on me. Willie Cheney, Arthur Clapp, Lyman Goff, Freddie Cheney. I received callers from three to five oclock . . .

*

At this distance of time and knowing nothing else of the relations between the child and her grandfather, it is impossible to say whether the letter represents a solemn joke, a game, or a childish imitation of the social customs of her elders. In New York and Boston, and so, no doubt, in Pawtucket and Norwalk, ladies held formal At Homes on New Year's afternoon, and gentlemen went from one to another from early afternoon until midnight unless they were earlier overcome by too much punch. Whatever its precise meaning, the letter indicates several interesting things about the Woolleys' family life. Mrs. Woolley was not holding her own reception. Her punch would, of course, have had to be nonalcoholic, but it would have been quite possible for her to receive guests in the hotel parlor. The eleven-year-old May was aware of the social custom, whether she was making fun of it or imitating it, and she was beginning already to gather the nucleus of the group of suitors that would be absolutely essential to her success as an adolescent.

Little Gracie had died in the previous summer, and Mrs. Woolley was nursing her grief. It had probably been a rather unhappy Christmas, although another of May's letters of the same period lists a number of small gifts from the Jilsons and their boarders as well as from the immediate family — a photograph album, handkerchiefs, stationery, cuffs, two bottles of cologne, a workbox, a "roman" necktie, a book, and money. In another letter she offers an invitation to visit "when we get in our new house." The change was clearly of importance to her.

Her next school, Mrs. Davis's Private School for Young Ladies, was a further step in the direction of conventional social success. It was, in her own words, "a long step forward into young ladyhood." It also offered her her first contact with a woman college graduate. Miss Lois Green, who taught Latin, held an A.B. degree from Vassar, by this time more than ten years old.

Miss Green must have been a subject of intense interest to the young ladies. The magazines had begun to print many articles on the subject of college education for women. Both Smith and Wellesley became colleges in 1875, and descriptions of their lavish endowments and elegant quarters alternated with articles about the hidden dangers of attending them. Miss Green was in her limited way an argument against college education for women, since she was a college graduate who had not married, and Mrs. Davis's young ladies were quite determined on advantageous marriages for themselves. On the other hand Miss Green had a vivid personality and an attractive physical appearance: "of medium height with crinkly black hair, a firm mouth, serious expression, and steady black eyes that could look right through one." Perhaps most important of all is the unstated implication that she liked teaching and was doing it because she thought it was important, not because she had small children or a widowed mother to support. She taught May the rudiments of Latin grammar, which would be of very little use to a young lady in society but which turned out to have substantial value for the career in which this young lady eventually found herself.

When she was fifteen May's youngest brother was born and somewhat restored her mother's spirits. Mary Augusta named him Frank after a favorite brother of her own and babied him to an extent he never outgrew. May herself continued to treat him as her baby brother to the end of his life.

J. J. Woolley's father Joseph joined the family for his declining years and Mary Augusta's duties became fairly burdensome with both an old man and an infant to care for. She had help, sometimes a maid-of-all-work and sometimes both a cook and a maid, but housewives of her class complained of the ignorance and laziness of the available girls, most of them immigrants from Ireland or Scotland. Also troubles within the church were accumulating. The young pastor was more popular in the town than in his own church. He would go wherever he was needed to attend the sick or the dying; he took food to the needy, and he converted a substantial number of the Catholic immigrants. They called him "Father Woolley," which scandalized his own conservative parishioners, and they came to his church and sometimes sat in the pews for which the established members had paid a yearly rent. Always there was the Reverend Constantine Blodgett, kind, wise, loving, and fatherly, to point out how much better the old ways were and to counsel discretion.

After a year or two at Mrs. Davis's May was transferred to the Providence High School, where she was enrolled in the Classical Department. I use the passive voice advisedly; all decisions about her education were made by her father without consultation with either May or her mother. No reason for the transfer from Mrs. Davis's school is offered in the autobiographical notes, but it may have been that her brother Erving was ready for high school that year and their father thought his daughter should have as good an education as his son, at least up to the closed doors of the university.

Providence High School had an admirable record in co-education, having opened its doors to girls from the time of its establishment in 1838, but in Mary Woolley's class girls were in a minority.

... a small group of girls in a room full of boys; no social life; and no informal "give and take" in the classroom. One certainly had to be on one's toes mentally, in Greek and Latin and mathematics, the three subjects on which I spent my days and part of my nights. It was good discipline for the girl who had always known the sympathetic atmosphere of the informal classroom. Of the three men whom we had as teachers, Mr. Peck, the principal ... did occasionally give a fraction of a second to collect one's thoughts — but Mr. Webster, who took classes in Latin and Greek on alternate days, allowed never an instant of grace. An immediate answer — or next! ... Two distinguished citizens of a later day — George Pierce Baker of Harvard and Yale, and Theodore Francis Green, Governor of Rhode Island and United States Senator — I remember vividly as boys at the blackboard successfully solving the "originals" which had laid low most of the class.

*

She spent less than a year at the high school. Early in 1882 the unpleasantness in the church came to a head. Like many church quarrels, it fostered a bitterness hard for the uninvolved spectator to understand. The major issue appears to have been that of pew rentals, but this was merely the focal point for the quarrel between rich and poor. J. J. Woolley believed himself to be on the side of God in the controversy, a dangerous certainty even when it lends needed strength to the arm of flesh. He suffered from insomnia and a burning sense of outrage at the injustice of those who disagreed with him. The unhappiness he felt pervaded his home. His old father died during the course of the quarrel, and Mrs. Woolley, with the infant Frank in her arms, suffered a fall that lamed her for life. The family always held that nervous excitement over what was happening in the church was the real cause of the accident.

In the spring of 1882 J. J. Woolley resigned or was dismissed from his pastorate and left for Europe to recover from what amounted to a nervous breakdown. The record is not clear as to whether the severance was a forced resignation or a dismissal. By tradition the precipitating event was a sermon in which Mr. Woolley said that he believed a soul on Water Street was as precious to God as one on Walcott Street. This opinion, although it had ample theological backing, was so offensive to the inhabitants of the big houses on Walcott Street that they could no longer accept the ministry of a man who held it.

There is no mention of any of this in Mary Woolley's autobiographical sketch nor in an article about her father that she later wrote for publication. All her accounts of her family life then and later were rigidly conventional — unclouded happiness, success, love, charity. The public image, important to her in girlhood because of the peculiar prominence forced on the child of a Protestant minister, became more and more so as her own career developed. She says only that her father's departure for Europe meant her own separation from the Providence High School. Mrs. Woolley with the three children, May eighteen, Erving fifteen, and

Frank four, went back again to South Norwalk. There May studied French and music (instructors unspecified), enjoyed her freedom, and considered her education complete.

Here the autobiographical notes suffer one of their most unfortunate lacunae. She was going on nineteen, and by the accepted standards of her society her education was adequately completed. The one pressing duty of her life at this point was to find a husband. She was living in the house where her father had courted her mother and among daily inescapable reminders of the fact that it was now time for someone to come courting her.

In the fierce competition of the marriage market, what had she to offer? Her grandfather manufactured hats, a business which, in the rapid industrialization of New England in its postwar years, might have made him a millionaire but hadn't. He was prosperous enough to maintain a hospitable home to which his children and grandchildren constantly returned, but he was not a rich man.

A grandfather in trade, a father in a highly respectable profession but of doubtful success at this point in his life, no money to inherit, no useful family influence for an ambitious young man. The suitors Mary Woolley could hope for must be motivated by true love alone. There are no extant pictures of her at this age; in her youthful maturity some years later she was a strikingly handsome woman, but it seems unlikely that at nineteen she was conventionally pretty. She was adequately accomplished: French, music, deportment, fine needlework, plus rudimentary Greek, Latin, and mathematics. A younger girl cousin testified in later years that May liked to dress up with her girl friends and parade the streets of Norwalk, Japanese parasols poised over their heads, but no record survives of any young man having nibbled at the bait thus offered.

It is perhaps surprising that the tragedy of the unmarried woman in nineteenth-century America has never been celebrated in fiction. A substantial portion of the "scribbling women" of whose competition Hawthorne complained must have suffered the agony and shame of being passed over in the market, but they did not write about it. The more lonely and frustrated their personal lives, the fuller and more romantic their fantasy ones. Louisa Alcott's Laurie and Professor Bhaer no less than Emily Brontë's Heathcliff both busied and satisfied their authors, and Miss Alcott's creations also brought her more fame and fortune than any flesh-and-blood lover or husband would have been likely to do. It is perhaps posterity's loss that she chose to invent them rather than write about the real life of an unmarried woman in her day, but again perhaps not.

For most unmarried women there was a family legend of tragedy more romantic than losing a race: a fiancé dead in early youth of a wasting disease or a spectacular accident; a hopeless love for a married man bravely conquered; family interference that had driven away an impecunious suitor who later became rich and famous.

Years later when Mary Woolley became widely known it might have been expected that a few happily married men should have said, "She was my girl once." But as far as the record goes, no one ever did. Nor is there any mention in the autobiographical record of even the most brief and fleeting affair of the heart.

When Pastor Woolley left the Pawtucket Congregational Church, one hundred and twenty of its members left with him. The months in Europe may have been motivated partly by a desire to make clear that he had not by his own action fostered a disastrous split within the church. In his absence the hundred and twenty met each Sunday in private homes or the Music Hall. Many of them were the immigrant mill hands the Pawtucket church had considered undesirable, but there were a useful and devoted few from Walcott Street. On his return in August he found a letter waiting from them inviting him to assume the pastorate of the new Park Place Congregational Church. It is probable that some letters had been exchanged while he was abroad and that he was quite aware of what would be waiting for him on his return, but, although the records of his denomination credit him with having established the new church, he was always careful then and later to make clear that it had originated in the spontaneous action of its members. Park Place Church is now recorded in Congregational Church history as a missionary offshoot of the Pawtucket Congregational Church, but the old bitterness has frustrated three attempts in a hundred years to reunite the two.

When her father's return and assumption of his new pastorate brought the family together again in Pawtucket, Mary Emma, now nineteen, would have been happy to keep on with her French and music and her presumably fruitless quest for a husband, but her father decided otherwise.

"You are going to Wheaton," he told her.

She did not think of contesting his decision or asking his reasons for it.

Wheaton was a well-regarded seminary at Norton, Massachusetts, twenty miles from Pawtucket. The magazine articles about the dangers of higher education for women were in full swing, and a New England father who was willing to run the risk of ignoring them could have sent his daughter to Harvard Annex, just opened, or to Smith or Vassar or Wellesley or Wells, or, indeed, to Oberlin, Cornell, Michigan, Wisconsin, or any of several other universities. Alice Freeman, a graduate of the University of Michigan, had become president of Wellesley the previous year at the age of twenty-six.

The seminaries occupied a position somewhere between classical high schools and four-year colleges. They were in some ways comparable to twentieth-century junior colleges, although the curricula vary so widely from those of the twentieth century that it is difficult to make comparisons. The more rigid and ambitious of the seminaries were open to the same objections that were being made to colleges for women, but many of them made no pretensions to any scholarly status and served simply as finishing schools. All of them carried rather more social prestige than the high schools that admitted girls. Relief at the discovery that he still had a parish and a dependable income may have been in Mr. Woolley's mind.

Whatever his reasons, he decided to send May to Wheaton, and she accepted his decision without the necessity of
making one of her own.

Wheaton Female Seminary had been founded a year or
two before Mount Holyoke and on much the same principles. Its endowment was the gift of Judge Laban N. Wheaton in memory of a beloved daughter and its emphasis rather
more on feminine graces and less on religion than that of
the sister seminary, but they were alike in offering a demanding intellectual program.

In 1882 Wheaton still maintained in many ways the atmosphere of a Victorian school for young ladies. The social
affairs, limited to Friday evenings, were lectures, receptions,
or musicales. Males were not excluded from these; the
Brown glee club came once or twice a year, and May Woolley's father was several times an invited lecturer. Indoor
calisthenics and etiquette were a part of the curriculum.
Miss Woolley remembered sixty years later the prescription
for entering a reception without embarrassment. "In the
dressing room, swing arms vigorously and then let them
come to a rest." She did not say whether she had ever
tested the method for herself. Walking, tennis, and croquet
were the approved forms of exercise.

Mary Woolley would seem on the whole to have matured
rather slowly, just as many years later she maintained the
health and vigor of mature life well into old age. At nineteen, even with advanced standing at Wheaton, she was
associated mainly with girls two or three years her junior.
She does not appear to have resented submitting to the
restrictions designed for younger girls. Her sense of propriety and of family pride was already strong; she remembered
later that the talks on manners indicated that the way the
girls ate their soup showed what kind of homes they came
from. She resolutely spooned hers away from her and re-
frained from tilting the bowl to get the last drop.

But along with the restricted social life she found an
intellectual life richer than any she had yet known. The
curriculum included, to follow Miss Woolley's own order of

listing, ethics, astronomy, physics, chemistry, zoology, botany, geology, mental arithmetic, Latin, world literature, and contemporary novelists. The sciences were all taught by an evidently omniscient Miss Pike, with the aid of a biennial lecture course in astronomy by Professor Charles Young of Princeton and in geology by a Professor Wright, not further identified in the autobiography. The world literature course under Frances Emerson included the Mahabharata, Ramayana, and Homer, Dante, and Goethe, all in translation and, one must assume, suitably edited for the perusal of young ladies.

Heloise Hersey lectured on the work of George Eliot, George Meredith, and "contemporary novelists" unspecified. It would be interesting to know whether the young ladies actually read these books or merely listened to lectures about them. Mary Woolley does not say. Clearly, however, in one way or another, "the woman question" was being called to the attention of these young women.

The course Mary Woolley remembered most vividly fifty-five years later was the one in ethics taught by Mrs. A. E. Stanton, the head of the school. The text was Mark Hopkins' *The Law of Love and Love as a Law*, a book which does a good deal to unsettle the concept of Professor Hopkins on that famous log. The subtitle is *Moral Science, Theoretical and Practical*, and it proposes to reconcile the natural moral law with revealed religion as exhibited in the Christian ethic. This effort entails ignoring the fact that there are any religions other than Christianity, and every time he encounters a really knotty philosophical problem Professor Hopkins unravels it by asserting flatly that God wanted things the way they are. His attitude is strictly Protestant and authoritarian, and his ethical system is not really applicable to anyone except an upper-middle-class New Englander.

Within this framework he had comparatively little to say about women; his book was widely used as a text in colleges for men, and he made little or no allowance for the fact that women might also read it. In the chapter called "Relation of the Sexes: Chastity" he offers the usual warning as to the relation of masturbation to insanity, but so delicately that a young woman could easily read the chapter without having any idea what he was talking about. As to illicit heterosexual relations his warning is directed entirely toward young men, but he says in passing:

There is no ruin and degradation like that which these sins bring upon the woman.

In discussing the rights and duties of both sexes in relation to marriage he says:

... And here the one duty of those whose affections are yet free is to withhold themselves from any attempt to awaken affection in another except with a view to marriage. This will be hard where there is conscious beauty and power; vanity and pride will plead strongly, and many will go as far as they can or dare ... Only when there is a view to marriage may that more intimate acquaintance be sought which will justify an engagement. Once engaged in a relationship only less sacred than that of marriage ... it will be criminal in either of them to seek the affection of another ...

Once married they are to recognize "the reciprocal rights and duties of husbands and wives ... If God has made, as He has, by nature and by revelation, the husband the head of the house, then the truest and best happiness of the wife will be found only in recognizing him in that relation." Of the possibilities of any other than heterosexual relationships in male or female he says nothing. George Meredith and George Eliot could have told these girls rather more about what they had to look forward to.

Mary Woolley spent two happy years in this idyllic if restricted environment, almost totally feminine. Her earliest publications date from these years. In the archives of Mount Holyoke College there is an essay, "Respect," written at the Providence High School. Inscribed in a copperplate hand, neatly bound in booklet form, and tied with white ribbon, it bears proudly on its cover a richly deserved A. It is eminently correct, proper, and well organized, but it shows nothing of its author's character or interests beyond an ability to follow directions and a sense of structure.

Her two publications in the Wheaton magazine, while not above the level of student magazine literature, do show both expanding interests and a genuinely personal response to her reading. Her editorial in the fall issue for 1883 makes ladylike fun of some of the things she has learned.

. . . our teachers do not encourage the use of slang, and yet [the textbook] says "That form of language is most excellent, which yields its continued idea with the least expenditure of mental power." We think that every sensible person will admit that it requires less expenditure of mental power to understand the phrase "I had a jolly time last night" than the sentence, "The effect upon my sensibilities occasioned by the events which occurred on the preceding day, after the descent of the solar luminary below the western horizon were of an extremely felicitous character."

. . . We are very sure that we shall continue our Astronomical observations after graduation. The experience of former classes has assured us that moonlight drives and sails often prove a more valuable incentive to the study of the Science than the observatory or the telescope . . .

So there *were* some mild flirtations!

. . . Every metaphysician seems to have a different opinion, so by believing all that each one says, we have something to suit every condition. When we are next afflicted with a toothache we are going to remember that Bishop Berkeley says there is no matter but only ideas, consequently we have no teeth, and hence no toothache. The mercury is near zero, the wind blowing furiously, and we must take one hour and a half of exercise, but do not stop to put on your idea of a cloak. Those snow drifts which you think you see exist only in your mind, and anyway, a dotted swiss idea will keep you as warm as a fur one. When we are studying in our Senior parlor, we are not going to be troubled by the amateur vocalists who are practising near

by. Berkeley says there is no sound, and we trust him implicitly, scorning those lower natures who say "If Bishop Berkeley says it is no matter, it is no matter what Bishop Berkeley says . . ."

. . . If we wish to have a little longer vacation at the Holidays, we are going to remember that Kant says that "All time is one and the same time." Therefore January 10th is the same time as January 3d and surely we are at liberty to stay home a week longer without rebuke . . . We would like to have the trustees remember on examination day, that Dr. Hopkins says "Some things in the mind pass beyond the recall of the will," and take it for granted that our knowledge is all there, although we cannot show it . . .

There is foreshadowed here the eminently practical woman whose administrative ability was to shape Mount Holyoke College into its twentieth-century form.

Portraits of Our Grandmothers, a series of brief sketches of women through the ages, always in their domestic relations, is, perhaps, as Jeannette Marks has pointed out, the first indication of Mary Woolley's intellectual acceptance of herself as a woman, but if so it shows no desire to blaze new trails for her sex.

During May's two years at Wheaton the prophets of doom were fully occupied with forecasts of what the overintellectualization of women would do to the race.

Unquestionably the great business of a girl is to grow pretty and amiable and nice, and train herself to be a good sweetheart, wife, and mother. Unquestionably also a girl who overstrains her mental powers may be laying up the seeds of nervous and other disorders.

So wrote an anonymous contributor to *All the Year Round* in February 1883. Dr. T. S. Clouston in *Popular Science Monthly* in December of the same year was almost as gloomy as Dr. Clarke.

If you have the vital energy doing the work of building the bones and muscles and brain during the year that a girl

grows two inches in height and gains a stone in weight you
cannot have it that year for the acquisition of knowledge
and for study . . . Why should we spoil a good mother by
making an ordinary grammarian?

Dr. Clouston makes no comment on the vital energy that
a boy needs for growing at the same period in his life, nor
on what is to become of the women who are not destined
to be mothers.

At the time of her graduation in 1884, May Woolley for
the second time in her life thought of her education as
completed. She was twenty-one years old and, so far as the
record shows, entertained no serious ambitions of any
kind. As the young lady daughter of the family at home on
Summit Avenue in Pawtucket she had plenty of activity to
keep her occupied. She was adequately educated to become
a good sweetheart, wife, and mother — perhaps a trifle
overeducated for the purpose, but not seriously so. The year
and a half she spent at home in 1884–85 is passed over in
her autobiographical sketch as lightly as the months at
South Norwalk in 1882. It requires a close reading even to
become aware that there was a hiatus between her student
days at Wheaton and her teaching ones. Again, however, it
was an important hiatus.

The new church was now two years old as an institution
but still homeless. In 1883 the congregation had purchased
a lot fronting on the little triangular park that gave Park
Place its name, and the cornerstone for a new building was
laid there on September 10, 1884. The location, across the
river from the old church and at a somewhat superior
height, might have been taken as symbolic. Raising funds
for the new building required a series of bazaars, fairs, and
oyster suppers that kept the ladies of the congregation
busy. Whichever side God may have been on, Mr. Woolley
was on the side of the future, a few years ahead of his time,
but not so far as to destroy his usefulness or his career. The
"social gospel" was coming into its own across America,
and the Park Place Congregational Church of Pawtucket
was in the forefront. There was plenty of work for the

pastor's wife and daughter in the Sunday school, the missionary society, and charities which would today be described as social work. This was in addition to all the baking, canning, ironing, sewing, and housecleaning which had to be done by the lady of the house and her daughter even when they kept help for the heavier work. As preparation for marriage, the year and a half she spent at home was probably more useful than anything else in her education. But no marriage ensued.

Eighteen-year-old Erving Woolley entered Brown University in the fall of 1884. Six-year-old Frank was at home being babied by both mother and sister. May was simply marking time.

In January of 1886 she was invited to come back to Wheaton for one semester as a substitute teacher. As such she was not expected to claim any superior expertise in a particular subject; she taught what was required, first mathematics, then Latin, and finally history, which became "her" subject. The semester as a substitute was followed by a regular appointment as a teacher of history, and she felt that she had, again in her own words, "found her career."

Everything that had happened to Mary Woolley up to this time had been without initiative on her own part; she went where her father directed her and did what her teachers told her. But now as a teacher herself she was required to show a certain amount of initiative, and the experience contributed to her slow maturing.

The love affair of Alice Freeman, later Palmer, in 1886 and '87 must have had a profound effect on the young teachers and professors of the seminaries and new women's colleges. In 1881 Alice had become president of Wellesley College. An intensely ambitious and aggressive girl, she had gone from an academy in western New York State to the University of Michigan at seventeen as one of its first female students. After her graduation there she taught for a year or two in a Saginaw high school and then moved on to Wellesley as professor of history at twenty-four. Two years later she became president, and in the course of her duties met Professor George Herbert Palmer of Harvard, who came to Wellesley to read his new translation of the *Odyssey*. His courtship ran through a year and a half; at the end of 1887 she resigned her position at Wellesley and they were married. Various alternatives to her resignation were proposed; she had been highly successful at Wellesley, and the college wanted to keep her. The presidency was offered to Professor Palmer, apparently on the theory that as the president's wife Mrs. Palmer could contribute quite as much to the college as Miss Freeman had done as president. This he refused; a Harvard professor did not lightly resign to become president of a mere college for women. Mrs. Durant, the widow of the founder of Wellesley, offered to build them a "cottage" (this term in the nineteenth century was used to describe residences that, when they survive into the twentieth, are denominated mansions) near the railroad station so that Professor Palmer could commute to his work in Cambridge while Mrs. Palmer continued hers at Wellesley. This offer also was refused. Miss Freeman felt that the title of wife was the highest to which any woman could aspire and that its functions would demand the totality of her best efforts. She was willing to give up her own salary of $4000 and live on her husband's $3500.

So far as her personal career was concerned, the choice was probably a wise one. As Alice Freeman Palmer she became much more widely known than Alice Freeman had ever been; she was made a trustee of Wellesley and an officer in several national organizations of women, and she was in great demand as a speaker throughout the nation. Moreover her social position was clearly raised, and the demands of her social life were such as to absorb much of her energy. She wrote her mother that the trousseau contained four dresses for receptions, a red velvet and a blue one, a white lace, and a yellow satin. The wedding was at the home of the governor of the state, and afterward Professor and Mrs. Palmer started a round of social activity that included making three hundred and forty afternoon calls

— the professor kept tabs in his notebook — and being guests of honor at a supper party given by President and Mrs. Eliot for the entire Harvard faculty, all of whom would entertain them in turn. As president of Wellesley, Miss Freeman could scarcely have aspired even to meet President Eliot of Harvard, whose distaste for women as professors grew as they proliferated. (Delivering the Commencement address to Smith's first graduating class in 1879, he congratulated the college on having had the good sense to employ male professors exclusively. "In President Eliot's otherwise luminous intelligence, women's education is the dark spot," M. Carey Thomas of Bryn Mawr remarked some years later.)

Whether Mrs. Palmer's desertion of Wellesley helped or hindered the cause of education for women would not be easy to say. It demonstrated beyond the reach of successful contradiction that a college education did not unfit a woman for marriage nor make her feel herself superior to its duties. She remained childless, although she was only thirty-three at the time of her marriage. A question might quite legitimately have been raised as to whether this was by choice or by misfortune, since the answer bore directly on the disputed point of what a college education did to a woman's potential for motherhood. Victorian delicacy, however, while it permitted free discussion of this question in general terms, forbade that it should be asked directly of a distinguished lady who was also the wife of a Harvard professor.

Professor Palmer always believed that his wife's work during her last semester at Wellesley in the fall of 1887 had shortened her life; he had wanted her to marry him in the summer of that year instead of waiting until Christmas. Alice Palmer lived some fifteen years after her marriage, during most of which she enjoyed vigorous health. She and her husband bicycled through Europe on his sabbatical, and she kept up a strenuous social and public life in Cambridge, but along with this she suffered the evidently obligatory ailments of the Victorian lady, headaches and nerves. She died in 1902 following an operation in France for an intestinal ailment.

During the years Miss Woolley was teaching at Wheaton, Bryn Mawr College opened in a Philadelphia suburb. M. Carey Thomas, its dean, had earned a Ph.D. summa cum laude from the University of Leipzig in 1882, an achievement far beyond that of Mrs. Palmer or any woman college president then in office. Although Miss Thomas took second place in the new college to a male president, James E. Rhoads, much of the work of organization fell to her. She visited Vassar and the New England colleges for women to study their curricula, and then deliberately set entrance examinations more difficult than any of them required. She apparently shared with many critics a suspicion that they were not really equivalent to the men's colleges, and she wanted to make Bryn Mawr a standard at which all of them might aim. Bryn Mawr did promptly assume an enviable position among the women's colleges, and her alumnae were eagerly sought for teaching positions in the others.

Miss Woolley's autobiographical sketch and Miss Marks' biography of her slide smoothly over these Wheaton years, peaceful, uneventful, busy, apparently happy. There was no obvious reason why May's life should not continue in the same path to its end. She was popular with the students; the girls in her hall gave afternoon fêtes in the apple orchard, serving strawberries, ices, and cake on tables decorated with flowers. She liked history and she liked her girls. But new forces were stirring in her as well as in the world at large. Wheaton graduates began going to college: Martha Alvord to Harvard Annex, Chedie Connor to Cornell, Mary Lynde to Smith. Miss Lowell of the Literature Department took a leave of absence to study at Harvard Annex. Almost all of the new women's colleges had special provisions for teachers who wanted to upgrade their education; it would be as easy for Mary Woolley as for her students to attend one of them.

Her brother Erving took his degree from Brown in 1888 and shortly afterward, having launched on his career as a banker, married a daughter of the governor of Rhode Island. The Park Place Congregational Church, completed in 1885 and flourishing, carried J. J. Woolley to an important position in the professional life of Pawtucket and Providence. In the spring of 1889 he had a second trip abroad, this time to the Holy Land with one of his deacons, leaving Mrs. Woolley and ten-year-old Frank at home in Pawtucket.

One advantage of being a teacher instead of a wife and mother was that May had money of her own and could, by the summer of 1890, pay for her own trip to Europe instead of looking to father or husband to do it for her. According to her own account it was the European vacation in the summer of 1890 that aroused in her a desire to go to college. It seems probable that the seed had been sown somewhat earlier and that the trip itself was the first sign of its sprouting. Four teachers from Wheaton went with a party from the Smith College faculty. The Wheaton group included the omniscient Miss Pike, a Miss Hopkins, and Miss Elizabeth Palmer, who had a degree from Wellesley and taught Latin. They were escorted by Professor Benjamin C. Blodgett, professor of music at Smith, and his wife, and accompanied by several other members of the Smith faculty. It was only the professorial rank that was preempted by men there; like the other women's colleges Smith had a number of women teachers. Very few of the Wheaton teachers were college graduates, thus this was Mary Woolley's first opportunity to associate with women who had attended college and to observe and compare their life style with her own. Professor Blodgett may have been a son of the Reverend Constantine; in any case he provided a thoroughly safe, respectable, and not unfamiliar guide and protector.

The party covered an astonishing amount of ground in view of the fact that the aeroplane was still in the undreamed-of future. They crossed the Atlantic in the *Aurania* of the Cunard Line, followed by the public prayers of Wheaton faculty friends. On land they traveled by excellent fast trains, luxuriously equipped, and by horse-drawn vehicles of various sorts. In this way they saw England, Edinburgh and Glasgow, Ireland, Paris, Cologne and the Rhine, Wiesbaden, Munich, Nuremberg, Lucerne, the Alps, Geneva, Lake Como, and finally the Passion Play at Oberammergau, all in about two months.

What the trip meant in the way of intellectual awakening is probably not easy for our generation to grasp. The museums, churches, art galleries, palaces, and landscapes they were seeing were all enriched for these learned young ladies by years of reading and study. They knew their Shakespeare, Milton, Pope, Macaulay, and Tennyson better than their native poets and playwrights; they had looked for years at reproductions of the pictures and architectural structures they were now seeing in the original. They probably visited the English universities as well, for May Woolley came home and told her father she would like to go to Oxford to earn a degree. The account of subsequent events is compressed into a few lines in her autobiographical narrative. According to that, her father mentioned her wish to President Andrews of Brown when they were dining together in Providence. President Andrews asked, "Why doesn't she come here?" and the thing was done. Other sources suggest that the matter was not quite so simple.

It is interesting to speculate as to why Mary Woolley in her old age understated the difficulties of her admission to Brown. The story as she tells it increases her father's importance and the power of his friend President Andrews, but it greatly discounts her own courage, ability, and determination. If she simply wanted a college degree she could have gone to Wellesley, where young teachers were admitted as special students and formed a substantial minority of the variegated student body. If, as Jeannette Marks claims, she "wanted to come in contact with men's minds," she could have entered Harvard Annex on a similar arrangement. The coveted residence at Oxford, while difficult and expensive, would not have been impossible. Vida Scudder, later to be a colleague at Wellesley, had gone there with

Clara French in 1884. The Association of Collegiate
Alumnae, forerunner of the American Association of University Women, had more than a thousand women as members by 1890, graduates of Oberlin, Cornell, Vassar, Michigan, Wisconsin, Boston, Smith, Wellesley, M.I.T., Wesleyan,
Syracuse, Kansas, Northwestern, and other colleges and
universities. To go to college was no longer a pioneering
adventure, but to open the doors of the local university to
her sex may have had a special personal meaning for her.
On the other hand Brown may have been chosen simply as
the cheapest and easiest place to go.

In 1890 J. J. Woolley, along with twenty other parents of
young women, put his signature to a petition requesting
that their daughters be allowed to enter and "pursue the
same course of study in Brown University on the same
conditions as the young men." Harvard had had its Harvard
Annex for eleven years, and Columbia had just opened Barnard as a separate college for women, to say nothing of the
coeducational colleges. Most of the Brown faculty were
opposed to admitting women, and the all-male undergraduate body wanted very much to remain so.

Here as at several earlier points dates must be scanned
closely to provide an understanding of what was happening. The autobiography clearly implies that May entered
Brown immediately after the European trip and her father's
conversation with President Andrews. Actually she went
back to Wheaton for another year before entering Brown
with the first freshman class of girls in 1891. In the mean-
time, however, she may have attended Professor Franklin
Jameson's lectures in history as his guest. She did actually
enter a Brown classroom first in this status, but whether a
full year or only a few weeks before the freshman girls
entered is not entirely clear. For Professor Jameson to invite
her in this way was not precedent-shattering, although it
was a strong entering wedge for women in the university.
The biological laboratories had for some time been open to
women teachers; that the history lectures should be also
followed reasonably enough.

*

More than forty years later Professor Jameson wrote his recollections of Mary Woolley's first appearance in his classroom.

I remember well the day she first came into the class — came in without bashfulness and without forwardness, quite as if it had been her daily habit, and as if unconscious of traditions to the contrary that had prevailed since 1763 . . . Still more vividly I remember the first occasion when, after some days, I asked her to answer a question or discuss a matter. She answered it or discussed it with so much fulness and exactness and skill that I could see the young fellows on the front seat glancing at each other with a smile, as much as to say, 'Who but a girl would get a thing up to so fine a point as that?' . . . I do not need to say that the introduction of women into Brown University after so many years of their absence was, in principle, not welcomed by the male undergraduates, but in this first case of Miss Woolley, it immediately appeared to them that it deserved toleration, and I do not think that she was ever treated otherwise than with due respect.

May herself testified on the same point.

I do not know how they [the male students] felt [about a women's college] but I can tell you how they acted. During the four years I received nothing but the utmost courtesy from any student at Brown.

The irony would appear to be unintentional, but with Miss Woolley can one ever be sure? Certainly she received neither friendship, comradeship, nor intellectual stimulation from her fellow students, except from the girls who shortly followed her.

In the fall of 1891 President Andrews found that it was possible to assemble a group of six young ladies to undertake the work of the freshman year in a separate class and without any guarantee that they would be allowed even to take examinations, much less apply for degrees. Their work for the first year was to consist of daily classes in French, Greek, Latin, and mathematics. Miss Woolley resigned or took a leave of absence from Wheaton — she continued a limited amount of work there until she went to Wellesley in 1895 — and joined the new class in the study of Latin while continuing to attend lectures in the men's college. The girls met in the University Grammar School after its regular occupants had left for the day. They were tutored by regular members of the Brown University faculty undertaking the class as extra labor for extra remuneration. Miss Woolley had been exempted from Latin at Wheaton because of the excellence of her preparation in the Providence High School; she was therefore on a level with the younger high school graduates in this field. A year later, when the university officially accepted women as candidates for degrees, she studied sophomore Greek and Latin with them and freshman Greek and mathematics with the new entering class. Meanwhile she was attending Professor Jameson's lectures in American and English history, President Andrews' in philosophy, and Dr. James R. Jewett's in Oriental history. During the first "guest" year there was no charge except for examinations; after that tuition for women was set at approximately $150.

Thus, while the Young Ladies' Class both was and wasn't a part of the university, Mary Woolley both was and wasn't a part of the Young Ladies' Class. As cicerone, however, she was valuable both to the girls and to the future of the Women's College they were helping to establish. They were the same age as the students she had been teaching at Wheaton, and she could remind them that they were "carrying on their shoulders the academic fate of future generations of females." She could also set them an example of how to cross the campus in front of the young men seated on the steps of Manning Hall singing, "Here she comes / There she goes / All dressed up / In her Sunday clothes," without seeming to notice.

In 1895 an undergraduate wrote in the *Brunonian*:

I'm glad Brown isn't co-ed because if I met on the campus and in recitation and in society, the right kind of girls — the womanly, tender, emotional kind — I am afraid I might

get interested in something besides study, but if we had a
lot of those coldly intellectual females — those prospective
old maid doctors and lawyers who are all very useful mem-
bers of society no doubt — the glorious "co-ed" influence
in polishing my manners etc. would amount to just about
nothing at all, for I don't admire a manly woman or a
womanly man.

The term "male chauvinism" had not yet been invented,
but clearly it was going to have to be.

In spite of such prejudice May Woolley achieved a degree
of acceptance that was a landmark in the history of the
university. In the spring of 1892 she published an article in
the *Brown Magazine*. This was followed by two more, and
by her senior year she was elected a member of the staff
with her own department, although she was not included
in the group photograph of the editors taken for the
yearbook.

Her sketches in "Etchings," the department she edited,
are probably the high-water mark of her lighter writing, and
suggest that she might have aspired to a career in literature had she so chosen. Her subjects were New England
"characters" and her foreign travel (in which she used
the masculine pronoun to denominate the "Foreign
Correspondent." The articles were signed only by
initials). Witty and entertaining, they compare very favorably with the journalism in national magazines of the
period.

When the Alpha Beta fraternity was formed for junior and
senior women she became its first president and addressed
it on "The Repeal of the Silver Bill." According to her own
account it functioned also as a social club to fill the gap left
by the indifference or hostility of male students. There
were class suppers, amateur dramatics, impromptu musicales and dances — with the girls dancing with each other?
— receptions, teas, and daily impromptu lunches.

Under Professor Jameson's friendly tutelage she also prepared and published two historical articles, "The Early History of the Colonial Post Office" in the publications of the
Rhode Island Historical Society, and "The Development of

the Love of Romantic Scenery in America" in the *American Historical Review*. The former has been recently republished as a solid if small contribution to American history. The latter is curious in that her examples are all taken from private diaries, official reports, or class poems at various colleges; she does not cite a single American author of any repute.

Mary Woolley was awarded an A.B. degree in 1894 with honors in history and Latin, one of the first two women graduated from Brown. The following year she again taught history at Wheaton for two days a week while working for her M.A. After that Professor Jameson thought he could help her to secure a fellowship for advanced research, but President Andrews secured a more attractive offer. Through his good offices Wellesley College offered her the post of instructor in Biblical history. She was invited to lunch at President Andrews' house with President Julia Irvine of Wellesley, and then to a reception at the home of ex-Governor Claflin in Cambridge, where she could be inspected by Alice Freeman Palmer and other Wellesley trustees. Perhaps her Wheaton training in how to keep calm at a reception stood her in good stead now; in any case she passed inspection, and in the fall of 1895 she entered on her duties at Wellesley.

III

Wellesley

IN THE SAME SEPTEMBER in which Mary Woolley started her work at Wellesley, Jeannette Marks entered as a freshman. Only five years after Miss Woolley had pioneered at Brown, going to college was no longer a difficult achievement for a girl. Wellesley's entering class of two hundred included young teachers on leave of absence from their schools, missionaries' daughters sent home for their education, gold or oil heiresses from the West bent on attaining culture, Boston and New York debutantes, girls from families which had traditionally sent their sons to college and their daughters to seminary. Almost all of them white Anglo-Saxon Protestants some years before anyone would think of calling them WASPs, these young women represented a much more heterogeneous social and economic background than any society Mary Woolley had previously encountered.

Also they were almost completely free of the pressures of male-dominated society. Henry Durant, the founder who had followed the fortunes of the college with obsessive attention, was now dead; his strong-willed widow and the carefully selected women to whom he had entrusted the administrative and teaching duties of the college were in control. This society of women had an enormous attraction for young women who had suffered in the restricted life of genteel little girls and rebellious adolescents. Jeannette Marks was one of these.

Born in 1875 into a family of wealth and privilege, she had grown to maturity under almost every handicap a Krafft-Ebing could have imagined. Her father had wanted her to be a boy, and alternately treated her like one and rejected her completely. Her mother was gentle, sweet, pretty, accomplished, and desperately unhappy. The unsuccessful marriage was held together for the sake of propriety, although husband and wife lived apart for increasingly long periods over the years. Jeannette and her sister always remained with their mother. Their education was spotty, conducted largely by governesses, some of whom were incompetent, some uncongenial, and some both. The year before Jeannette came to college her mother died, and shortly thereafter she quarreled bitterly and finally with her father.

William Dennis Marks was a man of considerable distinction, a college professor of engineering who left that work first to direct the great Philadelphia electrical exhibition of 1884 and then to head the Philadelphia Edison Company in the years during which electricity was being introduced into the everyday life of America.

A Yale graduate, he met and married Jeannette Colwell during a temporary stint of running a small factory making blast furnaces in Tennessee. His first daughter was born in a boardinghouse in Chattanooga on August 16, 1875. According to her own account she was originally named Augusta du Bois in honor of a professor at Yale whom her father had admired. She was christened, however, Jeannette Augustus, and during her childhood was always called Gussie. Thus at the very beginning of her life Jeannette's father would seem to have expressed his disappointment in her sex and his determination to ignore it, her mother to have won a Pyrrhic victory. The younger Jeannette throughout her life continued to use the masculine form of her middle name, although in later years she shortened it to the initial A.

The blast-furnace factory failed, and Mr. Marks went to

Lehigh University as an instructor in mechanical engineering and a year later to the University of Pennsylvania, where he became Whitney Professor of Dynamic Engineering. His second daughter, Mabel, was born in Philadelphia in December of 1876. Toward this little sister, whom she saw as pretty, feminine, and petted, Gussie was to remain strongly ambivalent throughout her life.

The young Markses lived in Philadelphia on Walnut Street. Gussie could remember sitting on the curbstone there, grieving over the death of Emerson, which occurred when she was seven years old. She could not remember how she happened to have heard of it or what she knew of Emerson at the time. She also remembered going to Wanamaker's at the age of thirteen to purchase a bookcase with thirteen dollars her grandmother had sent her as a birthday present. In the intervening years, however, her parents had built the house on Lake Champlain that was to serve as her home for most of her life and to be the center of her emotional life. By family tradition Mrs. Marks fell in love with the site on a vacation trip and begged, "Oh, Will, Will, set me down here and never take me away again!" Even after he achieved professorial status William Dennis Marks tended to lean heavily on the financial assistance of his wealthy parents, who had retired from St. Louis to a Georgia plantation. He spoke to them of Mrs. Marks' longing for "a little country home," and they provided both financial assistance toward purchase of the land and Georgia pine from their own property as the lumber. The "cottage" that rose on the shore of the lake, still standing in 1977, has nineteen rooms on two floors, an enormous attic, and a stone-walled cellar that has become the wonder and admiration of twentieth-century masons and architects. There Mrs. Marks and the children spent first their summers and over the years increasingly larger parts of their winters as well. Originally the house had neither central heating nor electric light: there were open fireplaces in most of the rooms. The one in the living room, with a six-foot mantel, was designed by Mr. Marks, that in the dining room by his wife.

The children were not allowed to go to the local public school in Westport, New York, W. D. Marks seeing himself as a country squire superior to his neighbors in education as in wealth. The two girls were thus thrown on each other and the servants for society. They romped and invented pranks together, learned to swim, to handle a boat, and to ride. Gussie was superior at the aquatic sports, but Mabel was an excellent horsewoman like their mother. Mrs. Marks played the zither and was an accomplished pianist; Gussie started taking piano lessons at seven but in early adolescence suddenly and unaccountably "forgot" everything she had learned. (Later she regained her competence, and music was a pleasure to her throughout her life.) Mabel painted and wrote romantic stories in the style of "The Duchess"; Gussie considered herself bright but untalented. She impressed strangers and even her parents with her remarkable vocabulary, but what good was a remarkable vocabulary to a girl? Gussie was tall, lanky, and, except in sports, awkward; Mabel was small — throughout her life the older sister was almost never able to refer to her without the adjective "petite" — with enormous blue eyes which she early learned to use with telling effect.

Mother and daughters spent two years in Germany with the family of a professional associate of Mr. Marks; he did not accompany them but provided first-class staterooms for the Atlantic crossing and a school in Germany for Mabel. Gussie was suffering from rheumatic fever and not considered able to attend school; she had the same German governess she had disliked in America, and was permitted to leave her bed only for daily expeditions to a milk station and for occasional tours of art galleries or other sights of conventional tourist interest.

Back in Westport life settled into a pattern. Papa would come up from Philadelphia most weekends, arriving by sleeper in the early morning. Sometimes Mama would meet him at the station driving a matched team of handsome horses; more often, if she were not well, one of the men would take the buckboard. Papa would get another hour or two of sleep in his own small downstairs bedroom and then come into the dining room for a lavish breakfast featuring freshly caught fish from the lake. Lucy, the black cook, had been Mama's mammy in Tennessee, and maintained the traditional southern relationship to her white family; she fussed over the breakfasts for Professor Marks and supervised the children's diet and manners in the absence of their mother.

Throughout her long life Gussie remembered the morning when she had been appointed by her mother to pour her father's coffee. Mabel came in uninvited and begged some fish, a request Papa granted, overruling Lucy, who attempted to enforce Mama's ban on eating between meals. Gussie sided with Mama, Lucy, and constituted authority, but in the end she was cruelly reminded that constituted authority really lay with the absentee father. "You are stupid in the morning and conceited all the rest of the day," he said to her. "Mabel, would you like some fish?"

So things continued until Mama's health grew so bad that it was necessary for her to retire to a sanitarium. Papa carried her in his arms onto the train. Gussie went off to a Boston boarding school and then, her preparation for Wellesley being still inadequate, to Dana Hall, a spin-off from the old preparatory department of Wellesley College. Mabel engaged herself to two young men simultaneously and found occupation in extricating herself from this dilemma. Mrs. Marks died in her sanitarium; Professor Marks, despite the rumors of "other women" in his life, did not remarry.

Shortly after her twentieth birthday Gussie entered Wellesley and became Jeannette or Miss Marks. She was a strikingly handsome girl with an aureole of reddish hair and the look of a pre-Raphaelite angel. She still thought of herself, however, as a gawky adolescent, too tall and thin for beauty or even conventional prettiness.

The luxuries of the Wellesley campus, which retained the atmosphere of the gentleman's estate it had been twenty years earlier, were no novelty to her. The main building, like a Victorian castle out of the Tennysonian imagination, outdid the splendors of *The Princess*.

> *The porch that sang*
> *All round with laurel, issued in a court*
> *Compact of lucid marbles, boss'd with lengths*
> *Of classic frieze, with ample awnings gay*
> *Betwixt the pillars, and with great urns of flowers.*
> *The Muses and the Graces, group'd in threes,*
> *Enring'd a billowing fountain in the midst;*
> *And here and there on lattice edges lay*
> *Or book or lute.*

The available sports included the solitary ones in which Jeannette was already skilled: rowing, skating, "wheeling" (bicycling), walking, and such competitive ones as hockey, tennis, and golf.

It was the society of the college, however, that enriched and delighted her. Wellesley, like Jeannette herself, was just twenty years old, and had almost come of age. The daring girls who had gone to college in the seventies and eighties, despite dire warnings of the dangers to their health, their sanity, and their potential for motherhood, had become women. Many of them were teaching at Wellesley. They were brilliant, tough, competent, gay, and deeply feminine in a sense of the word she had never encountered. Here were women professors with careers as distinguished and titles as honorable as Papa's; the musicians among them did not languish in loneliness over piano and zither, but performed in public and handed their skills along to a younger generation. Here were women who established and maintained hospitable homes without the support of an absentee male or the physical presence of one. Katharine Lee Bates of the English Department and Katharine Coman of Economics maintained such a home, always open to students and made more inviting to Jeannette by the presence of a beloved collie. The two women traveled together and worked together: Miss Coman's photographs illustrated Miss Bates' *From Gretna Green to Land's End: A Literary Journey in England*. Vida Scudder, an avowed socialist with

an Oxford degree, chose to live most of the time in a settlement house in New York. Margaret Sherwood had just
published her first novel. Jeannette sought the friendship
of all of these older women, partly as obvious substitutes
for the dead mother, partly as less obvious substitutes for
the rejecting father. Among her own classmates she made
few friends; Helen Cady, from nearby Mansfield, was the
closest and the one whose friendship endured the longest.

She also sought out Mary Woolley, who taught her required freshman Bible course. She was impressed by the
new instructor's reputation for erudition — it was said she
could read and write Hebrew, Greek, and Latin — and by
her youth and vigor and "well-cut tweeds." She was also
impressed at the second meeting of the class by the fact
that Miss Woolley addressed each young lady by name without reference to her roll book.*

Miss Woolley had been teaching young girls for a decade;
she was used to their admiration and affection and responded gracefully if somewhat distantly. She took to Jeannette rather more warmly than she had to the others. Her
affection was, by her own later account, partly motherly;
she was sorry for the orphan girl and ready to share her own
happy home.

Before long she took Jeannette with her for a weekend in
the parental home in Pawtucket. Miss Marks' own account
of this weekend, written many years later, has some curious
omissions. She describes Mr. and Mrs. Woolley, "Mother
Woolley" and "the Chaplain," but says nothing about
Frank, who, at seventeen, must certainly have made his
presence felt in the household. Even more strangely she
says nothing about going to church, a duty from which few

---

* The feat is more remarkable when it is remembered that Jeannette's
section was one of ten and she herself one of 243 entering freshmen, all of
whom Miss Woolley taught and remembered. It was a skill which she
perfected over the years and used with telling effect; in all parts of the
world she was to amaze and flatter Mount Holyoke alumnae accidentally
encountered by remembering their names and something about their personal lives. She would never confess to having worked to perfect this
ability, which must have been at least in part a natural gift, but which
must have required careful attention and cultivation.

visitors at the parsonage could have been exempted, or about "the Chaplain" in his pastoral relations. She was more interested in his relations with his dog, Rags. She liked both dog and master, but with Mrs. Woolley she quickly settled into a mutual icily polite hostility. Jeannette never mentioned her without a reference to her lameness, a result of the fall when Frank was a baby and which most people found negligible.

Mrs. Woolley, on her side, was quite unable to put a name to her uneasiness about the friendship. She had long given up hope that May might marry, but the academic distinction she had earned was a substantial consolation. The mother was pleased, of course, that May's students liked her, and she could not disapprove of kindness to a motherless girl or be rude to a guest in her own house, but she did not take much trouble to conceal her distaste for Jeannette.

What thoughts May herself may have had about marriage and children of her own were never recorded, but all the depths of affection in her nature were tapped by this new friendship, which grew slowly but inexorably. She made many new friends and acquaintances at Wellesley; she was genial and popular with all of them, but tenderness, warmth, intimacy, were all reserved for Jeannette, and even with Jeannette were not openly recognized and acknowledged until several years had passed.

One striking change in Mary Woolley's life, which may or may not have been connected with this emotional awakening, was the marked burgeoning of her powers. She had been a good teacher at Wheaton, an excellent student at Brown, but at Wellesley she first showed unusual executive ability. After a single year as instructor she became associate professor of Biblical history; the next year she was a full professor engaged in reorganizing the department. She employed two men from nearby divinity schools as parttime instructors, and although she must have enjoyed this role reversal, she was able to handle it so tactfully that they did not resent her.

Jeannette's interests were quite different; throughout

their lifelong intimacy neither woman was to show much understanding of or sympathy for the other's work. As a Wellesley freshman Jeannette wanted intensely to be famous but did not really care a great deal how that end was to be achieved. She toyed with the idea of becoming a doctor, but she was on the whole more attracted to the field of authorship. Both professions were among the limited number then open to women. A college degree was not required for admission to medical school; some women took an M.D. first and an A.B. later. One young wife, at Brigham Young's behest, came from Utah in the seventies to study at the Woman's Medical College of Pennsylvania, and returned three years later, established a practice, and trained midwives in the intervals of bringing up her own large family.

The discipline of the sciences, however, never attracted Jeannette, and she made no practical moves in the direction of preparation for becoming a doctor. Her interest in medicine became eventually a subsidiary of her literary interests; she wrote on medical subjects and made close friends of several doctors, chiefly those dealing with problems in psychiatry and psychology.

As an author she could set to work at once. This was an area in which the "scribbling women" of whose competition Hawthorne complained had already established a substantial beachhead. About a third of the contributors to the *Atlantic Monthly* in 1895 were women, most of them with triple names to attest to the fact that, like Harriet Beecher Stowe, they had husbands as well as literary talent.

In Jeannette's first semester at college a recent Wellesley graduate, Abbie Carter Goodloe of the class of 1889, published *College Girls*, "an unassuming volume of Wellesley sketches," which Katharine Lee Bates reviewed somewhat acidly in the *Wellesley Magazine*. The plots were simple: a young man waiting to meet his sister and starting in the interim a mild flirtation with a pretty girl who turns out to be a professor of mathematics; a shy gauche freshman being snubbed by a socialite upperclassman she admires and later making a "good" marriage and snubbing in her turn; an elderly professor musing on what she has missed in life and envying her married sister the affection of husband and children, while the sister muses in the same way about the intellectual life forever closed to her. Professor Bates objected to such expressions as "he don't," "he's no good," "terribly swell," and the like in the mouths of the characters, even though she admitted grudgingly that Henry James was guilty of a similar "lapse in linguistic morals." She suggested also that the young ladies represented as having "New York manners and clothes," "social ease and distinction," or "servants and carriages and conservatories" would probably go to Smith rather than Wellesley. For her Wellesley was a community of women scholars, and she resented the intrusion of those without genuine scholarly interests.

Despite this professorial disapproval, however, the book did very well; it was illustrated by Charles Dana Gibson; its first edition sold out within its first season and was followed by several more beyond the turn of the century. Miss Goodloe, unlike the married three-name ladies, dropped her first one and became Carter Goodloe on several romantic novels during the next decade. Jeannette, apparently, was never tempted to sign herself Augustus Marks; a woman writer no longer needed a male pseudonym unless she actually preferred one, and Wellesley encouraged achievement in one's proper feminine person.

Early in her sophomore year Jeannette began contributing to the *Wellesley Magazine*. Her short stories were lugubrious in tone and generally concerned with death; a newsboy run over by a streetcar, an old lady living a lonely life in a boardinghouse and dying unlamented from a fall on the ice, a Negro child succumbing to a neglected illness, a shipwreck in which not only all the human beings concerned but even a kitten were drowned. The poems were generally celebrations of the beauties of nature with philosophical overtones in the manner of Bryant's *Thanatopsis*. An essay-sketch described a nightmare following upon intensive study of Goethe's *Iphigenie*. There was no suggestion of any awareness of the possibility that the nightmare resulted from the fact that Iphigenia was murdered by her father for the sake of his own success.

In the spring of her junior year Miss Marks made her first appearance in a magazine of national circulation with "Outdoor Life at Wellesley College" in *Outing* for May 1898. Miss Goodloe's "Undergraduate Life at Wellesley" appeared in *Scribner's* in the same month. She was an alumna of almost a decade and a published author, formidable competition for an undergraduate, but Jeannette's article is probably the better of the two. It shows, as nothing else she published ever did, how the life of Wellesley had set her free from her unhappy childhood. She spoke with warm appreciation of the three-hundred-acre campus where students might wander at will, and the lake on which they could row and skate, although swimming as a sport was closed to them as dangerous and "unfeminine." The annual rowing contests were judged entirely on form, not on speed, and Jeannette commented: "Till women know how to do good honest swimming as well as fancy floating, and until the ratio between fainting and endurance is changed, racing will never be and ought never to be allowed." Her own preference for solitary sports over competitive team ones is clear, but she does passing justice to golf, tennis, basketball, crew, and gymnastics, with a scornful reference to those students — chiefly freshmen — who found bloomers immodest. In winter coasting, snowshoeing, and "skeeing" were available.

The walking club had disbanded in favor of a wheeling one, but there were still students who walked five to ten miles every week by choice. The melancholy note so prominent in the stories is evident only in a comment on the graves of Emerson, Thoreau, and the Alcott sisters in Concord. Jeannette found that the peace of the Concord cemetery made death attractive, but the observation was preceded by a fifteen-mile bicycle ride and followed by a hearty meal in a tea shop and a fifteen-mile bicycle ride back to Wellesley with a group of friends. Wellesley was indeed "An Earthly Paradise" for students who cared for outdoor life, Jeannette concluded, and "since man is as rare and as hard to find as a needle in a haystack, nothing is present to revile." Abbie Goodloe in her article the same month said, "I once heard an extremely disagreeable man declare, with a deplorable use of figurative language, that, 'the country was strewn with the wrecks of Wellesley College.'"

The notion that higher education was a cause of neurosis in women was by no means dead. In the fall of her senior year Jeannette contributed another example to the statistics supporting this generalization. She suffered an attack of typhoid fever in November, for which she was treated at Massachusetts General Hospital, but the end of the acute illness found her physically and emotionally so depleted that she could not return to college. She spent a part of the winter at Thoreau House in Concord.* There Jeannette could indulge herself to the full in contemplation of the graves in the cemetery and could visit the Emerson and Alcott houses, the Old Manse, and Henry Thoreau's house in town and cabin at Walden Pond.

Helen Cady and her mother visited her in the hospital and at Concord, but Mary Woolley wrote that "the doctor" (she did not specify whether she meant her own or Jeannette's) had forbidden her to visit Jeannette.

After the months at Thoreau House Jeannette spent some time with Vida Scudder at the settlement house in New York and some with relatives in Philadelphia. The definitive quarrel with her father probably occurred at this time, for she returned to college in the fall of 1899 announcing that he refused to support the cost of any further education for her. He had suffered serious financial reverses since she entered college. In 1896 the Philadelphia Edison Company, of which he was general manager, was sold, and he set up as a private consultant to municipal governments in the matter of utility rates. He was again to be successful, but for a few years he was straitened. Whether his withdrawal

---

* The present Colonial Inn used this name for a few years around the turn of the century. Thoreau's grandfather had lived in a part of the long, rambling structure many years before, but Henry himself had no direct associations with the building.

of support was due to poverty or to hostility, Jeannette never forgave him. She was two years past twenty-one, and he may have felt it was time for her to be independent; he may have shared the still-widespread prejudice against college education for women or felt that it had been responsible for her breakdown; he may have blamed her for her failure to graduate with her class; he may have simply been unable to afford the expense of another year. Whatever the reason, she was dependent on herself and her Wellesley friends for the costs of her second senior year.

Katharine Lee Bates and Sophie Jewett rallied round, along with Mary Woolley and Vida Scudder, to help her get back on her feet. They provided tutoring, editing, and reporting jobs, along with much-needed moral support.

Mary Woolley afterward confessed that it was the separation during those months that first made her realize her emotional dependence on the affection of the younger woman. Her own career was moving steadily ahead. Under the new president, Caroline Hazard, she was a full professor in her department and also head of College Hall, a new administrative position roughly equivalent to a deanship. Gossip suggests, however, that all of this may have been a consolation prize and that she was disappointed when Miss Hazard instead of herself became the new president of Wellesley. Mrs. Irvine had first offered her resignation in the fall of 1897 and had been persuaded by the trustees to continue in office through an additional academic year up to June of 1899. During this interim a Search Committee was inaugurated, the first in Wellesley's history, as Miss Hazard was the first president not promoted from the faculty but invited from outside. During the academic years of 1897–98 and 1898–99 the question of the choice of a new president was thus one of considerable importance to the faculty and must have been hotly argued. The issues would be re-echoed in Miss Woolley's life forty years later. A male president was first proposed by Alice Freeman Palmer, whose marriage seems to have gone far toward converting her to Harvard's view of the competence of women scholars. Mrs. Durant, the widow of Wellesley's founder, promptly retorted, "If we get a man now we will never again have the place for a woman." Mrs. Palmer accepted the refusal as final and turned her attention to wealthy and influential women from outside the field of scholarship. Just as Mary Woolley's appointment to Wellesley had been approved at a reception where Mrs. Palmer had an opportunity to look her over, the presidency of Wellesley was first offered officially to Miss Hazard at a similar crowded affair and by the same influential trustee.

Miss Hazard, like Miss Woolley, was from Rhode Island and had been educated at private schools there. The important difference was that she was independently wealthy and, after Miss Shaw's School in Providence, had gone abroad for finishing. Since then she had been active in the business and philanthropic concerns of her family, had published several volumes of poetry, edited the philosophical and economic writings of her wool-manufacturing grandfather, and written a study of life in Narragansett in the eighteenth century. She held no college degree but had a wide acquaintance among prominent people in social, financial, literary, and musical circles.

Mrs. Irvine, in outlining the qualities necessary in her successor, had strongly stressed the necessity for securing additional endowment for the college; Wellesley ought to have, in her opinion, "a president who could command the confidence of the world of affairs and who could as a speaker or writer . . . secure the support of persons of substance. In order . . . to obtain funds . . . the College requires a president whose relation to the internal administration will be . . . different from that [of] a member of the faculty, and who will bring to the college new forces and new friends."

So much for the value of a college degree with honors. Mary Woolley never mentioned any disappointment she may have felt, but she applied for a leave of absence for 1900–01 to continue work toward her doctorate. The request was granted, but again, as five years earlier, a more attractive offer intervened. In December 1899, which the abortive autobiography calls the most critical month of her life, she was offered the deanship of Pembroke and the presidency of Mount Holyoke.

The choice was not altogether easy. At Pembroke she was already celebrated as the first graduate and an alumna active in fund-raising projects. There she would be close to the home to which she was still strongly attached, and in contact with men's minds, an advantage which Jeannette Marks later said always meant a great deal to her. Mount Holyoke, in central Massachusetts, was the Cinderella among Massachusetts colleges for women, still regarded by many, including some of its own alumnae, as an excellent seminary that had overreached itself in becoming a college.

Founded in 1837 by Mary Lyon, it had for fifty years held an enviable reputation for scholarship as well as a strong tradition of evangelical religion. It had trained teachers who scattered throughout the United States and missionaries who carried its name to the world at large. In spite of the evangelical tradition it had, through the years when religion and science were at war, maintained first-rate work in science equal or perhaps superior to that of the women's colleges. When in the mid-eighties it first applied for a charter as a college, both Smith and Wellesley opposed its granting on the ground that Massachusetts was already adequately supplied with colleges for women, and Professor George Herbert Palmer (Alice Freemen's husband) spoke against the proposal because, he said, Mount Holyoke lacked both the facilities and the funds needed by a college. The charter was nevertheless granted in 1888, and in the intervening twelve years much had been accomplished. Instructors from Smith, Oberlin, Wellesley, and Harvard Annex were added to the faculty, which, up to this time, had consisted largely of teachers trained in the seminary itself. Under Elizabeth Storrs Mead, the first president not so trained, academic standards had been raised and restrictive social rules eased. A great deal remained to be done, however, perhaps primarily in the area of establishing prestige to equal that of the other colleges.

Of the two opportunities the Mount Holyoke one clearly offered the greater challenge, to say nothing of the fact that a president outranked a dean. The formal offer was made by the trustees on January 4, 1900, and accepted by Miss Woolley on the fifteenth.

Wellesley reacted enthusiastically with serenades and soirees, garlands of flowers and original poetry. Miss Hazard graciously allowed her new colleague a generous amount of free time to visit Mount Holyoke and its alumnae. To have produced a president for a sister college was an important first for Wellesley.

The challenge brought, among other things, a new phase in the relationship between Mary Woolley and Jeannette Marks. Miss Woolley became aware of how painful the separation would be when Jeannette was graduated and she herself left Wellesley. She had had some experience of the pain of Jeannette's absence during her illness the previous year, but throughout that period both of them had looked forward to a resumption of relations. Now it appeared that the intimacy must come to an end.

Under this threat the two women made in March a mutual declaration of ardent and exclusive love. It seems probable that it was made in an innocence like that of the Garden of Eden. Mary Woolley used the language and imagery of the Bible, Jeannette Marks that of the English romantic poets.

Havelock Ellis' study of sexual inversion in women was published in English in 1897, its circulation confined to medical men. In it he commented on the difficulty of collecting data because of the ignorance and modesty of women. Most of the cases he cited were described as borderline: intensely emotional affection based on an often unrecognized sexuality and expressing itself in extravagant verbiage and very limited physical contact. The very existence of his work was in all probability unknown to both Miss Marks and Miss Woolley, who nevertheless fitted rather neatly into this borderline category. They exchanged tokens, a ring and a jeweled pin, with pledges of lifelong fidelity.

"If you knew what a lonely feeling I have every night when I do not see you, you would realize what the thought of our separation next year means to me. I have such a feeling of security in your love, Jeannette. I *know* that it will not change . . . I rest in your love in a way that makes me stronger and happier," Mary Woolley wrote in April, and again:

Your coming is my rest and refreshment and delight after my hours of work or "Sassiety" . . . Oh! my dear little girl, do you not know, can you not understand, that you do just as much for me as I can possibly do for you? I want to be what you think that I am, Jeannette — the fact that I love you makes me wish to be more in the world . . . you are an inspiration to me, dear, as well as my greatest comfort . . . Does it seem possible that it is only a few short weeks since we have felt that we could say all that we feel without restraint or constraint? Two such proud ladies, too, each one afraid that she felt more than the other and determined to keep her own self respect! . . . I am so glad that it is not a sudden "possessing," Jeannette, that for five years it has been coming surely to pass and that for almost three years I have realized that you were very dear to me, never as dear, however, as you are today.

And in July, before her birthday:

You know that you have given me this great birthday gift, one which will make this birthday different from any that I have ever spent. I shall thank God for it tomorrow as the great gift which this year has brought to me, my Treasure . . . I wonder whether it often falls to the lot of mortals to love as we do. My own Love, should we not be very thankful for this supreme gift which makes life so full and rich and deep and tender?

What she is expressing here is in one sense a commonplace of the experience of lovers everywhere, but in another she may be read as revealing an ignorance and naïveté almost impossible for the twentieth century to comprehend.

Meanwhile, in her public life, she was cultivating friendships and acquaintances that would be important in establishing the prestige of Mount Holyoke. In May she visited the college and was fêted at a reception attended by President and Mrs. Seelye of Smith and President Hazard of Wellesley, the heads of the two colleges which had opposed the admission of Mount Holyoke to their sisterhood. Further entertainment of the day included an organ recital by William Hammond, the new professor of music, a lecture on Goethe by Professor Thomas of Columbia University, and in the evening a serenade by students of the college. Miss Woolley's ability to endure and appear to enjoy such grueling days was to be an asset in her work for years to come. She presented Mrs. Mead with a huge bouquet of red roses as an expression of appreciation for that lady's willingness to serve for an additional six months so that her successor might start on January 1, 1901.

The reason she assigned for this delay was that she wanted time to visit and observe the British universities, but actually she seems to have had an almost superstitious feeling about the twentieth century as the coming of age of women. There was a fairly lively debate in the newspapers as to whether the new century actually began on January 1, 1900, or January 1, 1901, but since it was already too late to start on the earlier date, she opted for the later one. A beginning in the middle of the academic year was not altogether convenient for the college or for Mrs. Mead, who had already made personal plans, but both agreed.

Mary Woolley spent the summer at home in Pawtucket, writing daily to Jeannette in Philadelphia in addition to tackling a heavy load of official correspondence and the preparation of several magazine articles. Jeannette was considering graduate work at Wellesley or Radcliffe and trying halfheartedly for a teaching position in a preparatory school. She was hardly eligible for one at Mount Holyoke, with the ink barely dry on her A.B., but Miss Woolley found herself thinking more and more frequently of how it might be managed.

. . . if only the separation need not come! It will be so hard this coming year — first the ocean between me and all that I love, and then the new work among strangers! If only

you *were to be with me, dearest, if only!* ... *Besides, we cannot afford to be separated! We should be bankrupt in the stationery and postage line!*

And again:

I cannot grow reconciled to the thought of being away from you. Even a day or two is hard ... *Dearest, my dearest, it is hard not to have your good night kiss* ... *God in His Providence has given me this love when I most need it, when I am about to take up crushing responsibilities* ... *Do you realize what it means to have you, the heart of my life, to talk with you as I would with my own soul, to have nothing hid, to feel that we are one!* ... *I have spent the morning in writing letters about the "Literature Lady."*

The Department of English Literature at Mount Holyoke was to be headed that fall by Ada Brann, Wellesley '83, who would run it single-handedly with the assistance of Clara Stevens of the English Department in teaching one course. This splitting of one department into two closely related ones was practiced at Wellesley, where Katharine Lee Bates headed one and Margaret Stratton, an Oberlin graduate, the other.

"*The Dial* has already given judgement in favor of dividing English as a university subject into the science of linguistics and the art of literature," Professor Bates wrote in that magazine in 1894. With such specialists as George Pierce Baker to teach argumentation in the English Department, and Vida Scudder, Margaret Sherwood, and others, each with her own specialty in English Literature, the division perhaps made sense; at Mount Holyoke, with one person in English Literature and two in English, it made much less, and, over the years, would cause a good deal of difficulty. In time people came to believe that Miss Woolley had created the English Literature Department for Miss Marks, as she certainly perpetuated it for her. In 1900, however, the purpose of maintaining the two departments was probably to make the college's course offerings appear somewhat more impressive. Jeannette was not officially appointed to the department until after Miss Woolley took office on January 1, 1901, but the correspondence during the summer indicates that the spadework was done then.

In September Jeannette embarked on graduate work in English literature at Wellesley and Mary Woolley set sail for England with her cousin Helen Ferris. They visited Somerville, Lady Margaret and St. Hugh's, Newnham and Girton, Bedford and Royal Holloway. But neither the autobiography nor the letters indicate any very serious study of the British university system of education for women. Rather, the expedition carried the name of Mount Holyoke to these seats of learning where ten years earlier Mary Woolley had humbly aspired to be a student and now was an honored guest. The daily letters to Jeannette had little to say about the work of the journey; they were travelogues or repetitious expressions of affection.

The months of separation hardened Mary Woolley's determination to end it permanently. She returned in November on the *Kaiser Wilhelm*. It was a rough crossing, and on the twenty-second they ran aground in New York Harbor. Nevertheless May made it home for Thanksgiving in Pawtucket, where Jeannette joined her. The graduate work at Wellesley was desultory; Jeannette was more interested in her career as a writer. She was willing to come to Mount Holyoke if a place could be made for her that would allow her to continue her seminar in English drama with Katharine Lee Bates and her study of Browning with Vida Scudder, but she was not enthusiastic about the prospect.

May stayed in Pawtucket from Thanksgiving through Christmas, eschewing the opportunity to work with Mrs. Mead through the transition period. That lady tactfully withdrew from South Hadley at the beginning of the Christmas holidays, leaving time for the housekeeper to prepare the presidential suite in Brigham Hall for its new occupant. In scrupulous adherence to her plan for entering with the new century, Mary Woolley left Pawtucket by train on the morning of December 31, 1900. She left a note of farewell for Jeannette on the chiffonier in their bedroom in

Pawtucket, and sent another that same evening from her rooms in South Hadley.

My own Darling, the year has brought me no gift as great as your love.

Since the year also brought her appointment to the presidency of Mount Holyoke she would seem here, on the threshold of the century, to be stating her priorities. Through the rest of her life she remained faithful to that commitment.

IV

Mount Holyoke

A HUNDRED MILES due west of Boston, Mount Holyoke lies in the Connecticut Valley, separated by a notch in the Holyoke range from Amherst to the north and by the Connecticut River from Smith to the northwest. Excellent train service in 1900 made it readily accessible from eastern Massachusetts or Rhode Island. The traveler left the main line at Springfield, journeyed north by a branch to Holyoke, and took the trolley car for the last four miles from there to South Hadley. As a rather special traveler, Miss Woolley was met in Springfield. A. Lyman Williston, a trustee and member of a family important in the life of the college for three generations, accompanied by two members of the faculty, escorted her from Springfield to Holyoke, where they were joined by two more faculty members.

These five took her to the door of Mary Brigham Hall, her home for the next nine years.

The old all-purpose seminary building had burned to the ground four years earlier, and the college was now expanding with dormitories — "cottages," as they were then called — classroom, laboratory, library, museum, and service buildings throughout its hundred acres. Mary Brigham Hall, the first of the cottages, stood just south of the new central building, Mary Lyon Hall, which contained offices and the chapel. Brigham, named for the first president of the college, had been designed with a presidential suite and rooms for thirty seniors. It was only a few steps away from the presidential office in Mary Lyon.

On the broad steps of the front porch that ran the length of the building the new president and her escort were received by the housekeeper and Professor Louise Cowles of the Geology Department, who had served a brief term as acting president after the sudden death of Miss Brigham. Inside the building Miss Woolley found her first-floor suite prepared for her welcome, with a fire burning on the hearth and white roses, violets, a fern, and a blooming primrose decorating the sitting room. There was also a gift from Professor Henrietta Hooker, a basket with two new-laid eggs and an accompanying note:

Some nineteenth century eggs for a twentieth century breakfast.

After the welcoming committee left her alone there, she discovered in the desk a pile of stationery headed "Mount Holyoke College President's Office, South Hadley, Mass." Her last act in the old century was to use it to write Jeannette.

Eating her nineteenth-century eggs on the first morning of the twentieth century, Mary Woolley looked forward to a hundred years of progress for women as dazzlingly white and unbroken as the new-fallen snow that blanketed South Hadley. Higher education had opened all the doors that had been closed against them for centuries; there was nothing now to which a woman might not aspire. Accomplishment would require hard and dedicated work of her, just as it would of her brother, but sex would not be a factor in her achievement. Mary Woolley's own career over the last decade would have been quite incredible from the vantage point of January 1, 1891. Then she had been an old-maid schoolteacher, respectably and safely settled but an embarrassment to her family and condemned to a lifetime of dull and repetitious work preparing young girls for what she was never herself to enjoy. Today she was a college president, rather more than the professional peer of her father and brother, the friend and equal of male scholars and executives. The women over whom she would preside had also made their mark in a male society: Miss Hooker, donor of the eggs, had worked with botanist Leopold Kny in Germany; Cornelia Clapp had carried on biological research with the scientists of Woods Hole, and already there were many others known beyond the confines of the seminary-turned-college. There would be more; an important part of her own work would be to find and attract them.

The love that the last year of the old century had brought her was totally unlike what she had been taught to expect love could be, but in her own estimation it outweighed everything else she had gained in that crucial year. She expressed it in the Biblical terms she knew best. David had said of Jonathan, "Thy love to me was wonderful, passing the love of women," and she could say to Jeannette, "Thy love to me is wonderful, passing the love of men." It was a love that filled her whole being; it dwarfed the importance of her work at the same time that it stimulated her to meet its demands.

But my work is one *thing. I am interested in it; I intend to put myself into it, but it is not* myself. *You are that —*
my very heart — my Love.

On the other hand it made her almost helplessly dependent on Jeannette's physical presence; the months abroad had brought that fact home to her. As a college president she had it easily within her power to offer an instructorship; the difficulty was that Jeannette was not at all sure she wanted to accept one. She considered Mount Holyoke an anemic seminary that had overreached itself, and much preferred the ambiance of Boston with all its cultural opportunities to that of Springfield. The inducements that could bring her were affection and financial need, and on that New Year's morning Mary Woolley was hopeful, but by no means certain, as to what the decision would be. She did not bring out her new guest book for her callers in the afternoon; she wanted Jeannette Marks' to be the first name in it.

Most, but not all, of her callers that New Year's Day were women. There were four men on the Mount Holyoke faculty out of a total staff of sixty-six. The board of trustees, on the other hand, was almost entirely male, although it also included Mrs. Williston and three alumnae trustees. Mary Lyon had envisioned an institution run for and by women, but she had recognized that men controlled the power and the money necessary for its establishment. Byron Smith, an elderly gentleman with a gift of two red apples for teacher, could remember her, dead now for more than fifty years, as could a few of the women. Mary Woolley knew that one of her first tasks would be to retire older teachers and replace them with able and aggressive young scholars. Ruthlessness was one of the qualities required in her work. She did not enjoy it, but she could exercise it when necessary.

In the evening she telephoned Pawtucket and spoke to her mother and Jeannette. A long-distance telephone call was an item worthy of entry in her mother's diary as one of the wonders of the new century.

May went to Holyoke yesterday. May telephoned this evening from Holyoke such a pleasure.

New Year's Day fell on a Tuesday in 1901; on Wednesday the students returned from their Christmas holiday, and on Thursday she addressed them assembled in chapel for the first time. She wore her academic robes with appropriate dignity, and above them her young face glowed with a radiant serenity. She read from the Scriptures and spoke briefly from the text "We are laborers together with God." Her voice was warm, strong, and flexible, her speech without marked regional accent. To listen to her reading Scripture was an aesthetic as well as religious experience, and her speech, simple, friendly, and unpretentious, won the hearts of the girls. Afterward they scattered to classroom, library, and laboratory, and she went back to her new office, where she was served by a secretary with a typewriter.

The longed-for note from Jeannette accepting the appointment as instructor in the Department of English Literature did not arrive until the end of the second week of January; on Monday the fourteenth the new secretary typed a letter in purple ink, which was sent unsigned and with the spelling of Jeannette's name uncorrected.

Miss Jannette A. Marks, Boston, Mass. My dear Miss Marks — Your note of January the 11th accepting the position of instructor in the department of Literature for the coming semester I was very glad to receive . . . I should be glad to have you spend any night this week except Thursday at the college or come on Saturday and stay over Sunday. Believe me, Very sincerely yours, Mary Emma Woolley, dictated.

The naïve duplicity of this note set the pattern for the opposition between Miss Woolley's formal and her personal relationship with Miss Marks, which would grow more complex over the years. On this occasion Jeannette did not wait to receive the invitation but came to the college on the heels of her own note; her name on the first line of the guest book is dated January 15, 1901. She was assigned a room on the fourth floor of Brigham Hall, but she did not immediately settle in, returning instead to the Cadys' in Mansfield, where later that month she received a letter from Margaret Sherwood of the Wellesley Literature Department sympathizing with her about her "long hours."

Her schedule was indeed demanding; she was expected to teach a survey course in the history of English literature, one in American literature, one on the eighteenth century, and special courses on the works of Chaucer, Spenser, and Milton.

May wrote from beside the fire in her sitting room, noting that the trustees had appropriated $2500 for the library for books and periodicals and that the English Literature Department had not been ordering books. She added the information that the Springfield Public Library allowed books to be kept out for a month. All of this was evidently intended to make Mount Holyoke seem more attractive to Jeannette. Katharine Lee Bates was rather more hortatory than sympathetic:

Make the best of everything and be cheery. After all, you have a rare and noble opportunity. My love to that brand-new president.

It may indeed have been "a rare and noble opportunity," but Jeannette found herself unable to "make the best of everything and be cheery." Her students seemed to her ill prepared. According to the official college entrance requirements, they should have read *The Merchant of Venice* and *Macbeth*, four poems by Milton, a few books of Pope's *Iliad*, *Sir Roger de Coverley*, *The Vicar of Wakefield*, Macaulay on Milton and Addison, *The Ancient Mariner*, *Ivanhoe*, *Silas Marner*, and Tennyson's *The Princess* in their preparatory schools, but many of them by the time they were sophomores in college had forgotten most of what they had ever known about this curiously assorted list. Not all of the courses Jeannette was expected to teach were offered every year, but her load was sufficiently heavy to daunt the stoutest spirit. Nevertheless, she worked on plans for a course in nineteenth-century poetry and encouraged the presentation of obscure pre-Shakespearean and Elizabethan plays in addition to journalistic work designed to establish her career as a writer.

At the close of every evening Mary Woolley walked up three flights of stairs "to kiss Jeannette good night." The ritual did not pass without notice; some of those who remarked it found it embarrassing, some merely amusing, but it was generally held against Miss Marks rather than Miss Woolley. It would have been easy, of course, for Jeannette to come down rather than for May to go up for their final meeting of the day and would have caused less comment. The ritual as actually performed suggested something of a mother's concern for her child, and perhaps from the other side that Jeannette was enjoying her power over the president of the college. It furnished material for the only unfavorable criticism of Miss Woolley that developed during that initial semester.

In all other areas Mary Woolley was demonstrating a new (if not unsuspected) talent for what could only be called showmanship. She was an effective public speaker, and accepted all the invitations that came her way. Her speeches were not brilliant, and their very number forced her to be more or less repetitive, but they were always sound, intelligent, and carefully structured. Her platform presence was remarkable, and to her own ability as a speaker she added an unequaled talent for giving at least the appearance of thoughtful and absorbed attention to what the other speakers were saying, even the dullest of them. She must sometimes have been thinking of laundry lists or Jeannette or an impending academic appointment, but if so her manner never offered a clue. To Mount Holyoke's established tradition of austerity and hard work she added something of the gracious living tradition she had encountered at Wellesley. She empowered Professor Hammond to establish a robed choir that became one of Mount Holyoke's hallmarks. Jeannette Marks published an article about it in the *Congregationalist and Christian World,* and pictures of it appeared in connection with most mentions of the college in the public press, along with pictures of Miss Woolley herself, a charming embodiment of gracious womanhood.

Her formal inauguration into office was postponed until May, when South Hadley could be counted on to blossom with all the beauties of a New England springtime. Against this background was presented a carefully prepared pageant of academic dignity.

On May 15 there gathered not only former principals and teachers, alumnae, family, and personal friends, but academic dignitaries from New England and beyond. Colleges represented included Pembroke, Princeton, Williams, Tufts, Radcliffe, Bryn Mawr, Hartford Theological Seminary, the French-American College, Colby, Western, Wesleyan, Lake

Erie, the University of Chicago, Boston University, Barnard, Smith, Yale, Harvard, and Dartmouth. President Hazard of Wellesley, Dr. Harris of Amherst, President Taylor of Vassar, President Faunce of Brown, the Mount Holyoke trustees, and others mingled with Mrs. Fanny Augur, who had taught May Woolley how to spell "bowl" at age five, Father and Mother Woolley with Frank, now a conscious "enfant terrible" in his twenties, reporters from the *Congregationalist and Christian World* and other papers, and the students.

The ninety-member choir wore white surplices over black skirts; the marshals were in black with blue wands; the underclasses had pure white dresses with ribbon streamers in their class colors. The seniors, like the visiting dignitaries, wore academic robes, all except President Taylor of Vassar, who had evidently not been forewarned.

The apple trees were in bloom, and grass, trees, and shrubbery were showing the fresh young green of spring. Miss Woolley led the academic procession with Judson Smith, president of the board of trustees. If she had not been a pretty girl, she was now a handsome woman at the peak of her bloom, erect, dignified, gracious, glowing in her academic robes. The processional hymn was "Ancient of Days," and Miss Woolley's father, far back in the line of march, would offer the benediction.

When some months since this office fell vacant, the trustees made wide inquiry and diligent search for a woman qualified by natural gifts and generous culture and academic experience to assume its duties. A kindly Providence led us with singular unanimity and strength of conviction to select you, Miss Woolley, for this great service.

Thus spoke Judson Smith for the trustees. Miss Woolley replied with dignity and modesty.

It is with deep feeling that I stand here today and receive the insignia of the office to which you have called me. I

*can almost hear a voice saying, "The place whereon thou
standest is holy ground."*

She continued with a tribute to Mount Holyoke's past, "the
present with its unlimited opportunities for education, as
accessible to women as to men," and a projection of its
future, although, she said: "we look down the present century without daring to predict what it may bring forth."
Nevertheless, she predicted that women might now look
forward to and should prepare for careers in teaching, social
work, invention, scholarship, and the home. Teaching was
already a traditional career for women; she stressed its dignity, its importance, and the variety of fields and ap-
proaches. In social work, she saw woman ameliorating if
not eliminating the evils of poverty, intemperance, and social injustice. Under the term "invention" she included
science, in which women up to that time had done very
limited work; she briefly pointed out the possibilities and
continued with a consideration of pure science as
scholarship.

*Nor is she [woman] incapable of the broad generalizations
and wide outlook demanded of the scholar. She is interested in mathematics and philosophy, as well as in literature and art, and the time seems not far distant when it
will be conceded that the ability to master certain lines of
thought is a question of the individual and not of sex.*

Finally there was woman in the home; Miss Woolley was
clearly anxious to allay fears that a college education would
unfit her for this important occupation.

*It is not often asked whether college fits a man for home
or not, it is taken for granted that the education which
trains and develops his powers makes him better fitted for
all relations of life. Is it not equally true of the "education"
of women, that education in the real sense prepares them
to be better mothers and daughters and sisters and wives?
... the college ... must give the power of grasping the*

situation, of being equal to the emergency, of controlling circumstances rather than being controlled by them . . . I have emphasized the value of the logical, the disciplinary, in college training, that which may not be so peculiarly the heritage of woman as of the man . . . There should be equal emphasis upon the importance of cultivating characteristics which belong more distinctly in the feminine realm. Is there not danger of minimizing the value of "intuitions," of quick perceptions . . . ? The sacrifice of gracious womanhood is too high a price to pay for knowledge . . .

Here was a middle-of-the-road speech worthy of a college president; education was to open all the doors previously closed to women, but husbands, fathers, and suitors must not worry lest all this make women less feminine. The other college presidents represented expressed rather conflicting views on this point. President Taylor of Vassar spoke of the need for Mount Holyoke's traditional missionary spirit, an area which Miss Woolley's speech had perhaps rather conspicuously neglected. President Harris of Amherst in a somewhat facetious tone advocated the graces and accomplishments for women, placing chief emphasis on literature, music, and modern languages. President Faunce of Brown disagreed, but congratulated Mount Holyoke for developing an ideal that was frankly feminine.

The formal ceremonies of the inauguration were followed by a reception in the gymnasium, decorated for the occasion with apple blossoms and blue and white draperies. Mrs. Woolley wrote in her diary that night, "May's inauguration day. Bright and beautiful in every way."

Legend has it that Jeannette Marks absented herself from this occasion, spending the day in the Springfield library without telling anyone where she was going and thus making anxiety about her the one fly in Mary Woolley's ointment. The same legend reports that Mrs. Woolley said to Ada Snell, the new young instructor in the English Department, "I know very well that May can hold this job down and hold it down very well. The only one I fear is Jeannette."

*

It seems highly unlikely that Mrs. Woolley would have spoken in these terms to a comparative stranger on this important occasion, and the language of the remark has clearly been influenced by time and repetition, but there is doubtless some basis of truth in it. Miss Snell, like Miss Marks, was to have a long and influential career at Mount Holyoke, one that brought the two many times into conflict, sometimes open, sometimes politely concealed. While Mrs. Woolley was not likely to have put her feelings into words, her manner on this and other visits to the college must have made her attitude toward Jeannette sufficiently clear to anyone interested, as many of the members of the faculty were beginning to be, in the curious relationship.

Whether she heard the speech delivered or not, Jeannette certainly read it, quite possibly in manuscript. It may even have had something to do with her choosing to absent herself. The phrase "the sacrifice of gracious womanhood" particularly irritated her, and over the ensuing years she quoted it frequently, often out of context. Gracious womanhood did not seem to her an ideal at all comparable in importance to the pursuit of knowledge.

The twelve years' difference in their ages may have accounted in part for the fact that Miss Marks found higher education for women much less of a privilege than Miss Woolley did. Born in the year in which Wellesley College was founded, by the time Jeannette came of age she saw it as something that had always existed. Her interest in the cause of women looked forward to their being allowed to vote, a possibility Miss Woolley regarded with extreme caution. For her what mattered was to consolidate the gains made for the cause of women over the last quarter century and specifically to bring Mount Holyoke into the forefront of women's colleges. This project required care not to arouse the prejudices of the wealthy and powerful.

The official May Day, which was to become a college tradition, followed the inauguration, and on the weekend May and Jeannette went to Pawtucket together in all amity. By June, however, they were quarreling, and Jeannette went off to her sister's in New Jersey, where Miss Woolley's abject apologies followed her. Jeannette was not at all sure that she wanted to return to Mount Holyoke for another year. They were thus back in the situation of the preceding summer, except that Miss Woolley and some of her friends had come to realize that her contentment and peace of mind depended to an enormous extent on Jeannette's presence.

Jeannette herself was eager to get on with her career as a writer. She was attempting children's stories as well as journalism, and sold one called "The Pussy Story" to the *Congregationalist and Christian World* during the summer. She also consulted Katharine Lee Bates as to the possibility of publishing a volume of short stories. Miss Bates thought it unlikely that she would be able to find a publisher, and urged her to return to Mount Holyoke.

No one could really make Miss Woolley behave as she ought, but you may sometimes be able to burn her telegrams.

Vida Scudder urged her to return and to persuade Miss Woolley to introduce settlement work at Mount Holyoke. These old friends clearly recognized the power of Jeannette's influence and just as clearly accepted it as natural and perhaps even desirable.

She was present almost as a member of the family at the family celebration of May's thirty-eighth birthday in July. Erving and his wife were there, along with Frank and his fiancée; Jeannette's status, not clearly defined, was nevertheless accepted.

Nothing came of the volume of short stories, but a Pawtucket printer issued a pamphlet: *A Brief Outline of Books and Topics for the Study of American Literature* with Jeannette Marks' name prominently displayed as the author and a dedication "to M.E.W. . . ." The cost of printing may well have represented Miss Woolley's atonement for the quarrel and a further inducement to Jeannette to continue teaching; writing could develop as a side issue until there was a sufficient body of work to make it a viable career. In the event Jeannette returned for the 1901-02 year, but with a schedule that enabled her to continue work toward her M.A. at Wellesley as well as her writing.

By December she had produced two articles growing out of the Mount Holyoke situation, "Domestic Work in Women's Colleges" and "Society Life in Women's Colleges." These two subjects were to be of considerable concern to Miss Woolley for a decade; it was perhaps characteristic of Miss Marks that she plunged into them at its beginning. Wellesley had abolished domestic work on the part of students after Jeannette's freshman year, and the other women's colleges had never used it. Domestic work had been one of Mary Lyon's cherished projects from the very beginning of the seminary, although she was always careful to explain that its purpose was not to instruct young ladies in the domestic arts but to save money. It was also partly an answer to the critics who maintained that higher education would unfit a woman for the normal duties of her life. Mary Lyon was particularly careful to refer to her girls as young ladies in this context. Most of them would return from school to homes where there were servants but where the lady of the house had responsibilities of her own in supplementing as well as directing their work. Herself desperately poor throughout most of her life, Mary Lyon always insisted on the dignity of labor. Nevertheless, uneducated laboring women were hired for the heavier work. Emily Dickinson reported with pleasure and relief in 1847 that her share consisted of carrying the knives from two tiers of tables to the kitchen after breakfast and lunch, and washing and wiping the same number of knives in the evening, considerably less than she would have been expected to do at home.

The real problems, however, were those of the role of woman in society and of the prestige of the college. M. Carey Thomas of Bryn Mawr is reported to have begged the students not to make their own beds when a strike of the maids left them unattended. There were only four precious years free from household tasks in which the girls might cultivate their intellects, she pointed out, and they could not afford to waste a moment on mundane tasks. If Mount Holyoke were to assert social equality with Wellesley and intellectual parity with Bryn Mawr it would no doubt have to give up domestic work. But not only did domestic work keep its fees lower than those of the other colleges for women, the students also clung to the tradition with what appeared to be real affection.

"Society life" referred to the Greek-letter secret societies, which had existed at Mount Holyoke ever since it became a college. Most administrators in the women's colleges objected to such societies on the grounds that they were snobbish and divisive, that they intimidated and discouraged the girls who were not invited to join and demanded undue time and effort from those who were.

Miss Marks' outspoken views on these subjects did not enhance her popularity in the college, already undermined by her open preference for Wellesley and her position of favoritism with the president. Miss Woolley's own popularity was solidly established and growing. Her association with the students in the dormitory was close and friendly. She presided at a table in the dining room as she had done at Wheaton and at Wellesley, and found many occasions for informal socializing with the students.

There is a story dating from these years that she once interrupted an after-lights-out party of students by knocking on the door of the hostess, who called out:

"Who's there?"
"It's me — Miss Woolley."
"Oh, no it isn't," the quick-witted girl is supposed to have replied. "If it were Miss Woolley she'd say 'It is I.'"

By the time the girl got to the door there was no one in the hall.

That is the end of the story as it is told, but presumably the illicit party broke up quickly and quietly thereafter and no disciplinary action was necessary. Perhaps for those who didn't know Miss Woolley a necessary addendum to the story is that it would be impossible to fail to recognize her voice.

It is also in these years that the crocheted-slipper joke originated. Year after year gullible freshmen were told that Miss Woolley wore crocheted slippers to chapel. When by judicious choice of seats and craning of necks they discovered that she actually wore conventional black shoes appropriate to her academic robes, and reported back triumphantly, the upperclassmen would say: "Sure. Crow-shade slippers."

Her popularity with her increasing faculty was firmly grounded in their respect for her ability and dedication to her work. Gently and tactfully but very firmly, she persuaded the older members of the teaching staff who lacked graduate degrees to resign or retire; the younger ones she sent out to complete their preparation at the best graduate schools in the country and abroad. Her new appointments included Elizabeth Laird, Alma Hussey, Nellie Neilson, Dorothy Foster, Ellen Ellis; and Bertha Putnam from Bryn Mawr; Helen Bradford Thompson, Amy Hewes, and Alma Stokey from the University of Chicago; Mignon Talbot from Yale; and Ann Morgan from Cornell, among many others. All of those named except Miss Thompson remained for a lifetime and made distinguished careers at Mount Holyoke. In looking back years later over their memories of Miss Woolley they spoke of her fairness, her careful attention, her willingness to delegate authority, her dignity, her graciousness, her respect for the learning and intelligence of others.

Outside the college also she was making herself known. From the first she was a joiner, and for some years listed her affiliations annually in one of the college publications. By the time the list grew too long for convenient reprinting, styles in this matter had changed, but the organizational affiliations of her early years show a judicious concern for the reputation of the college. She was a trustee of Pembroke, a member of Phi Beta Kappa, the Rhode Island Society for the Collegiate Education of Women, the American Board of Commissioners for Foreign Missions, the College

Entrance Examination Board, the American Association for Maintaining a Woman's Table at Naples, the American Institute of Social Service, the Association of Collegiate Alumnae (later to become the American Association of University Women) and its Council for Accrediting Women in Foreign Universities, the Religious Education Association, the American Academy of Political and Social Sciences, the American Social Science Association, the Daughters of the American Revolution, the Board of Electors of the Hall of Fame, the Hellenic Travellers' Club, the Lyceum Club of London, the New England Association of College and Preparatory Schools, and the Young Women's Christian Association, before she joined the American Woman Suffrage Association in 1906.

She represented Mount Holyoke at the inaugurations of Nicholas Murray Butler at Columbia, Woodrow Wilson at Princeton, and President Edmund J. James at Northwestern, and she spoke at clubs in Providence and Pawtucket, at Tufts College, at the Chicago Mount Holyoke Alumnae Association, at the two-hundred-fiftieth anniversary of the First Congregational Church of Norwalk, at the Woman's Law Class in New York, and in numerous other places. In those early years the college was proud to have her in so much demand, and there was no criticism of the necessary absences from the campus, where, in any case, she was keeping things under excellent control.

As a not unimportant side issue, the trips frequently resulted in securing money for the college. Helen Miller Gould, who entertained Miss Woolley when she spoke for the Woman's Law Class, eventually gave $40,000 to endow a Chair of Biblical History. Her instructions for their meeting in New York give a delightful glimpse of a long-gone age. The visitor was to be met at Grand Central Station by a Miss Detwiler, and taken to 579 Fifth Avenue in "my automobile," an electric coupe, which would be waiting at the Vanderbilt Avenue entrance to the depot and presumably in no danger of getting a parking ticket. A year later, however, Miss Gould was writing the college to protest that the man engaged with the income from her gift was destructive in his criticism and swept away faith without putting anything in its place. She had intended, she said, that the chosen instructor should teach what the Bible said rather than going into higher criticism. She suggested that a replacement might be found through the Bible Teacher Training School in New York. Miss Woolley worked hard over her reply to that one. She first expressed her regret that Miss Gould should have been troubled about the department which owed so much to her and then very politely and deferentially refused to make any change in her arrangements for staffing it. Possibly as a result of this criticism, she herself taught a senior Bible class on, Difficulties Arising in Bible Study, for a short time in 1902, the only classroom teaching she did during her career at Mount Holyoke.

Two magazine articles during the summer of 1902 discussed Miss Woolley along with other female college presidents as samples of a new breed. An anonymous author in *Cosmopolitan* in May wrote:

. . . the getting of money has come to be one of the standards of his [sic] worth . . . The question of the health of women must surely be regarded as settled in view of the test of the past three decades . . . In considering women for professorships and college presidencies, however, the plea of maternity will undoubtedly be argued in their disfavor. As none but unmarried women has ever served or would probably ever care to serve these causes, the argument is irrelevant . . . Nor is Miss Woolley's administration at Mount Holyoke in any way impaired by threatened matrimony. Indeed Mt. Holyoke has about it an air of thrift and a spirit of unity which say much for the executive ability of women.

Shades of Tennyson's lactiferous doctor of philosophy haunt this commentary, but if Miss Woolley had ever worried about lack of sex appeal she did so no longer.

In August Mary A. Jordan commented in *Outlook*:

The woman head of a woman's college has first of all to take herself seriously . . . Frequent public appearance is

*coming to be more and more expected . . . At the same
time hardly less is expected of them in general accessibility
. . . She must acquire the habits of a devoted, interested,
competent, far-sighted woman of business . . . must manage in some way or other to maintain a sort of alter ego for
the purpose.*

Miss Woolley's alter ego was functioning splendidly, re-
freshed by the daily communion of her real ego with Jeannette. When the evening meeting on the top floor of
Brigham was not possible there were letters, and on her
return from a trip she would sometimes arrange for Jeannette to take a room in a Springfield hotel, where they could
be together quietly for a night before her return to the
demands of her public life.

Jeannette, however, was still not contented at Mount Holyoke. She was beginning to have some small success as a
writer, with children's stories appearing in such publications as the *Churchman, Young People,* and the *Youth's
Companion,* articles in *Pathfinder, Travel Magazine,* and
Metropolitan, and she was continuing a determined assault
on more important markets such as the *Atlantic Monthly.*
She was still, however, far from earning enough to get along
without Mount Holyoke's $750 annually plus board and
room. The relationship that satisfied all of Mary Woolley's
emotional needs was not enough for her; she did not like
dormitory life and begged that they might share a home.
Most troubling of all, Katharine Lee Bates wrote that her
graduate work at Wellesley was not going well; it was in-
accurate and careless. This letter went to Mary Woolley at
her parents' Pawtucket address; Miss Bates evidently did
not feel certain of privacy at the college.

Here was a really serious problem. Jeannette could not
possibly maintain her present status at Mount Holyoke,
willing or not, unless she could show at least an M.A. to
justify it. The solution Mary Woolley hit upon was to give
her a semester's leave of absence to work at Wellesley; her
place in the department would be held for her, and she
would return to it for the spring semester of 1903.

The English Literature Department was presenting more staffing problems than any other in the college. In 1903 Ada Brann resigned, her reason adequately and appropriately explained by the change of her name to Ada Brann Darling. Martha Pike Conant, Wellesley A.B. and A.M., came to take her place, but not until the second semester of 1903–04. In the interim Bertha Kedzie Young had been added to the department. A niece of Professor Mary Vance Young, chairman of the Romance Languages Department, she held an A.B. from Vassar, had taught at Wheaton, and had spent the academic year 1901–02 studying at Oxford. She thus brought to the department a needed distinction and was in the line of the other new appointments Miss Woolley was making. Friction with Jeannette Marks, however, developed almost immediately. Miss Woolley personally visited the registrar's office to arrange Jeannette's schedule so that she could spend a Thursday-to-Monday weekend regularly at Wellesley in the semester following her return from her leave, but this could be managed only by dividing with Miss Young the nineteenth-century poetry course, which both wanted to teach. The first problem Miss Conant faced, even before entering on her duties at the college, was the assignment of this course. She visited the college in the spring of 1903, when Jeannette was finishing the work for her M.A., was entertained by her, and assigned her the course. To complete Miss Young's chagrin, Miss Marks was awarded the coveted degree in June and named to serve as acting chairman of the department for the fall semester preceding Miss Conant's arrival in January 1904. (Miss Conant stayed for only two and a half years, resigning in 1906 to go to the Woman's College in Baltimore and eventually back to Wellesley at a lower rank than she had held at Mount Holyoke. Miss Young stayed on until the end of the decade.)

Some further inducements were offered to make life at the college even more attractive to Jeannette. The shared home for which she had been begging was an impossibility, but in the fall of 1903 Jeannette moved from the top floor of Brigham to an apartment of her own in Alvord House, one of the big old frame houses that the college was acquiring from village residents. Miss Woolley bought most of the furniture for it and promised that this would be the nucleus of a home they might someday share.

A Brief Historical Outline of English Literature from the Origins to the Close of the 18th Century was issued in the summer of 1902 by the same Pawtucket printer who had prepared the American literature one a year earlier. This time the dedication was to M.E.W. and H.M.C. (Helen Cady). In the summer of 1903 there was a Second Edition Newly Revised and Corrected. And that fall Miss Marks, with the ink scarcely dry on her M.A., was acting head of the department pending Professor Conant's arrival for the second semester. She had the apartment, the course she wanted, authority over her rival, and her name as author on two slim textbooks. Surely now she could be happy. It was to be many years before Mary Woolley could understand, if she ever did, that no gift in her power to bestow could make Jeannette happy. At this point in their lives her favoritism predictably boomeranged. Jeannette's was a difficult temperament; she did not make friends easily, and her position as pet and confidante of the president subjected her to the envy and fear of ambitious young academics in other departments as well as her own. She was nevertheless, as a result of her own efforts, becoming more content in her own work. The nineteenth-century poetry course for which she had fought was a solid satisfaction; students liked it and respected her work. Her affection for the poetry of the period was subjective and romantic, but she had a solid core of biographical and literary information to add to it, and students responded to the combination. Her master's thesis had been on the subject of English pastoral drama, and she undertook to direct student presentations of some unfamiliar plays for May Day and other occasions. Her production of *Noah and the Waning of the Flood* was made memorable by the uninvited entry of a wandering small dog into the ark where the other animals were being loaded. She adapted Beaumont and Fletcher's *Faithful Shepherdess* for student use and cut a scene from Shakespeare's *Winter's Tale*. She even appeared in a faculty play as Prince Collegian, object of the amorous desires of seven princesses, played by Helen Thompson, Ada Snell, Nellie Neilson, Natalie Wipplinger, Emma D. Sandford, Frances Fox, and Margaret Wardwell.

Far more important from her own point of view was that in 1904 she sold her first short story to an important national magazine. "Toedium Vitae" in the *New England Magazine* for July marked the opening of a new era in her life. Its theme and treatment suggest an intentional about-face. If she had been collecting her Wellesley stories in the hope of book publication, she may have been struck by their lugubrious tone, or some editor may have called it to her attention. "Toedium Vitae," a term she used in private correspondence to describe her own psychic state, is here a humorous story about a rural New England family steeped in gloom, and what happened to it when the daughter made a deliberate effort to behave more cheerfully.

That Miss Marks' major interest was eventually to be the drama is suggested in the opening scene and indeed in the structure of the story as a whole. At its beginning the family, old mother, son, and daughter, are gathered in the farmhouse kitchen bewailing their unhappy fates. They have been plagued by illness, death, insanity, financial loss, and the unexplained disappearance of their sea-captain husband and father. The following morning the scene in the kitchen has the daughter making popovers, placing a jelly glass of flowers on the table, and laughing hilariously at one of her brother's gloomy anecdotes. There is no immediate explanation of how she has been motivated. Mother and brother think she is losing her mind, but gradually the change in her communicates itself to them; the brother engages himself to be married, and at the end the long-lost father is seen coming up the front walk. It might be pointed out that Jeannette has changed her approach but not her themes and (if the story were important enough to bear the weight of Freudian analysis) that the return of the long-lost father is an obvious wish fulfillment.

In the same year she formed a personal and literary connection that was to be of great importance in the development of her career. That summer she sailed for Europe on June 25, to be followed six weeks later by Mary Woolley for their first shared European vacation. In London Jeannette encountered Ethel Arnold, youngest daughter of the Thomas Arnold whose reputation was overshadowed by those of his father Thomas and his brother Matthew. Miss Arnold in her turn lived in the shadow of towering reputations. Her oldest sister, Mrs. Humphry Ward, whose *Robert Elsmere* was already a worldwide best seller, was turning out book after book to follow it. Her brother Thomas had served as their father's biographer, and her sister Julia had married Dr. Leonard Huxley and borne two sons, Julian and Aldous, who would be famous in their turn.

Ethel herself had published a short novel and an edition of Tourgenieff's letters translated from the French, along with a few magazine articles. Her father, while not the best known of the Arnolds, was far from being the least interesting. He was plagued all his life by an imp of the perverse which compelled him, whatever he might choose to do, to be drawn as soon as he had done it to its opposite. He immigrated to New Zealand to get away from his family and then returned to England to be near them. He was converted from Protestantism to Catholicism and back again, with brief interludes of atheism in the process. His conversions always occurred at the point in his life where they could do the greatest damage to his career. He died in the Catholic faith and was buried in Ireland, where his final conversion had exiled him to a provincial university. His children thus grew up in New Zealand, England, and Ireland, spending long periods of time in the home of their Arnold grandparents, and encountering along the way many of the most interesting literary figures of the nineteenth century. Ethel was one of the little girls Lewis Carroll entertained in rowboats on the river and with imaginative tales and photographing parties, perhaps the only one in whom his interest continued after her adolescence. He took her to the theater in London when she was eighteen. She had seen and heard Wordsworth, Kingsley, Newman, Thomas Huxley, Tennyson, and Arthur Hugh Clough, among others.

That Jeannette Marks should have been enchanted at this meeting with her nineteenth-century poets at only one remove from the flesh is easy to understand. Miss Arnold responded graciously to the younger woman's enthusiastic admiration. She was, like Mary Woolley, about a dozen years older than Jeannette, and established in her own career. The attraction was mutual, and its first fruit was Jeannette's introduction to Wales. Miss Arnold took her to Beddgelert, some fifteen miles from Carnarvon, where her father had passed holidays with Clough. The scenery was wild and romantic, the people picturesque, the language melodious and baffling. Jeannette fell instantly in love with the place. Miss Woolley's letter carrying the notification from the June 21 meeting of the board of trustees that Jeannette had been promoted to associate professor and a salary of $800 was forwarded to her there. Miss Woolley herself followed in mid-August. She was not greatly attracted to either Miss Arnold or to Wales, but she always tried to like what Jeannette liked. The joint holiday was cut to a few brief weeks; on September third Miss Marks and Miss Woolley sailed for home and a fourth year at Mount Holyoke.

Helen Cady, a classmate of Jeannette's from Wellesley, came that fall as a part-time instructor in the English Department. She would remain for sixteen years, during which she was a conscientious if not an inspiring teacher, but throughout that time her impact on the college was slight and her published scholarly work negligible. The correspondence and her life at Mount Holyoke both suggest that she was brought in as a companion for Jeannette, a part of the campaign to keep her happy. She shared the apartment in Alvord House, which Jeannette had named the Ridgepole, and was admitted to a limited intimacy with the president.

A new friendship which was to be even longer lasting was

formed that year. Dorothy Foster, A.B., Bryn Mawr 1904, came as a reader in the English Literature Department, her services to be shared by Miss Marks and Miss Young. Brash, bright, outspoken, a good deal of an intellectual snob, she grew with the years into one of the most brilliant and beloved of Mount Holyoke professors — "Dotty" Foster to her admiring students well into old age. In 1904 she measured everything at Mount Holyoke by the yardstick of Bryn Mawr and found a great deal lacking. She was shocked at seeing students in mobcaps sweeping the halls before chapel — it was she who told the story of Miss Thomas' urging the Bryn Mawr students not to take time out to make their beds — and even more shocked to see emeritus professors sweeping the sidewalk in front of their small apartment over one of the village shops. She did not approve of secret societies, "the existence of which had never been tolerated at Bryn Mawr," and she thought it infra dig for Miss Woolley to live in a college dormitory and share meals with students. Her estimate of the state of the college is worth quoting.

The academic departments were chaired by energetic young scholars who found able assistants and offered courses comparable to those open to men undergraduates in the universities. Clearly Wellesley was a model for Mount Holyoke, for which Miss Woolley and a number of members of the faculty from Wellesley were responsible. But the Bryn Mawr group was large and making itself felt.

Of Miss Woolley herself she wrote:

She was natural, gracious, humorous, shrewd in appraising people, wise, strikingly attractive though not beautiful, with a fine voice that drew me to Vespers to hear her read the Scriptures. Here was distinction.

Such a tribute from one who had sat under M. Carey Thomas should not be underrated. Of all those who admired Miss Woolley, Miss Foster was almost if not quite alone in admiring Miss Marks as well. The nineteenth-century poetry course was "more brilliantly taught than any similar course at Bryn Mawr." The friendship became personal as well as professional. Like Miss Marks, she enjoyed strenuous walking expeditions; together they climbed the Holyoke and Tom ranges, found rare wildflowers, flowering trees and shrubs, looked out over the winding Connecticut River, and talked poetry and department shop. Miss Foster lived first in Brigham Hall and then in the home of two elderly professors, the Misses Clara and Alice Stevens, whom she rather enjoyed shocking by such bohemian practices as going in and out by the bedroom window instead of the front door or bringing a friend to spend the night in a sleeping bag on the floor or cooking her meals in a chafing dish instead of reporting to her table in Brigham. It must have been a relief to them when she decided to share with Jeannette Marks and Helen Cady in renting a small house in the village.

The one they chose was on the long, straggling road that led downhill from the college to the Connecticut River. It was painted green and promptly denominated the Green Pea. Even Miss Woolley used that name frequently in her daily notes from the presidential office or suite, although the address was officially listed in college publications as 50 Hadley Street. Here the three young women were able to enjoy a life style highly satisfactory to them and totally different from that of the older members of the faculty.

The ideal of gracious womanhood was still strongly stressed in the dormitories. The large majority of the faculty were still unmarried women who lived there and presided as hostesses at "their" tables. They guided the conversation, carved the roast, and made the meals an integral part of the education of their students. They were at the beginning of what one former student had aptly dubbed "the era of the great ladies," an era that would endure for more than twenty years. After dinner, over coffee in the lounge, they continued the ritual of gracious living with merriment. Their rooms were open to student visitors on a fairly formal basis; working hours were respected on both sides. The friendships they formed with students outside the classroom were close and meaningful and usually exerted a continuing influence on the students' lives.

Miss Woolley took the lead in all of this quite as a matter of course. Only a few short years earlier the friendship with Jeannette had blossomed while the girl was one of the students at "her" table at Wellesley. By now, however, other people than Dotty Foster were beginning to say that the dignity of a college president demanded that she should have a home of her own and more privacy than was possible in a dormitory.

It would be several years before this observation would result in a president's house, but meanwhile Miss Woolley could visit the Green Pea as a contrast, refreshing or otherwise, to her official life. It would appear that during the Green Pea years she called more frequently than she was called upon; there were many notes inviting her to lunch or dinner and replies from her touching on her obligations to "the table" at Brigham. When she went to the Green Pea she walked, the mode of transportation then most usual in South Hadley.

During these years Jeannette's attitude toward her changed markedly; her notes were teasing, disrespectful, deliberately provocative. Many of them were written in a sort of private "little language," reminiscent of Swift's with Stella, made up of slang, baby talk, deliberate misspelling, and the introduction of foreign words, chiefly German. The signatures were "Your own little girl," "Good-for-nothing," or "Taugenichts." The references to personal matters are deliberately obscure, but the tone is unmistakable. Mary Woolley reacted often with a natural anger, but she could never maintain it; even when she was very obviously not at fault it was she who would apologize. The two other young women in the house treated her with the courteous respect to which she was accustomed from her faculty, but the situation must frequently have been embarrassing for them.

It is at least possible that it was good for Miss Woolley. Her position and her natural dignity protected her from criticism in most of her relationships; the very fact that the majority of the trustees were men and she a woman meant that they would treat her with a courtliness that might possibly conceal real difference of opinion. Jeannette Marks was becoming the only person who ever ventured to take her off her high horse.

The guests at the Green Pea also represented a society from which Miss Woolley's work tended increasingly to isolate her. Vida Scudder came from Wellesley with Emily Greene Balch, who would eventually lose her place there because of her Socialist ties; they talked of suffrage for women and the Women's Trade Union League they had helped to form. A student reminiscing years later recalled that Miss Marks and the other occupants of the Green Pea "walked down College Street waving those yellow flags for women's rights."

Miss Woolley's first public endorsement of this cause did not occur until 1906. Beth Bradford Gilchrist of the class of 1902 had won a $75 prize offered by the College Equal Suffrage League for an essay on the subject. Her prize-winning entry, "Equal Suffrage as an Influence on the Individual and on the Race," was published as the lead article in the *Mount Holyoke* for January 1903, but Miss Woolley did not choose to make much of it as an honor brought to the college. Miss Gilchrist herself adopted a largely defensive tone; she had much less to say about the advantages that might accrue to the individual and the race from giving women the vote than about her certainty that enfranchising them would not unfeminize them. A passing reference suggests one of the problems that was to plague proponents of the Equal Rights Amendment for years to come:

That what men decree is for the interests of women may not be so adjudged by the women concerned is evinced by a single point in the factory laws of Massachusetts . . . To decree by law women shall work but fifty-eight hours a

week handicaps them in selling their labor . . . Their pos-
session of a quota of political power will doubtless bring
about many changes in legislation respecting women and
economics . . .

By the time women actually did win the vote the general
views of society and the participation of the laboring classes
in the democratic process had altered sufficiently to ensure
that this particular piece of protective legislation should not
be sacrificed.

When a year or two later the College Equal Suffrage
League wanted to send a speaker to Mount Holyoke, Miss
Woolley referred the request to the president of the Students' League, Susan Reed, who issued the invitation without any official support from the college. The speaker came,
but the publicity was inadequate, and the sparse audience
did not include Miss Woolley. It was several years later
that, under prodding from Jeannette and no doubt other
pressures as well, she came out definitely as favoring suffrage for women.

V

Author and Executive

IN AUGUST 1905, the *New England Magazine* carried a story by Jeannette Marks entitled "The New Trustee":

The Board of Trustees and the President of the Faculty sat in solemn conclave. College securities had depreciated and they needed money. They wanted a new chapel, a music hall, an added instructor in the Department of Ornithology, a porcelain bathtub for the president, a new stereopticon lantern and sand for the Geology Department, hairpins for the experiments made by the Department of Psychology, and some cats and a pair of steel forceps for the Zoology Department.

So it began. The trustees decided that their only course was to elect a new trustee of known wealth and liberality. Six names were considered. Objections revealed that one of them was heterodox in her religious beliefs (she doubted the authenticity of Jonah and the whale), one addicted to alcohol, one a man who had publicly expressed his disapproval of higher education for women, one divorced, one a sports enthusiast who would give money for nothing but gymnasiums and swimming pools. The single remaining name was that of Miss Louise Biddle, an independent heiress, uneducated but known to have strong interest in good works of all sorts. She was elected to the board without a dissenting vote.

Upon her arrival at the college with her maid, she was invited to dine with the president and any professors of her choice; she chose those of Pedagogy, Geology, Botany, and Literature. She had armed herself with encyclopedia and dictionary and prepared a few questions that she thought would establish rapport in those fields. Instead they turned the dinner party into a disaster:

"What is the diameter of the earth?" she asked the Professor of Geology and "When was Shakespeare born?" the Professor of Literature. Neither of them was able to answer, but the Professor of Pedagogy saved the day with a long, learned, and enthusiastic disquisition on the question of the ethical importance of geography and arithmetic. Miss Biddle gave the college everything it required except the porcelain bathtub, which the flustered president had neglected to list among the requisites.

At the end of the story Miss Biddle married the Professor of Pedagogy. The president of the college was her only attendant and she presented the bathtub as a delicate expression of gratitude.

The reaction of the Mount Holyoke community to this story can only be imagined; no reference to it ever found its way into print.

The names of the characters were Professor Alphonse Peabody, Anne Beckford, R. (for Rosalie) Chapin Johnson, and Susie Smith. Since the names of the women's colleges were Jones, Vanessa, Waverly, Brynton, and Hollywood, it seems a reasonable deduction that the names of the characters also have some relation to those of real people.

Certainly the positions did. President Maxwell, the gracious, charming, competent hostess and fund-raiser, was a recognizable portrait of Miss Woolley. The Professor of Botany was Henrietta Hooker, who had presented the nineteenth-century eggs for a twentieth-century breakfast. Her passion for Buff Orpington hens provided the college with some of its favorite anecdotes about professorial eccentricity; she had been known to bring them (live) to a dinner party and place them upon the table for the admiration of her guests. The Professor of Geology was diminutive Mignon Talbot, so like her older sister, the Professor of Philosophy, that they were often taken for twins. Tiny and shy as they were, they held Ph.D.s from Cornell and Yale respectively. The Professor of Literature was Miss Conant, head of Miss Marks' own department, and the Professor of Pedagogy was indeed one of the very small minority of males on the faculty.

By what could have only been a painful mischance, the story appeared a very few months after the death of Miss Woolley's mother, an event that had strained relations between the two women about as far as they could be strained. There is no point in saying "almost to the breaking point," as apparently there was no breaking point for Miss Woolley. In the early part of the year both Miss Woolley and Miss Marks had been ill, Miss Woolley at her parents' house in Pawtucket and Miss Marks at the Green Pea with Helen Cady. Jeannette had spent Christmas there also, though it had been her custom for some years to share the holidays with the Woolley family in Pawtucket. May returned to college on the twenty-third of January, but by the end of the month she was back in Pawtucket, still suffering from bronchitis and rheumatism. Before her return to the college at the end of the first week in February she noted that "Mama has intestinal indigestion," but that she was improving and had come downstairs to rest on the couch. Less than a month later Miss Woolley was back in Pawtucket, aware that her mother was dying. She wrote twice to Jeannette begging her to come, on March 24 and again on the twenty-seventh. Apparently the letters were never answered; certainly Jeannette never came. Mrs. Woolley died on the twenty-eighth.

Jeannette's letters on this occasion were so inappropriate as to suggest that she was on the verge of an emotional breakdown. There is scarcely a note of sympathy for Miss Woolley; she is full of self-pity and making violently ambivalent demands:

> . . . *if I say I will come next summer, will you take care of me and help give me a chance to do the work I long to do?* . . . *If I give all to you and give up the idea that I must protect myself from you, will you really care for my work as well as loving me?* . . . *I believe anybody seeing the dignified dependence of two people who love each other deeply is the better for it. One thing I have always admired in Miss S—— is the simple reserved evidence she always shows of her love for Miss S——. I despise conventionality . . . I would not take a kingdom for the proof at the dinner table as well as in the quiet of our bedroom that you depend upon me; there is no gift equal to the dignity you can confer on me in that way.*

The implication is clear that Miss Marks has become at least partially aware of the nature of their mutual feeling, but whether she is asking for an overt as well as an open relationship remains questionable.

She had probably learned a good deal from Ethel Arnold, who had literary ties in Paris as well as in London. On the Continent a lesbian society had already surfaced, although it would not be much talked about for another twenty years outside of a very limited circle. Miss Arnold's one novel was concerned with a lesbian relationship, not so described. *Platonics: A Study*, to which her publishers had felt it necessary to add the further explanatory subtitle *A Tale*, is the story of two women and a man involved in a rather unconventional triangle. Of the two women the "feminine" one is a widow considering remarriage. The suitor is a gentle and delicate young man; the woman friend an active boyish virgin. When these two meet for the first time, the widow has already given the ritually required refusal to the suitor's first proposal, which here, as in Richardson's *Clarissa*, frees the man to look elsewhere even though he realizes that a second proposal is expected and may not be refused. In *Platonics* he falls in love with the woman friend, who reciprocates heartily. They marry and leave the widow to die of a broken heart. Treated satirically or realistically, the story might have made its mark, but Miss Arnold could apparently not forget that she was Mrs. Humphry Ward's sister, and any point her novel might have had is lost in a turgid romanticism.

Miss Marks' attitude toward Miss Woolley during 1905 and later suggests that she was torn between recognizing and acknowledging her own sexual orientation and a powerful ethical rejection. The conflict was in all probability not fully conscious. She was to continue all her life strongly ambivalent not only toward Miss Woolley but toward all her close friends. Many of her warmest friendships would end in complete alienation; love and hate for her were never far apart.

Miss Woolley appears to have been entirely free from any such internal conflicts, although her love for Jeannette caused many practical difficulties. It was simple, outgoing, adequate, generous, undemanding — or it appears on the surface to have been all these things. Jeannette's struggles to be free of it suggest that she at least saw in it a subtle and peremptory demand.

The upshot of the 1905 correspondence was that Jeannette agreed to come to Pawtucket for the summer providing she could have May's room to herself and her breakfast served there on a tray. It was the best room in the house in which to work, and she needed to have her mornings uninterrupted. May agreed to all the terms, so the two must have been together in Pawtucket at the time "The New Trustee" appeared in the *New England Magazine.* The summer was evidently not altogether a success, for by September May was apologizing for not having made it a happier one. Nor would it appear from the publication record to have been a very fruitful one. In May the *Outlook* had published "Mors Triumphans," the first of a series of Welsh stories with which Miss Marks was eventually to make a name for herself, but no more of them were published that year or the next. The *Critic* in October carried "The American College Girl's Ignorance of Literature," a rather schoolmarmish complaint about her Mount Holyoke students, and the *Outlook* in January 1906 ran a conventional eulogy of Mount Holyoke under the title "A Study in Educational Service," which might have been her way of doing penance for "The New Trustee." *The Cheerful Cricket*, a children's book, bore a 1906 dateline but did not actually appear until 1907.

Miss Marks thus returned to the campus in the fall of 1905 laboring under a growing sense of failure and an almost conscious envy of the serene progress of Miss Woolley's successful career. The new library for which she had solicited funds from Andrew Carnegie to match those raised by students, faculty, and alumnae opened its doors that fall, but there was no rest in the business of raising money. She was already engaged in a campaign to get more money for a music building and for a student-alumnae hall. Retired teachers from the seminary were pressing for a building of their own so that they might end their days on the campus where they had spent their lives, and Jeannette was pressing for a president's house.

The President's House would not materialize until several years later, but the 1905–06 academic year saw a much more significant capitulation to Jeannette. In February 1906, Mary Woolley appeared on the platform with Susan B. Anthony at a suffrage rally in Baltimore. The other speakers included M. Carcy Thomas of Bryn Mawr and Julia Ward Howe. Miss Woolley spoke first:

The time will come when some of us will look back upon the arguments against the granting of the suffrage to women with as much incredulity as that with which we now read those against their education.

The timing and the staging of this about-face were characteristic of Mary Woolley. Suffrage for women was still unpopular with a large number of Mount Holyoke's supporters, both male and female. Miss Anthony, however, was an old woman who, in fact, would die within the year, and even the most conservative were willing to allow other women to pay tribute to her long and stormy career. Miss Woolley was not by any means merely riding the crest of a wave of popularity. More than a decade in which to work for the cause of suffrage for women lay ahead of her, and her endorsement of the cause was in itself a substantial contribution to its success. But she was not going out on a limb as Jeannette Marks so frequently did. Those who disapproved of Miss Woolley's action could add it to the growing list of grievances against Jeannette, and those who approved would within a very few years forget that she had not always been a supporter.

At the end of that academic year Martha Conant resigned her position at Mount Holyoke. This left Bertha Young and Jeannette Marks as obvious candidates for the department chairmanship unless someone were again to be brought in from outside. Both were associate professors; both held M.A. degrees, and their salaries ($850 a year) were equal. Their feuds were already notorious in the college. Dorothy Foster complained of the rival demands they made on her as a reader. One of the legendary stories that has survived about them is that a student assistant was required to carry notes from one to the other even when their desks were in the same room. On one occasion the recipient shook her head, and commented, "What a strange person she is!" before writing her answer. When the student carried the answer back to the other one, she read it, shook her head, and commented, "What a strange person she is!"

Why Miss Woolley should have chosen to make Miss Young department chairman rather than Miss Marks is a question wide open for speculation. Her handling of similar problems in other departments was notable for tact and use of competing skills and ambitions. The departments of History, Economics, Political Science, and Sociology performed a regular country dance of separation and reunion to accommodate their chairmen. Psychology separated from Philosophy when Helen Thompson's contribution in the former field became too important to allow her to remain an underling with a specialty of her own; Physical Chemistry would eventually separate from Chemistry for similar reasons. In every such case the subdivision strengthened the offerings of the college. English Literature was to provide a notable exception to this record.

Jeannette Marks served as acting chairman during the next few years for almost as many semesters as the titular chairman, and the college magazine referred to her as "senior professor of English Literature at Mount Holyoke" when she addressed the Woman's Club of New Britain on the work of William Morris. In 1907–08 she was acting head of the department for the first semester in Miss Young's absence, though she was herself on leave because of ill health the second semester. In 1908–09 she was acting head throughout the year while Miss Young studied in England for a graduate degree, and in 1909–10 she had a full year's leave herself for health and professional reasons. Miss Marks was influential in securing the appointment of Carrie Harper, who came from a preparatory school in Cambridge as an instructor in 1907. Miss Harper stayed at the Green Pea when she came to the college for an interview, and Jeannette reported enthusiastically on her congeniality and cheerfulness and later prodded Miss Woolley to hasten the appointment. Helen Cady transferred from the English to the English Literature Department so that it was possible to divide the required sophomore survey course among Miss Cady, Miss Foster, and Miss Harper, freeing Miss Marks from this drudgery for work which she preferred.

Jeannette went to Wales for the summer of 1906, and, when Chaplain Woolley died during her absence, refused, as she had refused a year before, to offer any helpful sympathy. The death of May's parents, who had been for more than a decade surrogate parents for Jeannette, stirred up her latent feelings about her own parents and made it impossible for her to share her friend's grief.

I love you in the same passionate demanding way I loved mama . . . I am jealous of you . . . The horrible years of my girlhood when there was no place for me return with a suspicion that after all you do not, rather cannot love me

. . . I am reminded of so much that has gone wrong in my life . . . It brings the old confusion into my mind. [She wrote in a nearly illegible letter.]

Jeannette's publications were becoming more frequent and more important. She went back to Wales again in the summer of 1907; she found the inn at Beddgelert a good place to work and the Welsh people good copy. "Mors Triumphans," which had appeared in *Outlook* in 1905, was the story of a man in a remote Welsh village who won a local election by purchasing a hearse for the benefit of his friends and neighbors. "Respice Finem" was her first appearance in the *Atlantic Monthly* and her last use of a Latin title for a Welsh story. It concerned an old man on his deathbed being coached to make a proper ending with a Scripture quotation. "Dreams in Jeopardy" in the *New England Magazine* was unique in that it did not touch on death; the plot was a simple one in which a maiden lady attempted to conceal from a belated suitor the fact that she wore a wig. "A Last Discipline" in the same magazine returned to the theme of death but was permitted a happy ending; the old woman who served as protagonist not only survived an operation in a strange hospital in Liverpool but reformed her stingy husband by alarming him with the prospect of her death.

These stories were not above the level of the magazine fiction of their period, but they were fully equal to it. Wales was a new and interesting locale at a time when local color was popular, and Miss Marks certainly caught something of the combination of rigid fanatical honesty and Celtic humor that characterized the Welsh.

In 1908 she published an adaptation of her Wellesley master's thesis, *English Pastoral Drama*. It was not well received, the reviewer in the *Nation* calling it "feeble and sophomoric" and the *Saturday Review*, "too much like an annotated catalogue." It was nevertheless reprinted in 1972 as a reference work that had not outlived its usefulness. The reviewers' scorn may have been at least partially a reaction to the claim for female scholarship, since the book carried on its title page an identification of the author as an associate professor of English literature at Mount Holyoke and a dedication to Katharine Lee Bates, Sophie Jewett, Vida Scudder, and Margaret Sherwood, four Wellesley professors. It was all very well for women to write children's books and sentimental stories, but to invade the masculine realm of scholarship or to claim for their new colleges equality with the great all-male universities was another matter altogether.

Miss Marks took the unkind reviews personally rather than as a slur on her sex and suffered profoundly. In the spring of 1908 she was ill and on leave of absence from her teaching duties although she remained at home in the Green Pea. Her health was to give her and Mary Woolley grave concern for at least another decade, but both were so secretive about the nature of her difficulties that it is impossible now, as it may well have been then, to say what ailed her. The correlation with her professional problems suggests that the illnesses were at least partially psychic in origin, but the temptation to a post-Freudian biographer to diagnose posthumously ought to be resisted. She suffered from painful and debilitating menstrual periods, the dread of which was almost as bad as the reality, but beyond that she never mentioned specific physical symptoms. Her complaints were of emotional storms and the fear that she might be losing her mind. When Bertha Young went off to study for her Ph.D., Jeannette rallied and served as acting chairman of the department for 1908–09, during which time she applied for a leave of absence of her own for the following year.

Meanwhile Mary Woolley's career was advancing steadily and without apparent difficulty. She was aligning herself with new national organizations, notably the Peace Congress of Women in 1907. Her speech for its meeting in New York on April 16 made headlines in the metropolitan papers, which announced that she said "the new woman" had come to stay. She was beginning to be elected to important offices in the organizations to which she belonged: vice president of the American Peace Society, a senator of Phi Beta Kappa, on the national board of the Y.W.C.A. Her work in this organization, as in many of the others, was tied closely to her work in the college. Since 1901 Mount Holyoke had had a Y.W.C.A. secretary as one of its administrative officers, and a delegation of students went annually to the Y.W.C.A. conference at Silver Bay on Lake George.

Until 1906 students were required to attend church services at the Congregational Church in the village. By that time the student body had grown too large to be accommodated in its building, and Miss Woolley initiated Sunday morning services in the college chapel. Distinguished ministers from all over the nation were invited to preach and from the already established all-college choir the best of the juniors were chosen to sing. Membership in Junior Choir became an honor to which freshmen and sophomores eagerly aspired. With William Hammond at the organ, services became musical events that enhanced the growing reputation of the college in this field. Miss Woolley always joined the visiting preacher on the platform and listened to what he had to say with the grave absorption characteristic of her. Generations of college girls carried away as one of their most vivid memories of her the composed figure erect in the high-backed chair, the face turned eagerly but soberly toward the speaker, whose every word she was clearly drinking in. Afterward she would entertain the visitor at Sunday dinner in Brigham Hall, where students might have an opportunity to meet him personally. Attendance at church was required, and in this way over their four years many students heard more outstanding preachers than they could expect to encounter during the remainder of their lives.

This changed only slightly when the President's House became a reality in 1909; thereafter the preacher took Sunday dinner in company with Miss Woolley and whoever else might be living in the house. If it were a man Miss Marks wanted to meet, she would join them at dinner; otherwise she was served with a tray in her third-floor apartment.

In the matter of attracting good faculty members, the careful work of the first few years was already paying off.

Having chosen able young scholars to head departments, Miss Woolley could rely on them for recruiting. They were not only competent in their fields but acquainted with colleagues in other colleges. Miss Marks' 1906 article listed holders of degrees from Barnard, Vassar, the universities of Chicago, Michigan, Berlin, and Paris, Massachusetts Institute of Technology, Columbia, Cambridge, Wellesley, Bryn Mawr, and Yale. Mount Holyoke alumnae who carried on the seminary tradition of coming back to teach where they had studied took time out for graduate work elsewhere: Emma Carr in chemistry, Ada Snell in English, and Julia Moody in zoology, among others. Graduate schools were coeducational even in all-male universities, and the recognition of Mount Holyoke faculty throughout the academic community of the nation was wide and growing. Miss Woolley's part in attracting new faculty members was being reduced to the important function of raising money to increase salaries. The need for money continued on every side: faculty salaries, buildings, endowment, equipment, and her skill and devotion at the task of raising it continued also to grow. She contributed in varying degrees to raising funds for the Music Building, Peterson Lodge for retired faculty members, and the President's House, all of which became realities in 1909.

According to the official record, the Alumnae Association actually initiated the building of the President's House at a meeting in Chicago in April 1907. Their memorandum to the board of trustees read:

The present household arrangements for our College President . . . are inadequate to conserve her energies, owing to the lack of privacy and the wear and tear of being housed in a large dormitory where she is constantly before the public gaze . . . [we propose] that a separate household befitting the status of our college be prepared and maintained for the use of our President.

The trustees replied that they recognized the need and had failed to act upon it only because of the pressing necessity of providing housing for students. At the November meeting that year Joseph Skinner, a new trustee, presented plans and a site, and pushed through a vote to appropriate the money and begin building.

The site chosen was across the road from Mary Lyon Hall, where Miss Woolley had her office, and to the rear of Pearsons Hall, one of the dormitories. This meant that Miss Woolley would be still only a few steps from her office and that the view from her front windows would be of kitchens and rear bedrooms. The problem was solved by screening the small front lawn with shrubbery and concentrating the windows and gardens at the rear, where the view of the mountains and across the Connecticut River was unobstructed. The house was to be of light brown stucco with dark brown cypress trim.

The *Mount Holyoke* carried a descriptive article about the house in June of 1909 when it was ready for occupancy:

All white and cool greens and buffs and blues inside, the house is indeed very charming. The reception room, which is just to the right of the white vestibule, is small and square and white. The walls are panels of white wood, and the furniture is mahogany upholstered in a green-figured brocade ... Less formal than this little room is the large living room which runs the whole width of the house on the left side of the entrance ... There are big brown wicker armchairs, and comfortable mission armchairs ... the fireplace occupies almost all of the wall space on the south side of the room and is built into the oak wainscoting ... Across the green and white hall is the white dining room with its round mahogany table and its built-in china closet with panes of leaded glass.

From the wide, pillared porch the Mount Tom range and a good part of the Mount Holyoke one could be seen beyond the terraced garden and its hedge. On the second floor were a study, a den, two bedrooms with a porch facing west toward the mountains and the river, and the servants' quarters with a separate stairway leading down to the kitchen and the servants' sitting room. The third floor had two more bedrooms and

. . . another study, a kind of oratory with its long, low-raftered ceiling and its pointed arches over its casement windows. There are bookcases along all the walls, and a big mission desk and chairs and a fireplace.

This "oratory" was designed with Jeannette Marks' taste in mind and became her study, living room, and occasional classroom for almost thirty years. She named it Attic Peace and had her stationery so engraved. She and Helen Cady moved into the house along with Miss Woolley in 1909, abandoning the Green Pea.

Miss Woolley's contract with the college had from the beginning included a provision for her living. At the time she came to the college this was a taken-for-granted part of all salaries. The seminary teachers had lived in the seminary as a matter of course and used their pittances for other needs or for charity. By 1901 there were four male members of the faculty, who obviously could not live in the dormitories, quite aside from the fact that some of them were married. Some of the older female professors had bought homes for themselves, and some of the younger ones, like Jeannette, preferred to find living quarters outside the college. Therefore, in 1906, the trustees voted an increase of $250 for each faculty salary, the same amount to be charged against the salaries of those living in college houses. In effect, this was a subsidy of $250 annually for those living outside the college. By the time the President's House was built this had been increased to $275, divided as $150 for board and $125 for room and laundry. Miss Cady and Miss Marks as tenants in the President's House had this amount deducted from their salaries of $1025 and $1250 respectively. The college made Miss Woolley the "usual off-campus house allowance" and contracted to supply the house with ice, lights, fuel, care of the furnace and grounds, and an allowance for electric lights used after 10 P.M. "when necessary" and during short vacations when the college dynamo was not in operation. The official record would thus seem to suggest that out of her $275 Miss Woolley had to pay the expense of house servants and of food for her two boarders as well as herself. Her salary plus living allowances had now passed $4000, more than double that of any professor, but it seems doubtful that the college would actually have imposed this financial burden on her.

Whatever its official status, Miss Woolley thought of the house as the home she and Jeannette had long hoped to share. She furnished it at her own expense, borrowing on her life insurance for the purpose. If the alumnae had really wanted to conserve her energies by providing privacy and a refuge from the public gaze they must have been disappointed, but in the aim of securing "a separate household befitting the status of our college" they had amply succeeded. The President's House would be hospitably open to trustees, faculty, students, alumnae, and distinguished guests of the college for many years to come. It seems to have occurred to no one, least of all to Jeannette Marks, that Miss Woolley was here assuming the responsibilities of a president's wife in addition to those of a president. The President's House furnished a model of gracious living for the students, a meeting place for the faculty, a symbol of prestige for the alumnae, a free private hotel for trustees and guests, and a home for Jeannette. If the last item was the most important for Miss Woolley, no one could complain that she slighted the others.

Two other buildings opened their doors in the same year as the President's House. The Music Building was placed at the southern extremity of the campus, where neither the practice scales of the students nor the concerts in the auditorium could disturb those who did not care to hear them. The only building close to it was Peterson Lodge, which would remove from public view the old ladies surviving from the teaching staff of the seminary. This had been funded largely by the gift of Mrs. P. S. Peterson, president of the Chicago Alumnae Association, for whom it was named. Miss Mary Nutting, librarian emeritus, was largely responsible for the planning and the solicitation of funds.

An ingenious design of private facilities surrounding a shared foyer provided for both independence and community at Peterson Lodge. Apartments not required by the valetudinarians were available for active faculty members; Dorothy Foster took one of them. It enabled her to cook her own meals at her own convenience and to meet with students outside of classroom hours on her own initiative. It was perhaps she who coined the *mot* that the building was for the accommodation of tired and retired faculty members.

The year 1909 brought to Jeannette Marks many satisfactions, personal and professional. *Through Welsh Doorways*, a collection of her Welsh stories, was published and favorably reviewed. The *Book Review Digest* described it as "eleven excellent stories ranging from the humorous to the pathetic" and quoted favorable reviews from the *Atlantic Monthly*, the *Literary Digest*, the *New York Times*, and other periodicals. She also published a second children's book, this one in collaboration with Julia Moody of the Zoology Department. Miss Moody earned her master's degree that year with a thesis on the anatomy and early embryology of *Cumingia tellinoides*. She furnished the scientific knowledge and Miss Marks the literary skill for the composition of *Little Busybodies: The Life of Crickets, Ants, Bees, and Other Busybodies*. Issued in Harper's Story-told Science series, it had a generally favorable reception, and Harper's commissioned another book for the following year: *A Holiday with the Birds*. The *Outlook* in February carried a travel article on Wales introducing the Spectator, a persona she would frequently use again. Miss Marks' poetry was appearing in a number of magazines; her name was becoming known to magazine editors, and sales were correspondingly easier. For her even more than for Mary Woolley the new President's House was the fulfillment of a cherished dream. Only in her work at the college did she still find cause for dissatisfaction.

In the late winter she brought Ethel Arnold to lecture at the college on Thomas and Matthew, her grandfather and uncle. The lecture was a success; the students thought

Miss Arnold had a charming personality, and Miss Woolley treated her cordially and invited her to return in the following year. But by then both Bertha Young and Carrie Harper had earned their Ph.D.s, Miss Harper's from Bryn Mawr with a dissertation on Spenser's *Faerie Queene*. Bertha Young would return in the fall to a five-year appointment as a full professor at a salary of $1525 the first year. Jeannette was still an associate professor on a three-year appointment at $1250, and while she outranked Miss Harper and Miss Foster, instructors earning less than $1000 a year in spite of the new Ph.D., Miss Young had pulled irretrievably ahead of her. Miss Marks applied for a leave of her own for 1909–10, though without any intention of working toward a further graduate degree. Her future as an author now looked definitely promising, and she planned to concentrate on it.

Her first action in the academic year 1909–10, however, while Miss Woolley and Helen Cady were settling in at the President's House, was to take a "cure" at Battle Creek. This was a fashionable and expensive institution heavily patronized by celebrities as a rest cure and by debutantes and their mothers as a beauty treatment.

Established by the Seventh-Day Adventist Church in 1866, it had devoted itself to the cure of disease by natural means: baths, diet, rest, exercise, and fresh air. Dr. John Harvey Kellogg had taken over the medical direction and split with the church, but he continued the therapy along the original lines. The diet was strictly vegetarian, with an interesting variety of chops, roasts, and steaks made of beans, nuts, and other unexpected ingredients. Liquor, tobacco, tea, coffee, condiments, and highly seasoned foods were all banned. No drugs of any sort were prescribed as medicines. Two hundred different kinds of baths, douches, and fomentations were offered along with phototherapy, one of several subjects on which Dr. Kellogg had written a book.

Furnishings and services were luxurious; the rich could count on being pampered while they improved their health. By 1909 the sanitarium was famous all over the

United States if not the world and was treating five thousand patients a year, many of them also famous. There was a handsome central palm garden where ambulatory patients could mingle, and lectures, concerts, and entertainments were offered every evening in the main lounge.

Jeannette Marks was always secretive about her ailments. She did not speak directly of the nature of this one, although some references in her later work are suggestive. She did continue all of her life to follow a modified form of the Battle Creek regime, eschewing meat or eating it very lightly, and speaking with disapproval of even such very mild stimulants as cocoa.

The cost of room and board at Battle Creek was from $35 to $40 a week, which would have exhausted Jeannette's annual salary in about six months providing she had had an annual salary. Since she was on leave that year without salary, the financial burden fell on Mary Woolley, who insisted that Jeannette must not worry, although as a matter of fact she had had to ask Mr. Williston, the college treasurer, for an advance on her own salary.

There are some indications that Jeannette Marks thought her health problems to be connected with her affection for Mary Woolley and that she discussed the matter with a psychiatrically oriented member of the Battle Creek staff. Miss Woolley wrote from South Hadley:

I am so happy to think that there is no organic disease and that you need only patience, wisdom, care, rest . . . It is just like having an unremitting pain, this having you away. There is a dull ache all the time, and I long, long for you . . . I think that you do not know, Dearie, how my real life is just bound up in you. Everything, my work, my happiness, has you as its center.

Jeannette's problem was thus curiously like that of the able wife of a successful man, whose own drive for achievement cannot be satisfied merely by contributing to his success.

Miss Marks returned to South Hadley with a supply of

corn flakes, then a novel health food. Miss Woolley ordered nuts, raisins, and whole-grain cereals from the S. S. Pierce Company in Boston, and she and Helen Cady devoted themselves, so far as their other duties would allow, to coddling the invalid in an effort to restore her health.

Miss Woolley herself spent less time away from the campus this year than in previous ones. Her associations outside the college were well established, and she could begin to expect people to come to her in South Hadley rather than requiring her to go to them in Boston, New York, or the West. She evidently felt also that the time had come to devote herself to some important internal problems in the college which she had recognized from the first but about which she had determined to move slowly. These were the abolition of required domestic work and of secret Greek-letter societies. The required domestic work kept Mount Holyoke's fees substantially lower than those of Wellesley and Smith, but Miss Woolley did not see this altogether as an advantage. She was concerned as much with the prestige of the college as with the solid achievement on which it was based. This is not to say that she neglected the solid achievement. She had devoted herself to it for eight years, and now she felt the time had come for the world to recognize what had been accomplished. As long as Mount Holyoke's fees remained lower than those of the other women's colleges, people were likely to think that its offerings were less valuable.

She seems also to have shared with M. Carey Thomas a strong antipathy to the idea that woman's place was in the home. Both of them saw woman's place as being in the office, the library, the laboratory, the classroom, the study, the public forum, quite as much as in the home, and both of them feared that stress on the domestic arts would weaken or undermine the progress that had been made in establishing her right to choose her own life style. Miss Woolley stoutly and stubbornly opposed all efforts to introduce courses in domestic science into Mount Holyoke's curriculum, entering on this issue into what was probably her first important controversy with one of her trustees.

Not that she had any objection, she was always careful to say, to the marriage of Mount Holyoke graduates or their subsequent devotion to a domestic career. College could make women better wives and mothers, she maintained, not by giving specific instruction in the necessary arts and skills but by enlarging their minds, instilling habits of order and discipline, helping them to know themselves. An article by Miss Woolley on this subject in the *Ladies' Home Journal* in October 1910 stressed the point that a college woman was a better companion for her husband, a wiser mother for her children than one who had not gone to college. What value the education held for the woman herself was condensed into one brief paragraph. *"Non ministrari sed ministrare"* was her motto in this field as in all others; the idea that the unexamined life was not worth living was less familiar to her. She was always too busy in her own active life to spare much time for contemplation; this was perhaps one of the reasons she valued Jeannette, who quite frankly admitted that she indulged altogether too much in introspection.

The passion with which the students clung to the tradition of domestic work is less easy to explain than Miss Woolley's opposition to it. It was one of the things that made Mount Holyoke unique, possibly even its last remaining claim to be so, but it must have been a nuisance, and girls in 1910 were presumably no tidier than those in 1970. The feeling was so strong, however, that Miss Woolley moved very slowly and cautiously in attempting to interfere with it.

In the matter of the Greek-letter societies the crisis was nearer at hand. The first of them had come in with the college in 1888, and several more had been established before, in 1902, their further increase was banned. They represented a small minority of the student body, which now stood at about 750, but their influence was pervasive. Miss Woolley and many members of the faculty considered it bad. In Miss Foster's vivid phrase, the sorority girls "scooted in and out" of the basement rooms that had been allotted to them. Rushing and initiation occupied a disproportionately large place in the adjustment problems of young girls living away from home for the first time; sorority duties robbed other college organizations of the services of many student leaders, and loyalty to the sororities sometimes superseded loyalty to the college, which greatly needed the support of all its alumnae.

In 1908 articles about the sororities, both pro and con, began appearing in the *Mount Holyoke*. As a partial answer to the criticisms, rushing was postponed from freshman to sophomore year, and a tradition was established that the societies should never be mentioned to freshmen. This imitation of the practice of the most prestigious secret societies at Harvard and Yale had precisely the same effect it had there: to whet enormously the curiosity and envy of those excluded. The postponement of rushing merely exaggerated the importance it assumed in the minds of freshmen. A girl who was passed over in the first weeks of her first year could console herself by the reflection that the sororities had had no opportunity to know her before they rejected her, but one who had tried throughout her freshman year to make her mark and was then ignored had to console herself in other ways.

The problem of loyalty to the college was illustrated by the reaction of the societies' alumnae to any talk of abolition. Their hostility to the suggestion was much stronger than that of the students who were currently members and was quite outspoken.

Whether or not Miss Marks had influenced Miss Woolley's thinking on this matter, she had expressed her opinion on the subject some years earlier and had continued to do so at every opportunity. Among the charges she leveled at secret societies were false social standards and silly ceremonies, but the one which stung was that they were "hotbeds of special sentimental friendships." Here was a well-aimed stone from a very conspicuous glass house, and it drew a volley in return.

Dorothy Foster, who was teaching the nineteenth-century poetry class that term, may have found occasion to point out that in Tennyson's *Princess* the real cause of the collapse of the college was not the intrusion of men but internal differences among the women. The Lady Blanche envied and resented the Lady Psyche; each wanted to be Princess Ida's closest confidante. Both of them discovered the masquerade before Ida did, and Blanche used the knowledge to attempt to destroy Psyche. She succeeded instead in destroying the college and hastening the princess's marriage (which would in any case have taken place eventually).

The intense anxiety the Woolley-Marks friendship stirred up among the faculty and the alumnae can only be explained by a growing sophistication in sexual matters and a fear that all same-sex friendships were tarred with the same brush. As the college grew and many of the women on the faculty moved out of the dormitories, a substantial number of them set up domestic twosomes. Where the two were sisters this arrangement presented no problems; where they were unrelated it was beginning to attract some unfavorable notice.

Such twosomes had been common at Wellesley when Jeannette Marks and Mary Woolley first met there, and at Bryn Mawr, where M. Carey Thomas had already faced down criticism of her relation with Mary Guinn and, after Miss Guinn's marriage, with Mary Garrett. At Mount Holyoke they were comparatively new as the atmosphere of the institution shifted gradually from that of a Protestant convent. The anxiety generated was partly a fear of social criticism, but its intensity suggests also that the relationship between Miss Woolley and Miss Marks was forcing repressed feelings into consciousness.

Miss Marks herself wrote an essay that winter entitled "Unwise College Friendships." Like much of her later work it showed a not entirely successful effort to resolve her personal problems through advice to others. Unwise college friendships in her expressed view were a form of illness against which prophylaxis was available, but she clearly thought of them more as a moral than a physical problem.

There are several peroxides I would recommend, any one of which is sure to help drive out an abnormal or senti-

mental condition: a sense of humor, confession, a vigorous prayer for self-control taken every day and as often as necessary throughout the day, and a careful investigation of and bettering of one's physical condition.

There is no suggestion anywhere in the essay that such friendships may be other than unwise or unwholesome, no mention of sublimation or repression. The article was prepared for publication but was submitted as being "by a College Professor" rather than over her own name. In view of her eagerness to establish her reputation as an author, this hiding of her individuality behind her professional status says a great deal about the social taboos surrounding the subject of homosexuality and perhaps even more about Jeannette Marks' own conflicting feelings.

Her opening paragraph suggests that the subject was being widely discussed sub rosa. She points out that homosexuality exists in men's colleges as well as in women's and does harm in both, expresses a strong reluctance to discuss so unpleasant a subject, and says that "the only justification for speaking at all is that one might be able to help."

The second paragraph shows a feeling hopelessly divided between psychological theory and personal experience.

What is needed is not psychological investigation but common sense . . . wholesome, straightforward, friendly talking . . . psychology has forgotten . . . the human cause at stake and acts as if scientific interest were the end-all and be-all of our existence.

She goes on to report the situation as she sees it in the contemporary college through conversations with a woman friend from outside the college community and with a student.

They [such friendships] cannot be fumigated out of the college because they are brought in from the outside world, from an incomplete or unwholesome home life, or as the result of ill health . . . from the general atmosphere of "hush" that is maintained upon the subject . . . what sound idea of moral relationships can a boy or girl be expected to get in a home where . . . there are two standards of morality — one for the man and one for the woman?

The student friend reports with a "half-amused, half-disgusted look upon her face":

The other night I went into a girl's room, she's a nice girl, too, and she and another girl were in there spooning with the lights turned out . . . I've noticed one thing, that when girls are silly that way they begin to get sick . . . I don't see what makes girls act that way.

I didn't tell her that I did [Miss Marks adds], or that my life has taught me many things about human nature that I did not wish to know . . . I know that it is hard sometimes to tell where right feeling, feeling that is sound and faithful, ends, and wrong feeling, feeling that is morbid, passionate, and transitory begins. . . . Of actual perverts in academic life, at the worst there can be only a few in many years; of mistakes there are many . . . These college girls need older people, their wisdom, their experience, their love . . . There is a difference between the physical and the spiritual . . . the only physical relationship that can fulfill itself and be complete is that between man and woman . . . we have to be on our guard sometimes to distinguish between what is a natural expression of affection and an unnatural attraction . . . to fling oneself into any intimacy is to take a great risk . . . a relationship that injures one's health is abnormal . . . a friendship that cannot be lived in the open may become a detestable influence.

All of this says more about Miss Marks' personal problem than about the problem of homosexuality in women's colleges, but it says a good deal about that as well. Granted her premise that any physical expression of homosexual love is bad physically or morally or both, the article is eminently sensible and practical. It did not, however, so impress her contemporaries. Two copies of the manuscript are in existence, both prepared for submission to editors, but there is no record of its ever having achieved publication.

Miss Marks' decision to suppress her own homosexual tendencies — not to repress them, for it was a fully conscious decision — underestimated the further difficulties she would have to face and the danger of distortions in her emotional life that would affect her work. The most obvious and perhaps the most naïve of these distortions is the idea that a young girl hovering on the verge of homosexual experience "needs older people, their wisdom, their experience, their love." Her efforts to help young women in this way throughout the rest of her life were invariably misinterpreted, or perhaps it would be more accurate to say that observers saw in these relationships what she failed to see herself.

The first of these friendships was with Eloise Robinson, a senior that year, 1909, in whom it was possible for Jeannette to see herself twelve years earlier. Eloise had literary ambitions and some talent, a middle western family with whom she was at odds, and a fondness for the outdoors and the strenuous life. She was impressed by Miss Marks' publication record and flattered at being invited first to the Green Pea and then to the President's House. Miss Marks could see a repetition of the early relationship between herself and Mary Woolley, and felt quite certain she could avoid the mistakes the older woman had made in that one.

As a part of the movement toward the abolition of the secret societies, Miss Woolley invited some of the most active and hostile of the alumnae members to visit South Hadley, see the new President's House, and discuss the problem with her. They came, but the gesture did not work as she had hoped it might. Seeing Jeannette Marks installed in the President's House exacerbated the criticism of her, and it was easy to blame Miss Woolley's objections to the societies altogether on Miss Marks' known views.

Miss Woolley was also starting work, a full three years in advance, on a celebration that was to outshine her inauguration and mark the triumphs of her first decade. Wellesley and Smith had celebrated their twenty-fifth anniversaries in 1900; Bryn Mawr was looking forward to doing so in 1910. Mount Holyoke's twenty-fifth as a college would not come until 1913, but in 1912 the institution would be seventy-five years old if seminary and college were viewed as one. Vigorously as Miss Woolley had worked to raise the status of the college above that of the seminary, she was ready now to grant that they had grown from the same root and represented different stages of a steady and uninterrupted progress. A seventy-fifth anniversary celebration would assert Mount Holyoke's claim to be the oldest of the women's colleges rather than one of the youngest and would rally alumnae support for the work still ahead. Perhaps the most important part of the plan was the doubling of the college endowment by the addition of $500,000. The General Education Board promised $100,000 if the other $400,000 were raised by October 1912. The sum seemed astronomical; the undertaking was fully the equal of Mary Lyon's seventy-five years earlier in raising $20,000 to establish the seminary.

Trustee committees and a faculty executive committee were appointed in the fall of 1909 in the midst of the furor over the abolition of the secret societies. The faculty committee included the dean, the registrar, and two faculty members, Professors Abby Turner and Ada Snell. At no time during the three years did Jeannette Marks show any interest in the matter, although the plans later developed included her special interests, drama and literature.

The study in which Miss Marks worked aptly symbolized the increasing difference between her own interests and those of the president of the college. Running the full depth of the house, it offered views of the campus to the east and the Connecticut River and the Mount Holyoke and Tom ranges to the west. An open fireplace in the south wall was flanked by bookcases on one side. The other, less conventionally, she enclosed with small-scale chicken wire to house tame birds. She could thus observe their habits at leisure while she worked on *A Holiday with the Birds*, which would be published the following year. The room's location on the top floor of the house, as her room at Brigham and her apartment in Alvord House had been, suggests as a subconscious motive a rather childish assumption of superiority to all others and particularly to the college president, but it also provided the very practical advantages of privacy and quiet. Miss Woolley would arrange to have Jeannette's meals served there on a tray whenever she was too busy or too tired to join the formal meals in the dining room.

It thus provided very nearly ideal working conditions for an author, but she did not manage to accomplish much in her first year as its tenant. The bird book with Julia Moody, articles based on her Welsh experiences in *Outlook* and the *Atlantic Monthly*, a few poems in *Outing*, *McClure's*, *Outlook*, and other magazines, and an essay in the *New England Magazine*, "The Crowded Hours of the College Girl," were her harvest for the year.

The essay throws light on the increasing divergence of her views from Miss Woolley's. What Jeannette found most objectionable in the crowded hours of the college girl was the amount of time devoted to meaningless social duties. She cited one girl who had spent fifteen hours in a single week on sorority work, but she objected also to receptions, church and prayer meetings, Bible classes, Y.W.C.A., student government, athletic meets, musical clubs, choir, dances, and games — not necessarily individually, but as they affected the time left for study and for healthful exercise. In all of this, of course, Miss Woolley was setting an example which the most ambitious of her girls could only regard with awe and respect. As Miss Marks was to comment in a later article, she was up before the housemaid in the morning and in bed far later in the evening. Her waking hours were filled with exactly the kinds of activity Miss Marks deplored for students. On the other hand, in the face of this demanding schedule and with almost no time for exercise, her health remained much better than that of Miss Marks, with her long walks, her health-food diet, and her ample leisure.

"The Crowded Hours" dealt also, though peripherally, with some of the more basic problems of the college woman at the end of the first decade of the twentieth century. The increase in the number and size of women's colleges and the opening of many universities to coeducation meant, of course, that a much larger proportion of the total female population between eighteen and twenty-two years of age was in college than had been in Miss Marks' or Miss Woolley's undergraduate years. Going to college was scarcely even an adventure any longer; it was in danger of becoming a fad. Under these circumstances Miss Marks thought that many girls were coming to college without either definite intellectual interests or a clear-cut plan for their lives.

The condition of a man's life is certainty; the condition of this girl's life uncertainty. Perhaps she will marry; perhaps she will stay at home; perhaps she will teach — if she must. In parental minds probably most of the vagueness about the exact purpose of college life for a girl is due to the conviction that a woman's economic value is bringing children into the world. In the girl's own consciousness marriage is present; but she does not under normal conditions think much about it; however she realizes that when it does come it will make a difference in her work. All the while a man is constantly expecting both to work and to marry. This instability of purpose on the part of the woman inevitably affects her attitude toward her work.

Theoretically Miss Marks had no connection with the college that year; her leave of absence might equally well have taken her to Battle Creek or to Wales. In practice, given her temperament, her residence in South Hadley, and the presence in the same house of the president of the college and a member of the English Literature Department, she found it quite impossible to avoid being involved. In January she quarreled with Bertha Young so seriously that Miss Young resigned. Miss Woolley promptly accepted the resignation and presented it to the board of trustees, who also approved it. Before the end of the year Miss Young offered to withdraw her resignation and presented letters from students and alumnae asking her to remain. Miss Woolley informed the trustees and later the petitioning students and alumnae that instructors had already been engaged to replace her and that the resignation would have to stand. Some years later, in a letter to a junior member of her department, Miss Marks wrote her own account of what had happened.

In the year 1910 Miss B. K. Young, head of the department, insisted on forcing Carrie Harper out . . . I told Miss Young that if she forced Carrie Harper out I would resign. We both did. In our concluding talk together Miss Young said the day would come when I would regret the position I had taken. The day came . . .

This is not entirely accurate. In the report Miss Woolley presented to the trustees in February, Miss Young had resigned and Miss Marks had requested an additional year's leave of absence. A $50 raise in salary to $1025 per annum was requested for Miss Harper with no mention of a promotion in rank. She was now in her third year at Mount Holyoke, still an instructor. During all of that time either Miss Young or Miss Marks had been on leave; it is possible that there might have been some question about the need for an additional member of the department when both of its senior ones were back at work. Miss Harper maintained a low profile throughout the controversy, and in the event stayed on at Mount Holyoke until her death in 1919. Her early intimacy with Jeannette Marks did not endure; her name had disappeared entirely from Jeannette's private correspondence by this time and did not recur.

Agitation about reversing the acceptance of Miss Young's resignation was thus added to the subjects for controversy in the spring of 1910. Miss Young was popular with her students and with her faculty colleagues; her scholarship was impeccable, and her aunt one of the most respected and influential of the senior professors in the college. A good many people must have seen in Miss Woolley's standing out against all this pressure from every side a determination worthy of a better cause. She began to get poison-pen letters from alumnae attacking her friendship with Miss Marks and Miss Marks' character. Everyone seems to have felt that except for this one weakness her own character was above criticism.

In the midst of the controversy Ethel Arnold came again to lecture at the college and was entertained at the President's House. This time her subjects were the political situation in England and her recollections of Lewis Carroll. She joined Miss Woolley and Miss Cady in their concern for Jeannette's health and spirits.

Eloise Robinson was graduated in the spring and awarded a Bardwell Memorial fellowship for graduate study. On the recommendation of Miss Marks and Miss Woolley she decided to use it in working for an M.A. at Wellesley. The recommendations went beyond the official, and as a result of their personal associations at Wellesley she was taken into the home of Katharine Lee Bates and Katharine Coman, who had, up to that time, lavished most of their unused maternal instincts on their collie, Sigurd.

Jeannette planned to spend a full year in Wales with Ethel Arnold in an all-out effort to establish herself and earn her living as a writer. The new President's House for which she had begged and Mary Woolley worked for so many years was to be left to the president and Helen Cady. Carrie Harper would run the Department of English Literature.

Mary Woolley went along to Wales in the summer and settled Jeannette in a house in Bettws-y-Coed with Miss Arnold, to whom it may have belonged. Letters addressed to Miss Marks there were often c/o Miss Arnold. Bettws-y-Coed was rather more of a tourist center than Beddgelert and had more comfortable accommodations as well as easy access to Carnarvon. There Jeannette settled in for a winter of hard, sustained work. She was finishing a novel, turning some of her Welsh short stories into one-act plays, writing travel sketches, juvenile articles, short stories, essays, and poems. Mary Woolley returned to South Hadley and to the unresolved problems of the previous year.

A curious three-sided correspondence ensued. May sent money, advice, reports on the activities of the college, and pleas to come home. Jeannette sent manuscripts to be placed, errands to be done, complaints about the discomforts of her life, and tortured efforts to explain her need for independence. Helen Cady interposed pleas in support of Miss Woolley's that Jeannette should return and added that she thought the separation was affecting Miss Woolley's health. If Ethel Arnold contributed to the correspondence, her letters have not survived. The winter was for her apparently some sort of cure. Her nerves were bad, and Jeannette complained that her illnesses disrupted the household, adding a perfunctory "poor dear."

For Jeannette, Ethel was an obvious substitute for May — an older woman whose ability and success she admired and who could give her both emotional support and practical assistance in her own work. For the work she really wanted to do Ethel was the more useful of the two; she could offer introductions to important literary figures and judge work in progress from a professional viewpoint. On the other hand she was much like Jeannette herself — neurotic, unpredictable, self-centered, and of very doubtful status in the literary world — whereas May was strong, sane, and by this time very powerful.

In South Hadley the matter of the Greek-letter societies was settled to Mary Woolley's satisfaction. The faculty first and then the trustees voted by large majorities for their abolition on the ground that "the welfare of the college demands that secret self-perpetuating societies should not exist in the college." Miss Woolley wrote to Wales that the disgruntled alumnae

cannot attribute my action to your influence, and could not even if you were here . . . I am receiving letters from alumnae . . . assuring me of support.

*

With that question settled she hoped that Jeannette could come back and take her place in the English Literature Department.

. . . you will find not a difficult situation but a very pleasant and congenial one. I suppose that I was so worn out by "things" in the spring that I unconsciously exaggerated . . . Every day I feel more convinced that to remain in the department is the thing for you to do, unless you really prefer to give all your time to the other line . . . The feeling engendered by Miss Young will take time to allay . . . [but] that we must ignore.

May was also sending money, since the "other line" had not yet proved adequately profitable — $100 from her first salary check with another $100 to follow from the second. Throughout September Jeannette worked hard and was reasonably content.

If only I can come home with some decent work done and people will let you and me alone, we'll be orsul happy, won't we?

"Orsul" was her usual little-language misspelling of "awful."

Mary Woolley wrote on October 21:

I do not care what has been written to you. I want you to come . . . If my work here depends upon your being away from me, it is not worth the keeping. If I have made no place for myself, if I have to ask a group of alumnae to approve of my choice of a friend, if my hold on the college depends upon pleasing them in a personal matter — I would better give up. There is nothing in our friendship for which to apologize . . . We have done no wrong. Dearest, there is no reason why we should be separated. Jealousy and prejudice ought not to be allowed to triumph . . .

Jeannette replied on November 1 with a long, impassioned, and frequently illegible letter presenting her pleas for independence.

Darlin' Muddie: Can't you see how much harder you are making it all for me? . . . What you report to me about the college does not reassure me although it does not disturb me. People usually get something of what they deserve, and no doubt I deserve in part all the vindictive and vicious criticism that has followed me. But there has been so much of it and for so long that I feel almost entirely indifferent. As an institution and because it is your work I feel an interest in the college, but I must find the best part of my life elsewhere ... The circumstances of my life are a constant humiliation to me; that at 35 my footing in the world of work should be so insecure, that people should misinterpret my whole attitude towards what does and does not count, that I should be financially crippled and unable to do anything for you.

I am a grown and growing woman, and however much the child in me may want coddling it could never be really content with coddling and shelter ... And, darlin' Muddie, although I want you to be one of the few great women in the world today and with a still greater future before you, can't you see that ... however little I may be in comparison with you, yet ... I must try to have a life of my own! ... Let me find you strong; stay on your pedestal, darlin' Muddie, and so will you be helping me most. Your own little girl.

A few days later she wrote again.

When I feel that it is right for me to come home I shall take the next ship. However, I am certain that it will be months before I shall feel that it would be right for me to return to South Hadley. I am feeling resolute and cheerful today, but this is only two days after one of the worst storms I have had. I don't pretend to understand myself — I introspect too much anyway — all I know is that these cyclonic disturbances are too horrible for words: they are madness, perhaps madness in a mild form, but nevertheless madness ... E is better on the whole although it is off again, on again, and "nerves," poor dear, that give her and everybody else no peace.

Exactly a week later she cabled to South Hadley for money enough for an immediate return, writing at the same time:

Every breath I draw now has become a pain to me, and I am afraid of going out of my mind if this continues. When I get home just let me be near you and Neddie and say nothing. Be kind to me, be gentle, be patient. I will stand on my own feet all I can and as soon as I can.

Miss Woolley cabled the money and replied without apparent anxiety as to the cause for this abrupt about-face.

My dearest little girl, I am so excited today I hardly know what I am doing. This morning your cable came "cable immediately 15 pounds for passage" and my heart jumps at the thought of you being at home for Christmas. I am not letting myself imagine that you are not well; I am simply thinking that in some blessed way you have found that it is best for you to come home, and I am too happy for words.

This bland refusal to recognize that something must have gone seriously wrong in Wales was the attitude she continued to maintain. What had happened was never again referred to in the correspondence, and Jeannette never went back to Wales. If the difficulty had been a quarrel with Ethel it was smoothed over; the next fall Miss Arnold came to South Hadley and delivered a series of lectures on nineteenth-century poetry, living as a guest in the President's House. In some of Jeannette Marks' later books and in correspondence some years later there are hints that perhaps the two of them had been experimenting with drugs.

At about this time Jeannette first made the acquaintance of Dr. Oscar Jennings, an association that was to be important and fruitful for her. He was a Fellow of the Royal Society of Medicine who practiced chiefly in Paris and claimed a record of unusual success in curing drug addiction. His *Morphia Habit and Its Voluntary Renunciation* rather more than hinted that he had been his own first patient and that his successful self-cure had set him on the road to treating others. His methods were unconventional and roused a good deal of opposition within the medical

profession, but the patients with whom he had been successful idolized him. They were generally well-to-do and
often prominent in the arts or in society; his treatment was
slow and expensive and thus not well adapted to the needs
of the ordinary workingman. Ethel Arnold would have been
a fairly typical patient for him, Jeannette Marks rather less
so. Throughout the rest of her life she always spoke of him
with warm affection and admiration, but never said where
they had met.

Dr. Jennings shared with the authorities at Battle Creek
a disapproval of the use of alcohol, tobacco, or stimulating
diet for a former addict, and encouraged the use of the
Turkish bath and of bicycling as an exercise. Jeannette's
first contact with him may have been through Battle Creek,
but it seems on the whole more probable that it was through
Ethel in 1910.

There is also the possibility that the traumatic Welsh
experience was an overt homosexual experience of some
kind.

Whatever had happened, Jeannette had capitulated in her
effort to have a life of her own and chosen to accept the
coddling with which she could never be really content. In
the following fall the *Outlook* carried a short story, "Mrs.
Llewellyn Jones' Sister," by Jeannette Marks. Mrs. Llewellyn Jones is a soloist who has won prizes at several Eis-
teddfods; her younger sister has lost all identity except
through her sister's fame. Even when she wins a singing
contest herself people refer to her as Mrs. Llewellyn Jones'
sister.

*Of late she had had an almost frenzied feeling, as if she
should lose her mind if she couldn't cease being her sister's
sister and be herself for a little while. Only to be satisfied
that she* was *herself, to be able to tie her shoestring in
public, laugh, cry, quarrel, and love, out of the limelight of
her sister's greatness!*

Only when she escapes to America and finds a suitor does
she become fully herself.

Mary Woolley as a young professor at Wellesley.
(*Wellesley College Archives*)

Jeannette Marks at Dana Hall 1892, aged seventeen.
(*Special Collections, Wellesley College*)

The Rotunda, Wellesley College, as it looked in 1895.

" . . . clocks and chimes like silver hammers falling
On silver anvils, and the splash and stir
Of fountains spouted up and showering down
In meshes of the jasmine and the rose."

Tennyson: *The Princess*

(*Wellesley College Archives*)

Crew of the ARGO, Wellesley College class of 1894, with the college in the
background. (*Wellesley College Archives*)

Jeannette Marks as a young woman.
(*Mount Holyoke College Library*)

President Woolley at her inauguration, 1901.
(*Mount Holyoke College Library*)

Jeannette Marks in Wales, 1905.
(*Special Collections, Wellesley College*)

The President's House, Mount Holyoke College, 1908.
(*Mount Holyoke College Library*)

The formal dining room in the President's House.
(*Mount Holyoke College Library*)

MOUNT HOLYOKE'S SEVENTY-FIFTH ANNIVERSARY, 1912
(*Thomas C. Hawkes, photographer, South Hadley Center,
Massachusetts, Mount Holyoke College Library*)
Academic Procession

The Pageant: "The Telegraph"

The Pageant: "Radium"

Mary Woolley with one of the collies.
(©*Bachrach; Mount Holyoke College Library*)

Jeannette Marks with one of the collies.
(*Special Collections, Wellesley College*)

President Mary E. Woolley of Mount Holyoke College.
(*Mount Holyoke College Library*)

Jeannette Marks, author. (*Mount Holyoke College Library*)

Mary Woolley and Jeannette Marks together at Fleur de Lys.
(*Mount Holyoke College Library*)

Jeannette Marks in Attic Peace.
(*Special Collections, Wellesley College*)

Mary Woolley returning from the Geneva Arms
Conference, 1932, with Senator Claude Swanson of
Virginia (left) and Norman Davis, former
Undersecretary of State. (©*International News
Photos, Inc.; Mount Holyoke College Library*)

Student-Alumnae Hall, Mount Holyoke College Library, later renamed
Mary E. Woolley Hall. (*Mount Holyoke College Library*)

Mount Holyoke's first Laboratory Theatre, built in 1928–29.
(*Mount Holyoke College Library*)

Jeannette Marks at work in the Laboratory Theatre.
(*Mount Holyoke College Library*)

Mary Woolley at her retirement, 1937.
(*MacCarthy*, Springfield Union; *Mount Holyoke College Library*)

Fleur de Lys on Lake George, where Mary Woolley and Jeannette Marks passed their old age together. (*Special Collections, Wellesley College*)

At Fleur de Lys with collies and a guest. (*Mount Holyoke College Library*)

For Jeannette the return to America was not an escape, and no suitor was waiting in the wings. She had, on the contrary, accepted a lifetime of being Mrs. Llewellyn Jones' sister. The consequences were important for Mount Holyoke as well as for herself and Miss Woolley.

Christmas 1910 was celebrated in the President's House with suitable dignified gaiety. Those of Miss Woolley's friends who approved of her association with Jeannette wrote to congratulate her on the return; the others were silent. Eloise Robinson came from Wellesley with greetings from Miss Bates and Miss Coman and a collie pup in a basket. He was named Lord Wellesley and was to be the first of a long line. Miss Marks had always liked dogs; it is possible to suspect that Miss Woolley merely tolerated them, but if so she tolerated them as energetically as she did everything else. For the rest of her life her house was full of them, and they were always beautifully cared for and much in evidence. They became a part of her public image; in later years this sometimes pleased and sometimes irritated Miss Marks.

Even though the year of hard work in Wales had been aborted, Jeannette Marks had a notable publication year in 1911. She published her first novel, *End of a Song*, received the Welsh National Theatre prize for two one-act plays, and appeared for the first time in *Who's Who*, an achievement which drew a congratulatory letter from her father, also listed therein.

End of a Song, a sentimental novel laid in Wales, received unanimous acclaim from reviewers. The *New York Times* called it "as sweet and fresh and blithe as the song of a bird in June" and spoke of its "exquisite imagery." The *Literary Digest* said that its author showed "literary skill and that kind of naturalness which is the highest order of sophistication." It was dedicated, as planned, to the Dearest of Friends, Ethel M. Arnold, Helen M. Cady, and Mary E. Woolley. The story concerns a stingy rich man and his generous wife, a development of an idea first used in one of the stories in *Through Welsh Doorways*. Miss Marks was thrifty in her use of material; the stories in that collection reappeared also as the prize-winning one-act plays.

End of a Song expresses some feminist ideas which had not previously appeared in Miss Marks' fiction.

It was his inheritance as much as anything else, that made him blind, generations of fond short-sighted motherhood which had bred in him selfishness in personal matters and obliviousness to little things which help in the smooth running of any life when lived with another.

and

She waited till Shon had finished his breakfast. How many wives have waited thus, perhaps indignant within but helpless without, till an auspicious moment gave them a chance to ask for what was theirs by every common right of burden bearing, labor, interest!

The wife wins her own way, however, by the age-old feminine wile of weakness; she falls ill and so frightens her husband that he gives her both pocket money and charge accounts and allows her to adopt two orphans.

A less important publication of the year was *A Girl's Student Days and After*, a collection of essays that had first been published in the *Girl's Companion* and *Young People's Weekly*. It carried a laudatory introduction by Mary Emma Woolley, LL.D., President of Mount Holyoke College, who referred to the "wise hints in the chapters which follow" as "invaluable."

Miss Marks had very definite ideas as to which of her works were potboilers and which serious artistic endeavors. The distinction is not always clear to the reader, and in this area her inspirational works are particularly puzzling. They are superficial, conventional, sententious, and yet it is impossible to dismiss them as trivia. In them she is wrestling not too successfully with her own emotional problems.

A Girl's Student Days is aimed at girls somewhat younger

and less sophisticated than college students. It deals with health (she considered two hours of outdoor exercise a day the minimum requisite), team spirit, study habits, loyalty, ambition, and other relevant subjects. The chapter on friendship does not borrow from "Unwise College Friendships" but does make some points that could have been included under that title. A school or college friendship, she says, should not be exclusive or too demanding, should not turn a girl away from her own family, should not develop "the less fine traits in one's character," and should contribute benefits to both participants, not to one alone. The chapter entitled "The Student's Room" presents some ideas that Miss Marks would use with her classes for many years. There was a plea first for light and air, the elimination of heavy curtains and drapes, and the clearing out of knickknacks, frippery, and "kitchen equipment" (chafing dishes, teapots and cups, ice cream freezers, dishcloths and the concomitant cream bottles, sardine tins, cracker boxes, paper bags full of stale biscuits, and fruit skins). She had adopted some ideas about beauty and utility from Ruskin and William Morris. For many years she used to require her students to make lists of all their possessions under the headings Useful, Beautiful, and Neither, and urged them to throw away anything that could not be fitted into the first two lists. Very little was ever thrown away, if I remember correctly, but we enjoyed making the lists. It might be noted in passing that the advice is all directed toward an exclusively feminine society. Men are mentioned a few times, and even the possibility of marriage is acknowledged for a vague and unspecified future, but the real world of the author is the world of women and girls.

The Welsh plays probably remained throughout her life the works by which Jeannette Marks was best known. They employed small casts and single sets and were in many ways ideal for amateurs. According to the publicity attending the awarding of the prize, they were submitted without her knowledge "by an acquaintance." The prize had been intended for a full-length play suitable for use by the Welsh

National Theatre, but since no satisfactory one was entered in the competition the award was made for the two one-act ones, *The Merry Merry Cuckoo* and *Welsh Honeymoon*. In the former a dying old man hopes to hear the first cuckoo of spring before he leaves the world. His wife practices until she can imitate the cuckoo's call well enough to deceive him; her minister tells her it will be a sin to do so, but she does anyway, and her husband dies happy. In *Welsh Honeymoon* an unhappily married couple each wishes the other dead. They go separately and secretly to the church porch on Halloween, each hoping to see the spirit of the objectionable partner, a sure sign that the person will die before the next Halloween. Naturally both wishes are fulfilled and they go home separately but feeling a certain amount of compunction. Since it is their last year together, they both resolve to make it a pleasant one, and by the following Halloween, the time at which the scene is set, each is dreading the expected death of the other in the course of the evening. The happy ending here is assured in advance. It is perhaps an interesting point that only the wife confesses, allowing the husband to forgive her nobly.

While one shudders to think of the variety of Welsh accents in which these plays have been presented in America, they gave pleasure to actors and audiences for many years and may even be doing so today.

With these successes to bolster her self-confidence, Jeannette Marks summoned up the courage to resign her associate professorship. In the president's formal acceptance of the resignation the hope was expressed that Miss Marks would someday return as a lecturer. Determination was one of Miss Woolley's most notable qualities.

VI

Seventy-fifth Anniversary

THE LAST DAY of 1910 marked the end of Miss Woolley's first decade at the college. In those ten years she had assembled a faculty of young, vigorous, and ambitious women with impressive scholarly qualifications to replace the seminary teachers as they retired and increased the size of the student body by about fifty percent. She had added six major buildings to the campus and increased endowment by $300,000. She herself was a trustee of three colleges, a senator of Phi Beta Kappa, a member of the National Board of the Y.W.C.A. and of the board of electors for the Hall of Fame and the College Entrance Examination Board, along with holding membership in societies ranging from the Massachusetts Equal Suffrage League to the D.A.R. Her personal prestige, demonstrated in all these ways, was important to the college, but her personal popularity was at a low ebb. Her anniversary would be celebrated in the spring with suitable ceremonies, but more attention was directed to the seventy-fifth anniversary of the seminary, which would come a year and a half later.

Mary Woolley put the difficult year of 1910 firmly behind her, but she did not forget its lessons. The seventy-fifth anniversary should draw together all the segments of the college and bury its feuds.

By the spring of 1911 committees had been set up, an October date in 1912 chosen, and the fund drive for half a million dollars' endowment was showing promise of success. Of the $400,000 required to meet the General Education Board's offer, Mrs. John Stewart Kennedy pledged $100,000 unconditionally, so that only $300,000 had to be raised by alumnae and friends. The building fund to which students and alumnae had been contributing for several years looking toward a student-alumnae building was counted as a part of this total. Everyone connected with the college from the president of the board of trustees down to the youngest freshman was thus involved in the fund-raising, and everyone would be involved also in the anniversary program — everyone, that is, except Jeannette Marks and possibly Professor Mignon Talbot of the Geology Department.

Miss Talbot was battling for permission to send her dinosaur to Yale or the Smithsonian Institution. She had discovered its fossil remains in a gravel pit between South Hadley and Holyoke. She and her sister, Professor Ellen Bliss Talbot of the Philosophy Department, were accustomed to walk the four miles into Holyoke rather than riding the trolley. On one such excursion they paused to look at a little hill that struck them as an appropriate site for the house they were thinking of building. It turned out, however, to be only a shell screening an abandoned gravel pit. In Miss Talbot's own words as reported in Frances Lester Warner's *On a New England Campus:*

At the bottom of the pit I saw two boulders of sandstone, and other boulders of granite. On one of the sandstone pieces was a streak of white that looked like a pick mark. I was pretty sure it was only a pick mark, but I went down to see. And I saw vertebrae, and I saw ribs, and I saw bones — and I said, "Oh, Ellen, come quick, come quick, I've found a real live fossil." And she said, "Have you lost your mind?"

Miss Talbot had been taught that no geologist had a right to collect for herself while she was chairman of a department but that she had a perfect right to collect for the college. The readiness of the farm's owner to allow her to take the fossil bothered her New England conscience a little.

I said, "But Mr. Boynton! It is really a pretty good speci-men, Mr. Boynton." And Mr. Boynton said, "I guess we won't quarrel over a piece of sandstone." He said he didn't care for it anyway.

It was removed intact and sent to Yale, where Dr. R. S. Lull confirmed Miss Talbot's opinion of the importance of her find. It was named *Podokesaurus holyokensis,* and her article about its discovery appeared in the *American Journal of Science* in June 1911. Dr. Lull had plaster casts made, and asked that the original fossil be given to Yale's Peabody Museum or the Natural History Museum in Washington.

Miss Woolley was pleased, naturally, by the discovery and the publication, but she was firm in her determination that the little skeleton must remain at Mount Holyoke. Whatever prestige it might carry belonged to the college that shared its name. The plaster casts went to New Haven and Washington, and *Podokesaurus holyokensis* to Williston Hall, Mount Holyoke's science building. Neither Miss Woolley nor Miss Talbot could possibly have known that hall and skeleton would be destroyed by fire in 1917, but Miss Talbot never forgave Miss Woolley.

Miss Marks was writing furiously in Attic Peace and casting about for a place in America remote and picturesque enough to serve as a substitute for Wales. In the spring she discovered a camp near Greenville, Maine, which appeared to be suitable for her purpose. Her taste in the choice of a place to work was strongly influenced by the romantic poets she admired; it must be wild, lonely, rugged, remote, picturesque, and preferably somewhat uncomfortable. In none of these respects was Maine as satisfactory as Wales, but it appears to have been the best available substitute. Mary Woolley rented the camp for the summer from a middle western clergyman, and Jeannette changed its name from Mr. Pattison's Camp to Camp Runway. It was, of course, far less suitable for Miss Woolley's purposes than for Miss Marks'. The former could spend at most a month in the summer there, while Jeannette went early and stayed late. Responsibility for it cut into the opportunity for European travel, which Miss Woolley greatly enjoyed. Also it worried her to have Jeannette alone at camp; she arranged for Helen Cady and Eloise Robinson to take turns as companion-guardians, and returned herself to a lonely house.

The loneliness was ameliorated by the temporary residence of Ethel Arnold, who was to give a series of ten lectures in connection with the nineteenth-century poetry course, taught that year by Dorothy Foster. Miss Arnold and Miss Woolley were not close friends, but both had been brought up in the tradition of late-Victorian good manners, which enabled them to share a home without friction. And in many ways Miss Arnold was a more agreeable companion than Jeannette Marks. She enjoyed meeting the celebrities who visited the house, and they were impressed by her. She spoiled Lord Wellesley, feeding him forbidden chocolate creams and relieving Miss Woolley of some share of responsibility for him. The students made her something of a figure of fun. They were amused by her accent, her mannerisms, and her attitude toward her distinguished family, "a long line of eminent ancestors who have been men of the pen and gown," and who had left her with a preference for the "obscuah."

In any case Miss Woolley was perhaps too busy to be lonely. The seventy-fifth anniversary was now only a year in the future. Two $50,000 gifts had been added to the $100,000 one, but it was still necessary to work hard for the smaller ones, and many of them came with attached conditions that required further work. There were endowment funds for the Zoology Department and for an art museum, and gifts of casts, reproductions, and photographs to be placed in the latter, $1000 earmarked for a plant physiology laboratory, a memorial gateway of brownstone and wrought iron, and many others, all of which had to be solicited, placed, and acknowledged. Students and faculty were working frantically on projects to raise money for the Student-

Alumnae Hall; the girls took in one another's laundry, shined shoes, put on shows, wore last year's dresses to this year's prom. And money was, of course, only a small part of what the anniversary would mean. Faculty committees were appointed to plan a pageant and musical performances, to keep records, to plan accommodations and invitations, to distribute tickets, to prepare an outdoor auditorium, to arrange for reception of guests, to decorate the campus, to inform newspapers and magazines, to provide ushers, to arrange a formal luncheon, to ensure that adequate academic costumes were available (Miss Woolley had not forgotten President Taylor at her inauguration), to plan programs, to handle emergencies, to make notices and maintain bulletin boards, to organize student assistance, and to marshal the academic procession. Miss Woolley was chairman of the executive committee to which all of these reported, and of the committees on selection of speakers, awarding of honorary degrees, and publication of the proceedings.

Also she was still adding to her responsibilities in the outside world. Although she had come rather late to the suffrage movement, she was now a firm if not very active supporter. She was an honorary vice president of the Massachusetts Woman's Suffrage League and encouraged the organization of a chapter of the Equal Suffrage League at the college. Two thirds of the faculty and nearly two hundred students joined this in its first year.

Miss Woolley was not quite so strongly supported in her dawning interest in world peace. She had been since 1908 a vice president of the American Peace Society; by 1911 she was also a vice president and member of the executive committee of the American School Peace League and a member of the committee on educational institutions of the Second National Peace Congress. In succeeding years she became an officer in the Massachusetts branch of the Peace Society, a charter member of the Church Peace League, and a member of the commission on peace and arbitration of the National Council of Women, and, after 1914, member of a number of organizations attempting to keep America uninvolved in the European war. Professor Ellen Ellis of the History Department, reminiscing in her old age, said:

I do not believe, though I cannot be sure that I am correct, that President Woolley was a pacifist in the full sense of that term . . . She saw the problem of war and peace primarily as a moral problem rather than as the political and legal problem which it in reality is.

Whether or not Professor Ellis was entirely correct in her analysis of what the problem of war and peace in reality is, she was probably altogether correct in her view of Miss Woolley as pacifist.

Jeannette Marks was always a more enthusiastic supporter of suffrage for women than Mary Woolley, but at this time she was not much more interested in the cause of world peace than in the seventy-fifth anniversary celebration. When cold weather drove her back from Camp Runway to South Hadley she became organizer for western Massachusetts of the Woman's Suffrage League, of which May was vice president. This was perhaps the first time in their professional lives that they had worked together on a project concerning which they were in agreement.

Jeannette was at work on a second novel, more ambitious and more serious in purpose than *End of a Song.* It was concerned with the problem of drug addiction and drew heavily on the work of Dr. Jennings. A good deal of further research was necessary; the book she planned would be an attack on the drug evil as well as a work of art. About careless prescribing and over-the-counter sale of dangerous sedatives she knew something, but it was necessary to get information also about the mechanics of the trade: production, transportation, and illegitimate sale. The scene of the novel was to be Philadelphia and the protagonist a young man not unlike her own father in his youth, a professor of mechanics specializing in transit.

Her flesh-and-blood father had returned to live in the old

summer home on Lake Champlain and wanted her to join him there as paid companion if she would come on no other terms. After leaving the Philadelphia Edison Company, he had set up as an adviser to municipalities on utility rates, working out of a New York office and doing well. With the curious contrariness that seems to have been a family trait, he chose to return, alone and in failing health, to the family home for which he had had little time when wife and children lived there. Jeannette seems not even to have considered his offer; her few meetings with him since 1895 had been brief and painful, and she wanted no more of them.

The new novel grew slowly; she made more satisfactory progress on a travel book about Wales, which included several articles already published in *Outlook* and the *Atlantic Monthly*.

In January of 1912 preparations for the celebration the following October began in good earnest. The executive committee of the faculty with Professor Abby H. Turner as chairman had been at work for a full year, and the publicity committee was sending notes about Mount Holyoke's history and the anniversary to newspapers in all sections of the country. In April announcements were sent to colleges and universities throughout the nation and abroad.

The Trustees and the Faculty of Mount Holyoke College desire to announce that the commemoration of the Seventy-fifth Anniversary of the founding of the Institution as a seminary will be held on Tuesday and Wednesday, the eighth and ninth of October, nineteen hundred and twelve.

It is hoped that your institution will be represented on this occasion by your president and a delegate. Formal invitations will be sent out at a later date. The committee will esteem it a favor if you will reply before the first of July, indicating your willingness to participate in these exercises and stating the name of your delegate.

Very truly yours

For the Anniversary Committee

This was followed by two thousand formal invitations, which would result in representation from fourteen foreign universities and colleges, including those of Greece, Japan, Syria, South Africa, Spain, England, and Constantinople, and from eighty-eight American ones.

Invitations went out also to more than six thousand alumnae, graduates and nongraduates from both seminary and college. At this time the nongraduates still outnumbered the graduates, as a great many girls had come, like Emily Dickinson, for a single year. Class representatives were secured for every year from 1837 to 1912. The Commissioners of Education for the United States and the State of Massachusetts were also to be present, along with representatives from Phi Beta Kappa and the New England College Entrance Certificate Board.

Jeannette finished *Gallant Little Wales* in Attic Peace in May. It was a pleasant travel book in the style then popular, retracing walking tours Miss Marks had made and describing villages, churches, cottages, castles, and abbeys, with a chapter about the Eisteddfod, one about "the city of the Prince of Wales," and accounts of Welsh folklore and Samuel Johnson's tour of North Wales. The frontispiece of the published book was a picture of the Ladies of Llangollen:

two dear, quaint, sentimental souls, with personalities sufficiently marked and fearless so that they were unafraid to be themselves . . . Lady Eleanor Butler was the daughter of the Earl of Ormond. She was born in Dublin and was both wealthy and beautiful. The Honourable Miss [Sarah] Ponsonby, a member of an ancient family, was an early friend of Lady Eleanor. She, too, was born in Dublin, and both lost their parents at the same time. They loved independence and did not love their suitors. Many things drew them together and, as Wordsworth aptly phrases it, they retired into notice in the Vale of Llangollen.

Miss Marks quotes with obvious distress the report of an earlier woman travel writer who found them "foolish, condescending, proud, vain, and pompous" and thoroughly disapproved of their friendship. She is happier with Wordsworth's sonnet which concludes:

Sisters in love, a love allowed to climb,
Even on this earth, above the reach of Time.

Her failure to develop the theme further, like her failure to publish "Unwise College Friendships," speaks both of the social taboos of her era and the extent to which she had internalized its standards.

The book was reviewed favorably but did not sell well. Miss Woolley used it as a going-away present for faculty members sailing for Europe that summer, but their polite letters of thanks gave Jeannette little satisfaction.

As soon as her work on it was finished she went to Camp Runway for the summer, leaving Miss Woolley to follow when her duties made it possible. Jeannette was suffering acutely from a sense of being Mrs. Llewellyn Jones' sister and took it out in a fractiousness that must have been excessively trying. With the help of her godmother, Helen Frances Kimball of Boston, she bought the camp after Miss Woolley had refused to do so, and embarked on an ambitious project of restoration. When Miss Woolley joined her at the end of June she brought along Helen Cady, a maid, one of the college workmen, and the now full-grown collie, Lord Wellesley. With this entourage May planned reasonably enough to make the trip by day train, but Jeannette insisted she should travel overnight, taking sleepers for all but Wellesley. "Give the porter a dollar," was her advice about him. They argued the matter through several exchanges of letters, Miss Woolley pointing out the inconvenience of the night train and Miss Marks that of meeting the day one. It was, as usual, Miss Woolley who yielded, but by the time she did so the sleepers for the chosen date were all sold. It is possible that she was beginning to apply some of her famous administrative skill to her relations with Jeannette; in any case the journey was made by day.

The camp was now crowded as well as Spartan in its accommodations, and before the summer was over Eloise Robinson was added to the party. She had finished her graduate work at Wellesley and taken her M.A. to an accompaniment of high praise from Katharine Lee Bates, who found her a dear child as well as an admirable scholar. Miss Marks should have been pleased at this satisfactory working out of a plan she had suggested, and perhaps was so, but she was even more irritable with Eloise than with the others. She was again worried about her own health, and talked of going back to Battle Creek.

Miss Woolley must have found her return to South Hadley in August and the final burst of effort in preparation for the anniversary something of a relief. Jeannette stayed on at the camp with a series of companions: first Helen Cady, then her own sister Mabel with husband and children, then Ethel Arnold, and finally Eloise. She quarreled with Ethel definitively and with Helen so seriously that the friendship was never entirely restored. Of Ethel she wrote Miss Woolley:

I did the very best I could and for two years set aside my own life and interests in trying to do for her and help her . . . I cannot stop grieving, but that too is a fait accompli. Poor dear, poor dear!

Miss Arnold lived on for some years, but had no further contact with Mount Holyoke or her friends there. The nineteenth-century poetry class reverted to Dorothy Foster.

Through September Jeannette's letters to South Hadley continued captious and provocative. She thought she ought to go to Battle Creek; she had earache; Eloise was impossible; she had earned only $50 by her writing in four months. Miss Woolley sent money, clothes, apologies, and urgent advice to go to Battle Creek or come home.

The anniversary is nothing in comparison . . . You could be quiet in your own rooms.

Both statements offer a measure of Miss Woolley's devotion. The anniversary, if not the most important event in Mount Holyoke's seventy-five-year history, was certainly the most ambitious and spectacular. The number of guests, distinguished and otherwise, was completely beyond the resources of South Hadley to entertain. Hotels in Amherst, Holyoke, Northampton, and Springfield were engaged in addition to all available rooms in the village. Students from three of the dormitories were to give up their rooms to alumnae and delegates, sleeping themselves on couches in other dormitories furnished for the occasion. A temporary kitchen was set up in the basement of the village church; extra streetcar service from Holyoke was arranged, and a few private automobiles were made available. These were reserved for the most distinguished of the distinguished guests; others were advised to use the streetcars, which ran every fifteen minutes to Holyoke and every half hour to Amherst, or buggies, which would be waiting in front of Mary Lyon Hall to drive people up Prospect Hill or to their boarding places for a charge of twenty-five cents.

That Jeannette Marks could have been quiet in her own rooms is doubtful, but it is to be noted that she did not offer to lend the unused space nor did Miss Woolley venture to suggest it, although faculty members who had houses of their own and many citizens of the village were making their spare rooms available. Helen Cady was a marshal, Dorothy Foster was chairman of the program committee, and Carrie Harper a member of the reception committee. Every member of the faculty served in some capacity, but Jeannette Marks was represented only by copies of *Gallant Little Wales* on sale in the college bookstore. On October 8, the day the celebration started, she wrote:

Don't get a swelled head this week. You are nicer when you are flexible, human, and no knee action.

Mail service was such in 1912 that a letter written in Maine on the eighth could have been delivered in South Hadley on the ninth. If it arrived on that morning Miss Woolley would certainly have taken time out to read it at once, even though she was to be fully occupied with public appearances from nine-thirty in the morning until evening.

The day would begin with an academic procession and end with a reception at the President's House. In between Mary Woolley would introduce six speakers, confer fourteen honorary degrees, listen to seven speeches in addition to the six she introduced, preside at a luncheon in the gymnasium, and amaze and delight an uncounted number of the more than three thousand alumnae, delegates, distinguished guests, newspaper reporters, parents, and other visitors by recognizing them, remembering their names, and having an appropriate remark for each. On the previous day she had introduced and listened to eight speakers, presided at another luncheon, watched the pageant that most visitors considered the highlight of the anniversary, and attended a song recital and a student serenade. Everyone who saw her commented on the serenity and ease with which she handled this schedule.

Mount Holyoke's seventy-fifth anniversary was more than an enormous collection of people and a staggering list of speeches. It knit together with great skill the history of the seminary and the growing reputation of the college. On the first day attention was directed to the alumnae, and the speeches concerned the life of the institution from 1837 onward. The pageant was scheduled for that afternoon with typical long-range planning; if it rained on the eighth the outdoor performance could be moved to the ninth. The weather, however, was perfect on the eighth. The New England Indian summer outdid itself with a blaze of sunshine that glorified the autumn foliage. The campus boasts a natural amphitheater facing a level, grassy lawn, a brook, and a grove of trees. Still in use for many occasions, it has been "improved" almost beyond recognition, but at the time of the seventy-fifth anniversary it served as a magnificent natural setting for the pageant in which every student in the college participated.

Each department had planned its own presentation within

a framework designed by Professor Louise Jewett of the Art Department. Elizabeth Crane Porter, who reported the affair for the *Outlook*, chose to emphasize the presentation of the Chemistry Department as particularly poetic and beautiful. Its subject was "The Chemical Element," and a quotation from Sir Humphry Davy headed its section of the program:

To inquire whether the elements be capable of being composed or decomposed is a grand object of true philosophy.

Ancient theories of matter were typified by the Alchemist, and definitions and discoveries of the elements by Robert Boyle, Antoine Laurent Lavoisier, Joseph Priestley, Sir Humphry Davy, and John Dalton. Not a woman among them, though Emma Perry Carr, the young professor of chemistry who helped to plan the pageant, was in midcentury to be the first winner of the Garvan Medal for the outstanding contribution of her sex to the field.

Perhaps any of the gentlemen would have considered the presentation of the subject particularly feminine, for after Dalton, who had enunciated the atomic theory, came Dmitri Ivanovitsch Mendelejeff, discoverer of the periodic law, followed by a bevy of dancers in graded tints of gray, pink, brown, green, yellow, blue, tan, and lavender. In the words of the program's commentator, Louise Whitfield Bray, 1912, they "danced in wild confusion to the music of a Russian folk dance."

Suddenly a commanding figure stood forth, Mendelejeff, the Russian scientist ... At his bidding the dancing elements fell into harmonious groups in order of their atomic weights ... Once more the eyes of the audience were entranced by a dancing figure, Radium, in a robe shimmering with silver threads ... With a quick gesture she cast aside her glittering robe and stood revealed, a gray-clad figure, Radium transformed into Helium.

This peculiarly Mount Holyoke version of the strip tease

the program denominated "modern alchemy." There is no mention of Uranium.

The Latin Department had forty Roman boys and girls escorting Augustus and Agrippa and chanting the *Carmen Saeculare.*

Give ear, O Apollo and Diana, to our prayer on the day of our holy festival; grant thou, Apollo, that nothing more glorious than Rome may ever be . . . That such is the purpose of Jove and all the gods we have full faith.

The presentation of the Economics Department started with primitive man and ended with the year 2000. A flock of real sheep in the pastoral scene behaved with remarkable docility. At dress rehearsal it had required fifty minutes to drive them across the stage. On the day of the performance a trail of salt was laid in the grass, and when the crucial moment came they behaved as if they all had Equity cards. This strategy suggests a firm grasp of economic motivation on the part of the planners.

The presentation, after running through the hunting, pastoral, agricultural, and handicraft stages of economic production, wound up with the stage of the machine. In the words of the program's commentator again:

The ideal stage of machine production was supposed to take place not in the present day, when human beings are slaves to the machine, but in the far future when they shall be masters of machinery. That stage was symbolized by a figure in white bearing a simple model of a machine, attached by gold cords to figures typifying steam, water, and electricity, and by a chariot of happy and prosperous workers on a holiday.

There were sixteen such presentations in all. Romance Languages doubled up, as did Philosophy and Psychology, Art and Archaeology; Geology, Botany, and Zoology; Physics and Astronomy.

In conclusion one hundred and fifty alumnae marched across the field two by two, dressed in costumes representing each of the seventy-five years from 1837 to 1912. The representative of the class of 1902 was Miss Frances Perkins, a lobbyist in Albany for the committee on safety of the City of New York. Emily Dickinson's class was represented by Miss Sarah I. Walker. There was no mention of either Miss Dickinson or Lucy Stone among the distinguished former students honored. These were primarily the missionaries for whom the seminary had long been famous, but Lucy Cope Shelmire, speaking of the daughters of Mount Holyoke, listed also physicians, surgeons, nurses, druggists, librarians, curators, authors, editors, playwrights, lecturers, translators, bibliographers, secretaries, matrons, farmers, real estate and insurance brokers, lawyers, artists, illustrators, photographers, draughtsmen, a bridge designer, chemists, a microanalyst, an importer, organists, pianists, a harpist, choir directors, soloists, an advertising manager, an interior decorator, a commercial traveler, a manufacturer of concrete machinery and automobile accessories, a bank director, and a number of mothers, including one of a President of the United States. The fields of activity open to women had been enormously enlarged in the twelve years since Miss Woolley had listed in her inaugural address teaching, social work, invention, scholarship, and the home.

Participants and spectators alike for the rest of their lives remembered the pageant as the outstanding event of the anniversary. The students had been assigned their parts before the close of the previous academic year, and many of them had spent the summer making costumes authentic in every detail. None ever seemed to think that this enormous labor for a single public appearance had been wasted.

The next day the more serious part of the program included the awarding of honorary degrees to thirteen women and one man, President Alexander Meiklejohn of Amherst. No explanation was offered as to why he was included in the otherwise all-female list. He was newly come to Amherst and was an old personal friend of Miss Woolley's; perhaps she included him merely to make clear that she had no prejudice against his sex. His speech of acceptance was brief, witty, and urbane. Feminists of a later generation might have found a trace of male chauvinism in it. He spoke of the "predominant femininity" and continued:

I was not so much disturbed by that feature as I might have been because I feel myself in these days very much an infant in this business of being a college president and I felt that here was my first exhibition to a cold world, and it was rather comforting to see the women folk about.

M. Carey Thomas of Bryn Mawr, as might have been expected, dealt forthrightly with the problem of enforced celibacy for the woman scholar.

Women have almost won the right to study what and where they please. They have today almost equal opportunities for study. But they have not yet won the rewards of study. They are still shut out from the incentives to scholarship . . . In all coeducational colleges and universities the number of women holding even subordinate teaching positions is jealously limited . . . Even in a women's college like Bryn Mawr there is a steady . . . pressure exerted by some of the men on our faculty to prevent the appointment of women to vacant professorships . . . Colleges for women, few and poorly endowed as they are, offer the only reward for women scholars . . . Women scholars have another and still more cruel handicap. They may have spent half a lifetime in fitting themselves for their chosen work and then may be asked to choose between it and marriage . . . The next advance in women's education is then to throw open to the competition of women scholars the rewards and prizes of a scholar's life and to allow women professors like men professors to marry, or not, as they see fit.

Miss Thomas may have been referring very obliquely to her own relationship successively with two women professors at Bryn Mawr. It seems unlikely that she meant she would have preferred to have marriage an option available to herself, but she may have been thinking of the fact that marriage had removed Mary Guinn from the academic community as it had Alice Freeman Palmer much earlier.

It is not fair to blame men . . . The life of the intellect and spirit has been lived only by men. The world of scholarship and research has been a man's world. Men distrust women's ability to breathe in this keener air . . . At Bryn Mawr we have never closed the engagement of a woman professor who wished to marry. Several years ago I persuaded a young woman scholar whose husband was called to Bryn Mawr to take up college teaching again. She told me afterwards that it was like paradise on earth to shut herself into her study in the college library among her books for long hours of intellectual work.

Few if any of her hearers could have grasped the fact that Miss Thomas was here sounding the death knell of women's education à la Tennyson's *Princess*. At Mount Holyoke as at Wellesley the ideal had been an all-feminine society. Both of them had cautiously admitted a few men, but both of them had accepted the necessity of parting, regretfully or otherwise, with any female scholars who chose to marry. Ada Brann Darling had left Mount Holyoke for this reason, as Helen Thompson and Helen Cady later would.

The suggestion that marriage and an academic career were not either-or choices was a revolutionary one. In the following year the students at Mount Holyoke produced an original musical comedy, *The Thirteenth Amendment*, based on the notion of a community without men.

>*Much as we doubt them*
>*Can't run without them*
>*Any community*

they sang, to enthusiastic applause from the college audience. The women who had chosen a celibate life for the sake of scholarship or who had been forced into it through lack of opportunity to marry saw this as a desertion from their standard, but there was nothing they could do to stop it. The tide had turned; if women were to be equal they could no longer be separate. Miss Woolley was mercifully spared a look into her own future. In writing to the class of 1906 about the anniversary festivities she predicted of the one hundredth to come:

I suspect that my part will be that of an old lady spectator, perhaps helped up onto the platform by some of you sprightly middle-aged matrons.

She was quite wrong, but her triumph of the moment was a decisive one. From that day on, Mount Holyoke's claim to be the oldest women's college in America was never seriously disputed. Wellesley might have the most charm, Bryn Mawr the most intellect, Smith and Vassar compete in their claims to wealth and fashion, but Mount Holyoke was the acknowledged mother of them all.

The gratified trustees voted Miss Woolley a $500 bonus, but Jeannette had still no word of congratulation to offer. Shortly after the conclusion of the celebration she wrote from camp:

Please send me immediately upon receipt of this letter Jennings' Morphia Habit (which you will find put away) . . . You must not leave South Hadley without doing this . . . also some typewritten documents anent opium — especially some records from Dr. Jennings . . . Please send separately by registered mail . . . Don't let anyone but yourself do this.

If she were condemned to a lifetime of being Mrs. Llewellyn Jones' sister, she could at least order Mrs. Llewellyn Jones about.

In the following June two articles about Miss Woolley appeared in national magazines, both by members of Mount

Holyoke's Department of English Literature. Jeannette Marks in *Harper's Bazaar* said:

The college president gets up before the servants do and goes to bed long after they are asleep. Mary E. Woolley . . . has both the strength and the common sense to meet the gigantic pressure of her position . . . Sturdy, hard working, sane, unimpulsive, saying neither too much nor too little, pleasant but tenacious, tender hearted yet rigid, always a good "mixer," a brilliant administrator, she goes her own way . . . No one who has watched the college wheels "go round" as the writer has through seven years of teaching, beheld committee within committee and the endless ramifications of courses; been conscious of the sound backing of work and money essential, down to the fraction of a cent's difference figured out in the cost of table napkins — no one can have seen all this daily commonplace of college life without acknowledging what a beautifully smooth-running effective machine the corporate college must be.

Carrie Harper in the *American Magazine* stressed the breadth of Miss Woolley's interests as a trustee (she said) of two colleges, member of thirty-five associations and clubs, and the only woman senator of Phi Beta Kappa. She mentioned leadership in the women's suffrage and peace movements and an interest in labor legislation. She told also a story of two Chicago reporters who had failed to cover a speech of Miss Woolley's and attempted to make up for it by interviewing her afterward.

"What did you say that was startling?"

"Nothing," Miss Woolley replied. "I never say things that are startling."

What was true of this speech is true of Miss Woolley's life, Miss Harper continued. There is nothing startling. Good health, absolute honesty, unflagging interest in a multitude of different activities, a sense of humor, and rare social tact were the qualities she enumerated in her summing up. "She seems never to have met with failure or serious friction."

Whatever their motivation and whatever their reticences, these two articles presented the public image that was to represent Miss Woolley to the world for at least a decade and to which she herself increasingly conformed.

VII

Together Again

THE BOOK for which Miss Marks had wanted Dr. Jennings' papers was published in 1913. From the point of view of effort and ambition it was her *chef d'oeuvre*; she had worked on it for more than two years. It had required a great deal of research and an enormous emotional commitment. Publishing it was an act of remarkable courage, for Miss Marks had been the target of gossip often enough to know that it would stimulate a good deal. She had been afraid to use her own name on even a very circumspect and conventional discussion of homosexuality; here was new material for scandal, but this time it was scandal that could not touch Miss Woolley.

The title was *Leviathan, The Record of a Struggle and a Triumph*. It is the story of John Dean, a brilliant young professor at Franklin University in the heart of Philadelphia. The opening scene is laid in his rooms at the university on an afternoon in June; he is scheduled that evening for an important public lecture, but his Negro manservant finds him, early in the afternoon, in what is obviously a drugged sleep. With the aid of almost superhuman effort by the manservant, ably abetted by his two dogs, he is brought into shape to deliver the lecture, which he does triumphantly. But afterward, still showing physical signs of his recent indulgence, he feels that he must confess to his fiancée, Margaret Richards, that he is an opium addict. Margaret takes the confession lightly and assures him that her love will suffice to cure him.

Margaret hastens the marriage so that she may immediately start to assist her husband in his cure. Established in separate bedrooms in a Hudson River town called Martin's Ferry — John is too gallant to impose himself on his wife until the cure is complete — they begin a regime of gradual reduction of the dose. Margaret prepares the injections daily, and on her husband's instructions "cheats" a little each time. She dislikes everything connected with this procedure — the syringe, the medicines, the physical act of injecting him, and the other physical intimacies involved — but she nobly continues even when it becomes clear that he is smuggling opium into the house in various forms and taking a great deal more than the reduced dose she allows him.

The deterioration of her health under the strain suggests that she is reacting normally to the physical deprivation of this very abnormal marriage, but she sees John's abstention from physical involvement not as impotence or a symptom of addiction but as nobility.

It was true that a sword lay between them but it was the still bright blade of his conscience . . . How many men would have had this kind of self-mastery? She recalled what he had said when they were on their way to Grey Cottage. "It would not be right for us to live together under the ordinary conditions of man and wife just now. I care too much for you."

The summer passes with financial worries, scenes of violence, an attempted suicide in which the dog Smuggler is killed. After this event Margaret despairs of her own efforts; with the aid of her cousin Geoffrey and the kindly old neighbors from whom the cottage is rented, she persuades John to enter a hospital in New York.

Here the point of view shifts, and we experience the agonies of the cure along with John. He suffers one relapse in which he escapes from the hospital and wanders around New York, a Walpurgisnacht that is a brilliant if dated *tour de force*. He later completes the cure successfully and resumes his work. By the time of the happy ending seven years later there are three children, Margaret is a contented wife and mother, and John a successful and popular professor.

Subplots involve the uncontrolled sale of paregoric for children, the entrapment of innocent victims through careless prescribing, and the corruption of honest tradesmen by the business of illicit distribution. There are chapters of undigested research: history of the drug trade, analysis of its causes, suggestions for its cure, statistics about the number of addicts and the social classes to which they belong.

John Dean is clearly William Dennis Marks in all his external relationships, whatever the truth about the weakness and dependency of his private character. Margaret, noble, long-suffering, patient, loving, strong, and, to the extent that she is believable, rather irritating, may be intended as a portrait of Jeannette's mother. Margaret's mother, Mrs. Richards, is probably a truer one, a faded southern belle of the type that has since been treated by Tennessee Williams (nobody in *her* family or her husband's has ever suffered from anything as disgraceful as drug addiction). There is no Jeannette Marks in the story unless John Dean serves a double function, as well he may.

The novel was not well received. Perhaps the kindest as well as the truest thing that was said about it was the *Independent*'s comment: "hardly above average as a novel, it is easily the best tract yet written against the drug evil." Its kinship was rather to *Ten Nights in a Barroom* than to the best sellers of its year, the work of Rex Beach, Harold Bell Wright, Robert W. Chambers, and Gene Stratton-Porter.

Miss Marks was appointed to the standing committee on habit-forming drugs of the American Public Health Asso-

ciation, and received many letters from the troubled families of drug addicts. She was patient and generous in an-
swering these. The book was in no sense a triumph
comparable to Mount Holyoke's seventy-fifth anniversary,
nor did it at all advance her standing with the Mount Holyoke faculty, but she nevertheless consented nearly three
years after her resignation to return as a lecturer in the
Department of English Literature.

The action could be seen as either an admission of failure
or a celebration of success, and Miss Marks herself probably
saw it in both lights. As a writer she was not earning
enough to support herself, and Mount Holyoke's $1400 a
year would be a very comfortable subsidy. A lectureship
left time for writing and offered every incentive to work at
it. On the other hand she was now an established author,
if not a brilliantly successful one, and could feel that she
had something to offer. The appointment need not be simply the gift of Miss Woolley's doting affection. Miss Marks
had published a dozen books and more than a hundred
magazine articles, poems, and stories. She belonged to the
Poetry Society of America and the Authors League; she was
acquainted with a number of writers she could now invite
to the college to speak to her students.

Carrie Harper had been promoted to associate professor
and was carrying the burden of the department chairmanship without a permanent appointment. She was making
a name for herself among her colleagues and students as a
striking personality; her dry wit enlivened faculty meetings,
and students admired her commanding presence in the
classroom, her knowledge of Shakespeare, and her effective
reading aloud. She was famed also for a somewhat eccentric
style of dress: she wore a green blazer with orange stripes,
a black velvet dog collar fastened with a jeweled pin, and
an assortment of gold chains that jingled as she moved. She
had founded and was serving as chairman of a literature
club at which faculty members of the literature departments
reported on their research; she was faculty adviser for the
student dramatic club, and from time to time she presented
evening readings of plays and poetry.

Jeannette Marks might well have resented her as she had Bertha Young, but she chose instead to imitate and eventually surpass her. Their salaries in the year of Miss Marks' return to the campus were the same; Miss Harper could scarcely have avoided resenting that fact, but there was never any open hostility on either side. Both of them had learned from the experience of Bertha Young.

Miss Marks' position was even more equivocal than it had been when she came to Mount Holyoke in the wake of the new president thirteen years before. Then she had been an unknown quantity; now the whole faculty knew the story of Miss Woolley's marked favoritism; new ones heard it from old even before they met her. Her old enemies and her few friends had read *Leviathan* and the lukewarm or hostile reviews; they knew that she had left the college to establish herself as an author and that she had returned with that ambition at best half satisfied. It was a hostile environment, but with a limited and cautious hostility. No one any longer ventured to criticize Miss Woolley; her public image and that of the college were inextricably intertwined, and to attack one would be to attack the other. Moreover, although no one was close to her, most people liked her; except with the friends or enemies of Miss Marks she was scrupulously fair; she was hard-working, devoted, gracious, impressive, a president to whom the world looked with respect and admiration.

By 1913 it was inevitable that the faculty of a college for women should be rather more sophisticated about the nature of such a relationship than in 1901. They were by no means unanimous in their opinion, but they were very near to being unanimous in their decision to accept the situation as one they could not change. They could choose to ignore the friendship, to defend it, to condone it, to condemn it, but they could not substantially alter it. Most of them regarded Miss Marks as a necessary evil, Miss Woolley's one unalterable weakness. In time they went beyond that; such faults as they were willing to recognize in Miss Woolley were ascribed to Miss Marks' influence; she became scapegoat and whipping boy. This attitude coexisted with a scrupulous formal courtesy in all professional relations, and no one on the faculty ever discussed the two women with students.

For Miss Marks this was not an altogether unsatisfactory situation; she rather enjoyed martyrdom, and she was eager to embrace unpopular causes. Suffrage for women was rapidly becoming too widely accepted to serve her purpose. By the end of 1913 Miss Woolley could write:

It is impossible to consider the question of civic responsibility without reference to the question of women suffrage. For those of us who have come slowly, perhaps, but convincingly to the affirmative side . . . the emphasis is no longer upon "rights" but upon "duty."

This was part of an article in the *Journal* of the Association of Collegiate Alumnae for January 1914, by which time the Equal Suffrage League of the college had enrolled two thirds of the faculty, and when the students wanted to schedule a debate on the subject no one could be found to support the negative side. In this matter as in many others the alumnae were rather more conservative than either faculty or students. The *New York Times* reported in November 1913 that a Miss Olcott, "one of the younger alumnae," made a suffrage speech at a fund-raising luncheon at the Hotel St. Denis. "This question has heretofore been taboo at Mount Holyoke gatherings, and its introduction on this occasion was not received with great enthusiasm by the alumnae."

Miss Marks, however, marched in suffrage parades in Springfield and Hartford and became an organizer of the National Woman's Party. The Woman's Party worked for equal suffrage by public demonstrations, including the picketing of the White House, disruption of public meetings, parades, and similar activities. Alice Paul, its director, had been arrested in England and carried on a hunger strike in a British jail. All of this appealed to Miss Marks' taste for martyrdom, although she did not herself go to any such extremes.

Along with the return of Miss Marks, Miss Woolley ventured in 1913 on the long-delayed abolition of required domestic work at Mount Holyoke. She had learned her lesson well from the secret societies; this time, although there was substantial opposition from both students and alumnae, the transformation was managed without personal bitterness.

Miss Woolley's arguments for the abolition were admirably sensible and persuasive. It was impossible to schedule both domestic and academic work in such a way that they would not interfere with one another; many of the domestic work jobs were trivial, and all of them were repetitive and boring, which meant that many of the girls did them carelessly; increasing numbers of servants were required for the heavy work which could not be managed in forty-five minutes a day; having all students contribute labor and thus keep down costs for all meant that there were fewer opportunities for employment for those who really needed work. The abolition of domestic work would raise the annual fee from $350 to $425, but there would be many available part-time jobs in the library and laboratories as well as waiting on table and similar domestic work.

It is well to point out, too, that domestic work in Mount Holyoke was never a form of domestic teaching. We have no courses in domestic science; we do not try to train our students in the practical details of "keeping house." I myself firmly believe that the Mount Holyoke girl — the average American College girl — is a good homemaker. I think that both the spirit and the education that makes for good home-making exists in Mount Holyoke. But it does not exist as a part of our domestic work schedule, and it never was the object of the household requirement in the college course.

What she did not say was that raising the fee to a parity with those of Wellesley, Vassar, and the other women's colleges would correspondingly raise the prestige of Mount Holyoke, nor did she mention the fact that the trustees had proposed that along with the abolition of domestic work household economics should be introduced as a curricular study. This she firmly and persistently if quietly opposed. Perhaps she thought that if she could run the President's House, including Jeannette Marks as tenant, without ever having studied household economics, her students ought to be able to meet any challenges they might encounter in their lives.

In January of 1914 William Dennis Marks died in the Champlain Valley Hospital, New York, without a reconciliation with his daughter. There is one reference in her papers that suggests she was rushing across a snowy New England to reach him, but the letters of the period do not bear this out. Whether she had tried or not, she was certainly not with him when death occurred. Settlement of the estate would appear to have involved a certain amount of controversy with her sister. Their letters have not survived, nor is W. D. Marks' will recorded in Westport, the seat of the county in which his house was located, but one unsold short story among Jeannette's papers for the period concerns a quarrel between sisters over the property of a parent who died intestate. Whatever difficulties may have been involved, she did in the end inherit the house she had not entered for twenty years. Her relationship with the sister remained distant but decently amicable.

The inheritance was at least as important an event in her emotional life as her return to the Mount Holyoke faculty. Gone were the years of being a guest or hanger-on in the homes of the Woolleys, the Cadys, Ethel Arnold, or more distant friends and relatives. The house was much too large for a single woman, and the estate expensive to maintain, but she gave no more than a passing thought to selling it. Instead she sold Camp Runway to her godmother, Helen Frances Kimball, who took it off her hands "rather grumpily." With the money thus realized, whatever cash she had inherited, her Mount Holyoke salary, and assistance from Mary Woolley, she undertook an extensive program of restoration. Along with this she began to weave about the house a fantasy that would obscure the facts of her unhappy childhood. She called it Fleur de Lys, a name she said had first been used by her mother in reference to the August lilies that grew in fragrant profusion around it. She allowed herself to remember romping on the wide porch that ran around three sides of the house, sliding on the rocks by the shore, learning to swim and handle a boat in the lake. She began occasionally to sign herself "Gussie," the childish nickname she had detested.

Her father's library filled all the built-in bookcases; she left it intact and added new cases for her own books. In his last years, in an effort to restore his health, he had farmed the land, working in the fields along with the hired men. Jeannette did not attempt to restore her mother's flower garden, but employed the same men to care for orchard and kitchen garden and to maintain the outbuildings. It was no longer possible to keep horses, but the open fields provided splendid spaces for the growing family of dogs to run after a winter cooped up in the President's House. Miss Marks was now, as her father had been, a country squire for one half the year, a college professor for the other.

The house was not yet ready to use by the summer of 1914, when she went again to Battle Creek, listing Mary Woolley as her next of kin and the President's House of the college as her home. Perhaps relevant to this visit to Battle Creek, briefer than the 1909 one, is the passage in *Leviathan* in which John Dean returns to consult with wise, tolerant Dr. James after his cure is completed.

The very fact that you return to me for talks when you have been overworking or you have reached the danger point in nervous depression or want advice about taking up new work, shows more than anything else that you are permanently cured.

It would be Miss Marks' last visit to Battle Creek, and whether or not she was "permanently cured," she took up her work in the Department of English Literature with a new spirit. The five years away from teaching, the limited successes as an author, and her new status as property owner had changed her. She was more mature, more certain of her own powers, perhaps more dictatorial and demanding than she had been as a girl, but in a different way. Now she was asserting her conviction of the rightness of her own views and quite deliberately trying to influence Mary Woolley's rather than merely playing on the older woman's affection for her.

She continued to accept the advantages offered by Miss Woolley's favoritism, but not as bribes to secure her physical presence. They were rather tools to be used in her re-creation of the Department of English Literature according to ideas of her own. She worked hard both at the college and on the estate, and she began to feel something like equality in her partnership with Miss Woolley. For the rest of their years at Mount Holyoke they spent their winters in the President's House, their summers at Fleur de Lys. And at Fleur de Lys Miss Marks was boss.

VIII

The First World War

I T IS A TRUISM to say that 1914 was the year after which
nothing was ever the same again, but the impact of the
European war on South Hadley was not immediately apparent in any very large way. A few faculty members were
caught in Europe at its outbreak and rather expected to be
torpedoed on the Atlantic on their way home, but all of
them arrived safely and devoted themselves to academic
matters. Miss Woolley said, in the *Congregationalist and
Christian World*:

*This is not a people's war; neither is it a woman's war.
Women have had little to do with the making of wars; they
have had much to suffer from wars that have been made.
The old argument that women should have no voice in
government because they could not bear arms to defend it
will give place to the new argument that they should have
a voice because their united voices will make for peace.*

She promoted the organization of a Women's Peace Party
at the college in an endeavor to "enlist all American women
in arousing the nations to respect the sacredness of human
life and to abolish war."

Jeannette Marks took a precisely opposite view.

Your "pacifists" are sentimentalists. To arms, I say, and put down this hyena Germany. After that, time enough to talk of peace. You can't oppose violence with anything else but violence.

On this matter both of them were to reverse themselves within a few years. Miss Woolley found a place for herself within the women's peace movement much more quickly than she had in the suffrage one. Many of the same women were active in both, but the peace movement in 1914 carried none of the stigma that had marked the suffrage cause a decade earlier. Militant women, religious women, feminine women, and feminist women joined hands in the belief that women as the custodians of human life were better able than men to preserve it and its values.

In 1914 Mary Woolley was a charter member of the Church Peace League of America, serving on its commission on peace and arbitration; by 1916 she had added memberships in the American League to Limit Armaments, the Boston Women's Peace Party, the Central Organization for a Durable Peace, the Church Peace Union, and the Peace Emergency Committee for Massachusetts, plus a vice presidency of the somewhat paradoxically named League to Enforce Peace.

Within the college there was some difference of opinion, stemming largely from a strong emotional bias toward the Allies. Professor Mary Vance Young of the Romance Languages Department headed a Belgian Relief Committee later enlarged to a War Relief Committee. Professor Nellie Neilson of the History Department set up a series of weekly lectures on the "background forces in which the conflict had been bred" and was privately reported to be highly annoyed at America's long delay in entering it.

Taking them all together, however, one of the most striking things about the years from 1914 to 1917 is how little attention the college community was paying to the war, in marked contrast to the central position it assumed in everyone's consciousness after the spring of 1917. Miss Woolley's major concerns in the three years preceding America's

entrance into the war were the unending task of fund-raising, the problem of introducing a full-time treasurer into
the college staff at the risk of offending the Willistons, two
generations of whom had served as volunteer or part-time
treasurers, the formation, with Vassar, Wellesley, and
Smith, of a four-college conference, which eventually became the Seven Sisters, and constant speechmaking on non-
controversial subjects.

Miss Marks' concerns were the suffrage movement, the
establishment of Poetry Shop Talks under the aegis of the
English Literature Department, and her own writing. She
published *Early English Hero Tales*, a collection of stories
for children, and polished the Welsh plays for book publication. She also expended a good deal of effort on several
full-length plays that never saw the light of day. For a time
she was very optimistic about *Old Lady Hudson, The Dan-
gling Man*, and *The Doctor*. She had a conference with John
Barrymore about one of them, and predicted gleefully that
she would earn enough money to buy Miss Woolley an
automobile. Nothing came of it, however, and Miss Woolley instead sent Earl Buss to meet her in Springfield on her
returns from Fleur de Lys to the college. The son of the
local grocer, he had "a nice little Dodge car and seems to be
a careful driver," as Miss Woolley reported. She had recently begun to hire him and his nice little Dodge car for
her own trips to Springfield or Northampton instead of relying on the streetcar. Eventually he became her regular
driver, so that later generations of students were never quite
sure whether Mr. Buss was his name or an appellation derived from his business.

As one fruit of her work on the plays, Miss Marks established a course in playwriting for a few carefully selected
students. The structure of the existing departments required that this should be a course in the English Department rather than the English Literature one. Such distinc-
tions never bothered Miss Marks; she simply told Miss
Woolley she wanted to teach the course and Miss Woolley
made all necessary arrangements. Thus technically Professor Ada Snell of the English Department became Miss

Marks' chairman for this portion of her work, as Carrie Harper was for the nineteenth-century poetry and other literature courses.

Membership in the playwriting course became a mark of prestige among the undergraduate literati in the college. There were never more than half a dozen of them at one time; they met in Attic Peace, overawed by the atmosphere of the President's House and by their own distinction in having won access to it.

The Poetry Shop Talks were on a much larger scale. Miss Harper's Sunday evening readings of Shakespeare and other poets had won a devoted following, but Miss Marks by-passed them in her planning. She invited poets of her acquaintance to come to the college to speak or read to the students. In the spring of 1916 Robert Frost, Grace Hazard Conkling, and Katharine Lee Bates came. Miss Marks was thus drawing not only on her literary associations but also on the resources of the neighborhood and on old friends. Robert Frost lived most of the year in Amherst and Grace Conkling in Northampton. Katharine Lee Bates, always genial and accommodating, came from Wellesley to crown the first series. Amy Lowell had promised to come in April but broke the engagement at the last minute with minimal apology. Two years later the series had become so well known that she wrote rather testily to inquire why she had not been invited to read. Miss Marks, who could be testy herself on occasion, wrote back with admirable courtesy and restraint, reminding Miss Lowell of the earlier commitment and inviting her to choose her own date for a second attempt. She came in May of 1918 to the satisfaction of all concerned.

Jeannette Marks used one of the smaller rooms in the new Student-Alumnae Hall for these meetings. The New York Room, financed and furnished by the New York alumnae, has comfortable cushioned window seats beneath mullioned windows, and easy chairs and couches arranged to give the effect of a lounge in a luxurious club. It can also in case of necessity be filled with serried ranks of folding chairs. Thus a sparsely attended meeting can be cozy and informal but the room can be rapidly arranged to meet the needs of a larger audience.

As a further insurance against the discouraging effect of light attendance, Miss Marks arranged that some of the meetings should be "closed"; these were open only to members of the nineteenth-century and modern poetry classes, past and present, the class in Verse Forms, the boards of the college publications and members of the honorary writers' club, to English and Literature majors, the staffs of the English Literature, English, Speech, Bible, foreign language, Art, and Music departments and of the library, and to all officers of the college. With this gentle hint as to who could be expected to attend, and possibly also with attendance required for certain classes, she made certain from the beginning of at least a respectable audience. After the series had become well established the "closed" meetings were dropped and all programs were opened to "all lovers of poetry in the Connecticut Valley and round about."

Miss Marks carried on all the wearisome correspondence necessary for making the arrangements for dates, transportation, entertainment, and remuneration. Most of the poets were invited to use the guest room in the President's House, but some, like Amy Lowell, who came with an entourage, had to be accommodated in hotels in Holyoke or Northampton since there was none in South Hadley.

For a fairly brief period Eloise Robinson served as Miss Marks' secretary, living at Fleur de Lys or in the President's House along with Helen Cady. She had embarked on a literary career of her own, publishing poems in the new magazine *Poetry* and short stories in *Harper's*. Whether because she found this competition distasteful or for some other reason, Miss Marks decided that Eloise was an unsatisfactory secretary and sent her back to her unsympathetic family in Ohio.

In 1916 Miss Marks' short story "The Sun Chaser," first published in the *Pictorial Review*, was chosen for Edward J. O'Brien's anthology, *The Best Short Stories of 1916*. It is a curious amalgam of local-color realism and symbolism. Wales having been abandoned as a background, her characters are not definitely placed in any social or geographical setting. The sun chaser is an alcoholic lamplighter whose vice has reduced his family to stringent poverty; his wife takes in laundry and his child lacks shoes. His obsession with the sun sees it reflected in the lamps he lights and the coins his wife earns. There is perhaps a faint echo here of Ibsen's *Ghosts*, but a more obvious influence is *Ten Nights in a Barroom*. In the end the child freezes to death outside the jail in which her father has been incarcerated.

The success of the story encouraged Miss Marks to elaborate it into a four-act play, which she published six years later. Its staging made almost impossible demands on the scene designer, and it appears never to have been presented by either professionals or amateurs.

The other direction in which her work was progressing was more fruitful. She began work on a study of the relationship between drug or alcohol addiction and creative power. Her book on the subject would not appear until the mid-twenties, but before starting it she published four articles in the *Yale Review* and *North American Review* which served as preliminary studies. Her attitude toward drug use in all of these is curiously ambivalent. In *Leviathan* she represented addiction as an unmitigated evil to be combatted by legislation, medical science, and individual will power; in these studies she recognizes the stimulus drugs may give to creative power and even claims to be able to recognize what drug has been used through its effect on word patterns, rhyme, rhythm, imagery, and sounds. Her disapproval on moral and physical grounds is unchanged, but she does not divide the subject, as De Quincey does, into the pleasure of opium and its pains; the two remain throughout in an uneasy balance.

Here in the chemistry of minds is some mystery — some added energy which liberates vision. Indeed there is the type of writer or artist who is inspired only when he is mad. It would often seem as if the world's history were made by the asylum and the hospital, by neuropaths and epileptics and consumptives, and that there was in this an argument in favor of asylum and hospital . . . It is in the morbid stimulation of protoplasm that toxins, drugs, alcohol enter in. Disorder reigns supreme, chaos, noise, nervousness, near madness . . . tea, coffee, drugs, alcohol seem temporarily at least to put the mental furniture in order, to bring harmony where there has been disorder . . .

In 1916 Miss Woolley's endorsement of Woodrow Wilson for reelection ("he kept us out of war") again brought her mention in the pages of the *New York Times.* But the pressures of the times were beginning to tell on her.

"Is that President of yours still a Pacifist? There ain't no such animal," Katharine Lee Bates wrote Jeannette Marks in March of 1917. She was almost right. The majority of the peace societies to which Miss Woolley belonged turned to support of the war as soon as it was declared or even sooner. The individuals who held out suffered for their opinions, and Jeannette Marks, who was always attracted by martyrdom, swung around to their side.

This is the university's last and only word of warning to any among us, if such there be, who are not with whole heart and mind and strength committed to fight with us to make the world safe for democracy.

Thus spoke Nicholas Murray Butler, president of the university and head of the Carnegie Endowment for International Peace, at the Columbia Commencement in 1917. Subsequently three Columbia professors were dismissed with wide publicity.

Miss Woolley's statement on this issue was much more circumspect and was made in conjunction with the presidents of eight other colleges.

Although we believe that the settlement of international difficulties by war is fundamentally wrong, we recognize

*that in a world crisis such as this it may become our
highest duty to defend by force the principles upon which
Christian civilization is founded.*

She was faced with practically no dissension within the
college. A few students belonged to the Collegiate Anti-
Militarism League, which used the name of the college on
its letterhead. At a general meeting of the student body the
league was officially requested to drop the name of Mount
Holyoke from its literature, with only five dissenting
votes. The five must have submitted, for no more was heard
of them.

Wellesley was not so fortunate. Professor Emily Greene
Balch of the Department of Economics and Sociology, a
trade unionist and social reformer, was deeply committed
to the cause of peace. In 1915 she attended the International
Congress of Women at The Hague, an assembly of women
from neutral and belligerent countries attempting, at the
cost of considerable physical danger as well as widespread
ridicule in the press, to protest against the war and take
counsel as to ways of preventing future ones. Later in the
same year she helped to organize the company for Henry
Ford's Peace Ship, although she did not herself sail on it. In
1916–17 she took a year's leave of absence from Wellesley,
which she spent in New York, serving as balance wheel for
the more radical organizations of young pacifists, and in the
spring of 1917 she was in Washington fighting a last-ditch
battle against the declaration of war.

Her separation from Wellesley did not come immediately;
she was that rather unusual anomaly, a genuinely pacific
pacifist. She voluntarily took an additional year's unpaid
leave in 1917–18 in order to spare the college embarrassment. The question of her reappointment came before the
board of trustees in 1918 and was postponed for a year; in
1919, six months after the end of the war, the trustees voted
over the protest of the president and many members of the
faculty not to reappoint her. By that time pacifism had
become disloyalty and disloyalty treason.

In 1975 the centennial history of Wellesley College said:

In the absence of detailed minutes we do not know whether this action was taken because of Miss Balch's activity as a pacifist or because of her long absences from the college to attend to her outside interests.

During the sixty-year interim Miss Balch had been awarded the Nobel Peace Prize and Wellesley was understandably willing to share the honor. In 1918–19, however, there was no doubt in the Wellesley faculty nor among Miss Balch's many friends in the world outside as to the reason for her dismissal. Both Katharine Lee Bates and Jeannette Marks were among the many who wrote the trustees protesting their action. Emily Balch's was the kind of courage or obstinacy that Jeannette particularly admired, and she was among the influences that eventually brought the younger woman to a stance of complete pacifism and identification with the Society of Friends. The two would meet again in support of Sacco and Vanzetti in the twenties.

Far more enthusiastically than they had supported the Women's Peace Party, the girls at Mount Holyoke now rallied around the war effort. On May 10, 1917, the entire college marched from the chapel to the steps of Skinner Hall, where a handsome new flag was raised, another gift of Joseph Skinner. "The entire college," according to the Springfield *Republican*, but in view of the record one wonders whether Jeannette Marks may have been absent at this time as she was on several other historic occasions. Miss Woolley spoke from the steps of the hall, and then all joined in a pledge of allegiance that had originated at Goucher and already been adopted at Wellesley and Vassar.

. . . prepare . . . physically, mentally, and so far as possible specifically, for usefulness in the war.

The specific ways in which Mount Holyoke students and faculty members could assist in the war effort were not, on the whole, such as to trouble the conscience of a pacifist. Nor was Miss Woolley in any case much given to introspection; her forte was action. In addition to Belgian and Polish relief, the major effort was a war garden, which proved picturesque and newsworthy and brought Mount Holyoke to public notice nationally. The physical energy no longer required for domestic work was now channeled enthusiastically into plowing, hoeing, weeding, picking beans and tomatoes, and digging potatoes. Turnips, Swiss chard, squash, radishes, peas, lettuce, corn, cauliflower, carrots, cabbage, cucumbers, and beets from the college farm graced the college tables as a result of the efforts of six hundred volunteers during the spring and sixty who stayed through the summer. Pictures of them in sun hats and knickers appeared in newspapers throughout the nation and inspired other war gardeners. A cash gift of $750 was used to prepare more land for the second summer, during which two thousand bushels of potatoes were harvested and seventeen thousand four hundred cans of vegetables processed. The preparations had been so enthusiastic that it was necessary to continue the garden on a reduced scale in the summer of 1919 in order to use up the cans that had been provided. The project was valuable for morale and for publicity and paid its own expenses, but there was no temptation to continue it beyond 1919.

Neither Miss Marks nor Miss Woolley made a token appearance among the gardeners. By 1917 Miss Marks had made substantial progress in refurbishing and modernizing Fleur de Lys and spent all her summers there. Miss Woolley joined her for as much time as she could spare from the college. Miss Marks was an enthusiastic gardener herself, and her efforts went into flourishing vegetable gardens and reestablished orchards in what she was coming increasingly to think of as her ancestral estate. Early in the war she also did some work as a member of the publicity committee of the War Camp Recreation Fund, but as the persecution of pacifists and "pro-Germans" increased, she swung more and more toward the position of Emily Balch and other martyrs to the cause of pacifism. She joined the Society of Friends and spoke at Friends' meetinghouses in the Philadelphia area in support of political prisoners.

Joseph Skinner, president of the board of trustees and generous donor to Mount Holyoke, called at the President's House in Miss Woolley's absence to protest this conduct. He told Miss Marks that her talks were harming the college, that she had been accused of being a Communist, and that she must stop speaking in support of political prisoners. She refused, but offered to resign instead. On Miss Woolley's return she reported the interview, in tears.

Miss Woolley's hold on the affection and respect of her faculty and alumnae had increased substantially since 1910, when she had written Jeannette privately that she would rather resign than separate. Now she said at least semiofficially to her board president: "If Jeannette Marks leaves Mount Holyoke I shall leave with her." It was a valid and serious threat. Mr. Skinner stopped bothering Miss Marks, as had most of her faculty colleagues; one more person had accepted her as a necessary evil attached to Miss Woolley's many excellencies.

In the overt and recognized lesbian relationships of the period the usual pattern was for a less talented woman to attach herself to one whose genius she revered and served, much as a wife would expect to serve a talented husband. Alice B. Toklas with Gertrude Stein and Una Troubridge with Radclyffe Hall furnish examples. The traditional roles of male and female were never divided between Miss Marks and Miss Woolley in any such way. In general Miss Woolley's was the masculine role; she was the major breadwinner, the executive, the head of the joint household, the public figure. Miss Marks was an appendage, and most of their acquaintances saw her as the friends of a famous man might regard his unfortunate marital choice — say, as a sort of Mary Todd Lincoln, to be respected and treated with courtesy because of her famous husband, who was, as far as possible, to be protected against her idiosyncrasies.

Miss Marks, however, never accepted the role of either the spoiled or the proper wife; she was neither Dora nor Agnes Copperfield. She privately considered her own talent rather more important than her friend's, and accepted any service to her professional needs as merely her due.

The relationship had settled into what one faculty member would describe to a visitor as "just like a marriage," but if so it was like a mid-twentieth-century one rather than any of the models presented before 1920. Perhaps the only way in which Jeannette Marks fitted into any contemporary conception of the wife's role was in being the power behind the throne. Increasingly over the coming years she influenced Miss Woolley's thinking on a number of issues. Those who recognized this fact during the lifetimes of the two considered the influence deleterious. A later generation may find cause to revise that estimate.

Having followed Woodrow Wilson ideologically into the war, Miss Woolley had no difficulty in following his postwar plans for ensuring that it should really be the war to end war. One of his justifications for his own change of views had been that it was necessary to take part in the war in order to have a voice in the eventual settlement. She now enthusiastically seconded his efforts to have an effective one. She believed in the justice and wisdom of his Fourteen Points and in the potentialities of the League of Nations. In these views she no longer found a united faculty behind her, although in October 1919 only two members of the faculty and nineteen students voted against the league and in December sixty of sixty-three members present at a faculty meeting voted to send a petition to the Senate urging early ratification. Such near-unanimity melted in the face of the various amendments and reservations proposed, and in the presidential elections of 1920 both students and faculty were substantially divided.

To whatever extent Miss Marks may have influenced Miss Woolley's pacifist views, she was not much interested in their political implementation, just as she was not much interested in the administrative problems with which Miss

Woolley daily wrestled. Miss Marks' health was still troublesome. In an effort to restore it she took in 1919 a leave of absence on very short notice. She had been at Fleur de Lys all summer trying to conquer insomnia and nervousness. The visible symptoms of her illness were an exceedingly bad temper and an increase of her normal arrogance. After Miss Woolley had returned to college in September Miss Marks wrote first that she wanted to be on half time for the year, then that she had decided irrevocably that she would return for full-time work.

Kindly spare me all fussing, all solicitude, all smothering. All I ask of you is that you see that your house runs.

Finally, on September 10, she wrote that she would not be back at all. Miss Woolley was faced with the necessity of asking Carrie Harper to chair the department for another year and of engaging people from outside to teach the nineteenth-century poetry and the playwriting courses. Miss Marks was not willing to trust them to any regular member of the English or English Literature departments. Grace Hazard Conkling took over the poetry course and Samuel Eliot the playwriting one. Miss Woolley asked Carrie Harper to assume the responsibilities of department chairman for another year. Miss Harper's note of September 12 in reply says:

I will do my best with the department next year . . . I am sorry that the summer has not restored Miss Marks' health.

Ironically enough, it was her own death that occurred within the year. If she had any concern about her own health in September she said nothing of it. On a Wednesday evening in December, after meeting her classes that day, she became ill; she was operated on the next day in the hospital in Greenfield, and on Saturday she died. Jeannette Marks did not come back in the spring term to help out in the emergency thus created, nor did she speak at the memorial service in February at which Dorothy Foster and others offered generous tribute to Miss Harper's memory. The following fall she took over the chairmanship of the department, which she held until after Miss Woolley's retirement in 1937.

Shortly after Carrie Harper's death Helen Cady married a widower with two little boys. A striking testimony to the nature of the society of which she had been a part at Mount Holyoke is that her name disappeared as completely as that of Carrie Harper; marriage, like death, cut one off entirely. At the time of her fiftieth reunion with her Wellesley class Miss Cady, then Mrs. Brainerd Taylor, wrote affectionately of her memories of her sixteen years at Mount Holyoke, but the sixteen-year intimacy with Miss Marks and Miss Woolley vanished without a trace. Shortly afterward Eloise Robinson married and similarly disappeared.

Two much younger women moved into the President's House. Harriet Newhall of the class of 1914 at Mount Holyoke was first Miss Woolley's secretary and later served the college in various capacities for the rest of her life. Ethel Barbara Dietrich of the class of 1913 at Vassar joined the Department of Economics and shortly afterward the presidential household. If the group is to be regarded as a family, their position in it was that of daughters or nieces.

The relationship between May and Jeannette settled into a very curious pattern. Miss Marks was the only person in the college who ventured to speak rudely to Miss Woolley, to make fun of her, or to issue orders to her. Miss Woolley had worked out a technique for handling this which, while it could not altogether relieve the embarrassment of unwilling spectators, seems to have made it endurable for her. Perhaps even she enjoyed it.

Thus they entered the crucial decade of the twenties.

IX

The Twenties

I F 1914 was the year after which things were never the same again, 1920 was the one in which that fact became apparent in the women's colleges. The young of those post-war years werc as strange and alarming to their elders as the young of the sixties to theirs. Bobbed hair, knickers, sexual freedom in speech perhaps rather more than in action, smoking, drinking, necking, the increased popularity and availability of the automobile, all presented problems for college deans and presidents as well as for parents.

The difficulties of the generation gap were increased by the fact that in this generation many more girls were going to college than had ever donc so bcforc and their attitude toward the experience was correspondingly changed. A college education was now a privilege of the socially or intellectually elite. Most Mount Holyoke students appreciated at least some of the values of what was offered to them, but few understood the personal sacrifices that these privileges had demanded of an earlier generation. Professor Amy Hewes of the Sociology Department expressed the difference in terms of her own discipline in an article in the *American Journal of Sociology* for September 1923.

College education for women of the generation of the students' mothers was less general than it is now and might

*be said to be due to a more definite intellectual interest
. . . The college or university woman of two generations ago
was a "blue-stocking" more differentiated intellectually
and professionally from other women than the college student of today can realize.*

Moreover Mount Holyoke had become fashionable — less
so, perhaps, than Smith or Vassar or Wellesley, but definitely of their kind. For girls from Ohio or Iowa, "going
east" carried much more prestige than attendance at the
local state university or denominational college. Sinclair
Lewis' Babbitt had a daughter at Bryn Mawr who came
home with a vague social consciousness and a habit of
ending all her sentences with "and so on and so forth." The
author seemed to find her intellectual pretensions as irritating as did her father. She may not have been a fair picture
of the eastern-college girl, but it was true that sending a
daughter to one of the Seven Sister colleges was a mark of
success for Babbitt, like his Buick or his house in the
Heights.

These young women were frankly interested in men and
in their chances for marriage. In the spring of 1920 the
Mount Holyoke magazine carried an unsigned article:
"Down with English." It began with a limerick.

> *There was an old maid of Peru*
> *Who thirty-one languages knew;*
> *With one pair of lungs*
> *She worked thirty-two tongues,*
> *I don't wonder she's single; do you!*

*No, of course we don't, [the anonymous student continued]
and now we think it behooves us college maidens to think
of our fate, for whether we will admit it or not, we all wear
the hidden tattoo (at least it is hidden in most cases) "Object, matrimony."*

Men had breached the walls of the citadel. They came
from Amherst and Williams and Dartmouth driving road-

sters with rumble seats and wearing coonskin coats with hip flasks in the pockets; they came from Harvard and Yale and Columbia with newly awarded Ph.D.s, willing to start their careers under women professors of the caliber they would encounter at Mount Holyoke. Miss Marks had one, Leslie Burgevin, in the English Literature Department; the English Department had Ralph Boas, and many, if not most, of the other departments had at least a token man. This made a difference in the Mount Holyoke life style; some of the men who came to teach had wives and children, and others added these appendages in the course of their careers. The great ladies of the Mount Holyoke faculty were no longer altogether desirable role models for most of their students. As to the life style in the President's House, few if any of them gave it a thought. They went there twice in a college generation, for a formal reception as freshmen and another one three and a half years later as seniors, and that was that.

The Nineteenth Amendment to the Constitution, for which their predecessors had fought so hard, meant little to these young women. Generally speaking they were more interested in the Eighteenth. Not that alcohol was a serious problem at Mount Holyoke; well-bred young girls were not yet accustomed to drinking at home or in public places, and there was little opportunity for acquiring the habit at the college. The nips from hip flasks were tokens of defiance and liberation, but drunkenness on the part of either the students or their guests was quite out of the question. Nor was sexual license much of a problem; the ten-o'clock curfew was generally respected, and both Mount Holyoke dances and visits to men's colleges were carefully chaperoned. The college stood frankly in loco parentis to its students; one girl was refused readmission because she married on the way home for Christmas vacation. It was explained that if she had waited until after reporting in at home the responsibility would have been her parents', but up until that time she was technically running away from college.

The one vice that offered an easy, safe, and comparatively harmless opportunity to express defiance of authority was smoking. The habit had just begun to spread to women; "Blow some my way," the pretty girl in the advertisement said to her cigarette-smoking escort. Miss Woolley's opposition to the indulgence was almost pathological. She did not object on grounds of health, as anticigarette propagandists had done earlier and would do again later, nor had she any objection to men's smoking. But for women, "I don't say that smoking is an evil habit," she exhorted the assembled students in chapel and individual miscreants in private, "but it is an indescribably *dirty* habit."

But the students of the twenties did not respond as the girls of 1910 and 1914 had to her views about the abolition of secret societies and of required domestic work. Smoking became the most serious of the discipline problems during the decade. To carry a pack of cigarettes down to the old cemetery and smoke behind the tombstones became the mark of a free spirit. It was also possible to smoke in one's own room, leaning on the windowsill with the window wide open. Under these limitations addiction to the habit was unlikely to develop, but during the decade a number of girls were suspended or dismissed from college for indulging.

There was also the problem of money. The half-million-dollar endowment that had seemed so splendid in 1912 was now negligible. During the war, fund-raising for the college had been suspended in favor of work on the sale of Liberty Bonds; when it was resumed the campaign aimed originally for a million and a half by June of 1921, a sum which was raised to three million by the end of 1920. The college needed new science buildings, new dormitories, a new gymnasium — the list of its needs, important and trivial, was still very much like the one Miss Marks had used in "The New Trustee" in 1905, but in the interim the cost of everything needed had risen astronomically. Students' fees were raised to $600 a year and then to $750. Faculty salaries were up — Miss Marks as department chairman earned $2000 a year — and so were the wages of maids, who nevertheless threatened to strike for more, something that could never have happened while the students were doing their own domestic work. The operating deficit reached $63,587.65 for the year 1920. The high cost of living in the postwar world was a topic of universal conversation and newspaper comment, referred to familiarly in headlines as the "h.c. of l."

With all of these problems to face, Miss Woolley was firmly in control. Her manner was always serene and unruffled; in her two decades at the helm she had brought the college to the forefront among colleges for women in America; her faculty liked, trusted, and respected her and had full confidence in her ability to steer the institution through the stormy times ahead. Most important of all for her, Jeannette was "back home" and settled for life.

The publication of *Willow Pollen* in 1921 brought together Miss Marks' verse contributions to magazines over the twenty years. The list of periodicals in which the poems had appeared was impressive in length and included *Poetry*, already important in its field, the *Bookman*, *Century*, *Forum*, *Nation*, *New Republic*, and *North American Review*, along with many less prestigious journals, but publication in book form did nothing to enhance the author's reputation. Reviews were lukewarm. For all her literary associations, Miss Marks was almost untouched by the new movements in poetry. Harriet Monroe came to speak at a Poetry Shop Talk in 1920, but she did not include any of Jeannette Marks' work in her anthology, *The New Poetry*, the text that was used in Miss Snell's class in verse forms. The Mount Holyoke faculty pounced gleefully on *Willow Pollen* as an opportunity for satire.

"Sleep Song," which appeared originally in *Poetry*, ran thus:

> *Shoo, Rose Toada, Shoo!*
> *Jewelled red eyes for you.*
> *Shoo, Rose Toada, Shoo.*
>
> *Hoosh, Rose Toada, hoosh!*
> *Little green snake in the bush.*
> *Hoosh, Rose Toada, hoosh!*

> *Bizz, Rose Toada, buzz!*
> *Gold on its wings and fuzz.*
> *Bizz, Rose Toada, buzz!*

A parody that circulated among the faculty was designed "to complete the vertebrate series evidently indicated by the amphibian reference in stanza 1, the reptilian reference in stanza 2, and the avian reference in stanza 3."

> *Splash, Rose Toada, Splash,*
> *Scales in the breakfast hash,*
> *Splash, Rose Toada, Splash.*

> *Mieow, Rose Toada, Mieow,*
> *Claws and hair in a row!*
> *Mieow, Rose Toada, Mieow.*

or alternatively

> *Bow-wow, Rose Toada, Bow-wow*
> *Five collie dogs jump at you!*
> *Bow-wow, Rose Toada, Bow-wow!*

> *"Boo-hoo," says Rose Toada, "Boo-hoo,*
> *Is that the best you can do?*
> *I won't go to sleep, would you?"* *

An Amherst student parody of the same poem was shorter and more pointed.

> *Shoo, Miss Marks, shoo,*
> *We like home brew too.*

The Mount Holyoke faculty at this time was also making fun of the work of Gertrude Stein and Amy Lowell, but this

---

* The family of collies in the President's House had increased from the original puppy, Lord Wellesley, by the addition of Ladybird Holyoke and assorted puppies until now and hereafter it numbered four or five. They were generally known as Miss Woolley's dogs and frequently accompanied her in publicity pictures, which was fair enough since she took a substantial share of the job of caring for them, but which often annoyed Miss Marks. And although they were well-bred and well-trained dogs, they did have a habit of assuming that all visitors were as fond of them as were their two mistresses.

could have been little comfort to Miss Marks, as neither of
the other two ladies had to live in South Hadley and work
with their critics as colleagues, and since, also, she had no
way of knowing which reputations would survive.

The copy of *Willow Pollen* in the Mount Holyoke College
library carries on its title page a holograph copy of a poem
not included in the text.

> *O, Jew Jesus, Jew Jesus,*
> *Wings in a world of love!*
> *The wind, the wind, the wind, the wind*
> *Cries like a bleeding dove!*
>
> *...*
>
> *O Jew Jesus, Jew Jesus,*
> *Small fellowship for you:*
> *The peace, the dream, the hope are wind,*
> *What can a poor dove do?*
>
> *O, Jew Jesus, Jew Jesus,*
> *Back to your tree again,*
> *The wind, the wind, the wind, the wind*
> *Whirls with a dove in pain.*

The self-pity and megalomania in this help to explain
Miss Marks' unpopularity with her colleagues, but serve
also to convey her unhappiness with painful clarity. The
reviews were less unkind: "always a little too personal,"
"a distinct disappointment" (which implied that better had
been and could be expected).

Whether because of the reception of the book or because
current taste had diverged from what she did best, Miss
Marks published no more poetry. All the force of her powerful personality was now turned into running the department, directing the work of her students. In her own writing she turned to scholarship, a field in which she had not
shown much early promise and in which the literary scholars on the Mount Holyoke faculty were sharply critical of
her work.

In the spring of 1921 Miss Woolley was invited to serve as a member of the China Educational Commission set up by the Foreign Missions Conference of North America to study Christian missionary schools in that country. The invitation represented her growing importance on the national scene as well as Mount Holyoke's distinguished record in providing missionary teachers and doctors over the years. During the summer she made a rather vague suggestion to Miss Marks as to how it might be possible to finance taking her along as a guest, but the idea was impracticable, and neither one of them seems to have taken it very seriously. Miss Marks was left instead as doyen of the President's House as well as chairman of the Department of English Literature, and Miss Woolley set out alone for China on August 12, 1921.

With the advantage of fifty-five years of hindsight it would be easy to fault her perceptions of what she saw in the Orient. Everywhere she went she encountered Mount Holyoke alumnae: college presidents and college professors or their wives, headmistresses, Y.W.C.A. secretaries. Of a lunch with Japanese women heads of schools, editors, and the like, she wrote back to Miss Marks that they were "as like a similar group in America as peas from the same pod . . . We were even one on the League of Nations and the folly of Militarism!" Her associations in Japan and Korea as well as in China were chiefly with Westerners and westernized Orientals. She made no effort to add Chinese to her Latin, Greek, and Hebrew, and one of her most frequent comments about the Orientals she met was on the excellence or weakness of their English.

Writing to Miss Marks many years later, after Miss Woolley's death, Margaret Burton, who had accompanied her father as his secretary, said:

One of my clearest memories is of the hosts of Holyoke alumnae, Chinese and American . . . They were all so proud because she knew every one of them by name and remembered all about each one. She lived at the Y.W.C.A.

hostess house, and its head used to tell of her coming home at half past ten or eleven and working until two or three in the morning in order to be ready for the commission meeting the next morning.

Busy as she was, however, she never failed to write the daily letter to South Hadley. A reader is reminded of the busy, successful executive writing home to his dear little wife. The things Miss Woolley finds worth mentioning in these letters are the decorations of the rooms where she sleeps and the menus of the restaurants where she eats.

You would love it here in my room with its soft deep cream walls and deeper woodwork, the lattice on the side near the hall and over the door, the sliding doors leading to clothespress and bath, covered with a gold grass paper with blue and gold leaves scattered over it, its matting with an occasional soft pink flower. The minute I came into the room I said — "This is just the kind of room Jeannette would like."

As for the actual work of the commission and what it accomplished, she says very little in these personal letters. After Japan and Korea she arrived in Mukden on September 12, en route to Peking. Mukden struck her primarily as dirty and smelly. She commented that the missionaries had space, fresh air, and order within their compound, and thought that they had "sights and sounds and smells enough outside to deserve comfort and something attractive when they reach their home."

The next day in Peking she attended a garden party given at the Summer Palace by the Chamber of Commerce and the Bankers' Association of Peking, a part of the ceremonies in connection with the dedication of the Medical College. The association of missionaries, teachers, and college professors with wealthy businessmen did not bother her at all; even in South Hadley improvements in the college plant and salary scale for professors depended on the good will of rich trustees. She seems never to have questioned the basic structure of American-style education in the Orient, with its imposition of American cultural patterns. She recognized the difficulties of extending these advantages to the lower classes but did not question the desirability of the attempt.

There were teas for Mount Holyoke alumnae in Peking and dinners with influential Chinese women active in the Red Cross, who were

... *quite like middle-aged American women of leisure and philanthropic instincts. Of the six younger women — I being the only foreigner present — two are American college graduates . . . and two are graduates of Ginling . . . Not only did they speak perfect English, but . . . they could easily be taken for attractive American college women . . . one cannot despair of China's future with a group of this sort.*

Like almost every other American who met her, Mary Woolley succumbed to the charm of Mayling Soong, Wellesley-educated "Madame Sun's sister," when she met her in Shanghai.

From Peking she went into the interior, crossing the Yangtze River in a sampan. In the Boone University compound in Wuchang she was again the guest of a Mount Holyoke alumna, class of '96. She dined with the president of the university and spoke, through an interpreter, to an all-male audience on education for women. Then again by river to Hankow and Kiukiang en route to Shanghai, where she found mail from home after a five-week famine. There were five letters from Jeannette written between September 15 and October 9 — about one fifth as frequent as her own daily ones.

The commission spent six weeks there at work on its report. Within a limited scope it is an excellent piece of work. Granting the assumption that American-style higher education will best serve the needs of Chinese young men and women, we find thoughtful and sensible recommendations for transferring it across the Pacific as economically and effectively as possible.

Miss Woolley worked hard on the report, but already she was counting the days until the sailing of the *Hoosier State* on January 20. She spent the lonely Christmas she had dreaded in bed recovering from a cold and sharing in fantasy the celebration in South Hadley. In 1922 the journey from China to Massachusetts allowed time for readjustment; it was February 20 before Mr. Buss met her in Springfield.

When they reached South Hadley, students lined the long driveway from the road to the President's House, with the overflow spilling out onto the lawn in front of Pearson's dormitory and stretching along the road toward Holyoke. They had composed new songs for the occasion, which they interspersed with the traditional college songs. Miss Marks and the other members of the presidential household had decorated the collies — four at that time — with ribbon bows; they were let out the front door just as Miss Woolley stepped from the car and flung themselves upon her in a satisfactorily theatrical welcome. It was a homecoming to remember, and one she did remember as long as she lived.

She found some changes as a result of her six-month absence. Perhaps the most significant to her was that Jeannette Marks had really taken hold of the management of the Department of English Literature. For most of her years as acting chairman she had been content to accept the appointment as a piece of blatant favoritism, but now, although Miss Woolley's motive in giving her the title might be unchanged, her own in accepting it was based on a conviction that her ability and her record entitled her to advancement. The issue came to a head within a couple of months of Miss Woolley's return, when Charlotte D'Evelyn, in Miss Marks' absence, went to the president for approval of a department lecture she wanted to secure. Miss Woolley approved, and arrangements had been completed when Miss Marks returned from New York.

Her subsequent temper tantrum over what must have

seemed to all the others involved a trivial matter served nevertheless to assert the new relationship. Her three-page single-spaced letter to Miss D'Evelyn recapitulated her connection with the department over the previous decade in a strongly defensive tone and with some inaccuracies, but it made its point.

It has been a matter of common local history — often distorted, I am certain — that since 1910 the English Literature Department has been run through the President's office . . . When I took up the management of the Department, I made up my mind that whatever mistakes we might make, they should be our own . . . May's relation to the Literature Department is neither more nor less than her relation to any other self-respecting department in the college . . . I have told May that if anything of this sort ever happens again, I will resign from the Department and leave the College.

This was a threat the effectiveness of which she well knew. There is a story to the effect that in subsequent faculty meetings (which Miss Marks seldom attended), when a problem in any way related to her department arose, Miss Woolley would say, "That is a question involving the Department of English Literature. Is the chairman of the department present?"

She would look solemnly about the assembly as if waiting for a reply, and when none came would move on to the next item of business.

Like all faculty-meeting stories this one must remain apocryphal, since faculty meetings are officially confidential. It illustrates, however, not only the relationship of Miss Woolley to Miss Marks in their professional lives, but the attitude of the faculty toward both. No one ever challenged Miss Woolley. No one so much as thought of saying, "You know perfectly well she isn't here." They all pretended that the emperor was handsomely clothed and saved their comments for private gossip sessions, in which Miss Marks' reputation was the one that suffered. It speaks well for Charlotte D'Evelyn, who was at the time young and new in the department, that she managed over the years to develop a good and fruitful working relationship with her crotchety chairman.

I myself entered Mount Holyoke as a sophomore in the fall of 1923, and I find it impossible to write this section of the book in any but the first person, just as I find it very difficult to imagine either of the two ladies except as they were at that time. It is as if the cinema film froze into a still picture of Miss Woolley at sixty, gracious, reserved, formidable, and Miss Marks at forty-eight, whimsical, capricious, domineering, and a powerful force in the lives of all the undergraduates with literary aspirations. All the best English majors took her playwriting course, which was "open to juniors after conference with the instructor." There were usually six or seven in the course, and to be admitted to it was a mark of prestige equivalent to appearing in the college magazine or winning one of the annual literary prizes. There is a story, easily to be believed, that three of the top literary lights in the class of 1922 got together and agreed not to register for the course, and that it was promptly canceled for that year. The nineteenth-century poetry course continued its general popularity, with a few non-English majors venturing to register for it each year just to see what their friends were talking about. For the most part they remained baffled and impervious to Miss Marks' appeal.

As to any connection between Miss Marks and Miss Woolley beyond the fact that they lived in the same house, most of us were unaware or uninterested or both. Here I must perforce generalize from my own individual memory, although I have had some opportunity over the past year to talk to classmates about theirs. We were aware of the hostile rivalry between the English and English Literature departments primarily as a duel between Miss Marks and Miss Snell. Most of us took courses with both, although a few enrolled in one camp or the other. My own literary ambitions were polymorphous, and I greedily enrolled for all the writing courses I could find: Miss Snell's Verse Forms, Miss Griffith's Short Story, Miss Marks' Playwriting. The title of the verse-forms course was a deliberately modest understatement; it was a rigorous study of prosody illustrated by wide reading, and it constituted my introduction to the poetry that was contemporary in 1923. Miss Helen Griffith was stoutly opposed to anything "popular"; her favorite method of damning with faint praise was to comment that one of our stories "might sell to the *Saturday Evening Post.*" Even in our ivory tower I was aware that this was not literally accurate and consequently downgraded Miss Griffith's opinion rather more than was justified.

One surprising thing about our attitude toward Miss Marks is how little we were impressed by her publication record. By the time I arrived, people had largely stopped talking about *Willow Pollen;* the Welsh plays that were then at the zenith of their popularity with amateurs seemed like something out of the dim past and rather childish, and I think few of us had heard of her other books. Of course we were all extremely self-centered and far more interested in our own future accomplishments than in those of our professors.

When I say that Miss Woolley was remote, I may seem to be ignoring the fact that she was woven into the fabric of our lives through daily appearances at chapel and weekly ones at church. Although we thought of ourselves as rebellious postwar types, there was surprisingly little objection to our highly structured lives; we took it for granted that each day should start with chapel immediately after breakfast, the seniors in cap and gown occupying the front center section of the chapel, Miss Woolley presiding also in academic dress with the famous crow-shade slippers, Mr. Hammond at the organ. On Sundays the Catholics went in to Holyoke to Mass; the rest of us attended the college church, where again Miss Woolley in her academic robes read the Scripture, introduced the preacher, and set an enviable example of rapt attention to every word he spoke.

On Sundays, too, the Junior Choir sang. Admission to this chorus was a distinction to which all the freshman and sophomore vocalists aspired. We less talented remembered its music all of our lives. All this we accepted almost without question, as we did the ten-o'clock curfew, although Miss Woolley commented sometimes on the number of lights still burning at eleven and the consequent waste of electricity.

In 1923 China was very frequently the subject of her chapel talks. She spoke often also on the League of Nations, of which she had become an ardent proponent. She was some years ahead of the twentieth century's prophets of doom in predicting that civilization could not survive another world war, the weapons had become so terrible. I can remember being a little surprised that the Second World War didn't wipe out mankind. China became a joke around the campus, but even so many of us learned almost all we were ever to know of that country from her speeches.

Her position also made her an instant expert on what was then called "the modern girl." She publicly defended the flapper, but behind that defense we had no trouble in recognizing her real opinion of our clothes and our manners. In the Faculty Show of 1924 she had only to appear chewing gum and wearing a coonskin coat and flapping galoshes to bring down the house; no witty lines were needed or supplied. On our side we rather admired her formal good manners, more like those of our grandmothers than our mothers. She was reported to have said that no lady could dress in less than half an hour, a remark that was quoted gleefully as we dashed in and out of the dormitory bathrooms. She never left the campus without wearing hat and gloves, and she never failed to greet us by name with a formal "good morning" or "good evening" when we passed on the campus. Sometimes if we saw her coming we turned off on an adjoining walk to avoid the greeting, which always made our own replies seem gauche and childish.

The *New York Times* for January 25, 1924, quoted her as defending the modern girl against the attack of Dr. Florence

H. Richards, medical director for the William Penn High School for Girls in Cleveland. According to the *Times* reporter, the issues of smoking, dress, and dancing were brought up in their relationship to morals.

There is a tendency for the modern girl to forget feminine frills a little too much [Miss Woolley is supposed to have said], and added: The college girl's mind is fine — superior to her mother's even. I know that they are not so hampered by tradition as girls of twenty years ago were. Girls found blowing smoke rings on Mount Holyoke green are "campussed" if they get caught, but not because it is immoral. Not at all. It just isn't quite smart, and the nicest girls aren't doing it.

In reply to this Miss Woolley wrote:

The account of an imaginary "long-distance debate" with Dr. Richards reminds me of the story of the would-be speaker called down by a long-suffering chairman. "Before I take my seat," he said, "I should like to remark that what I did not say had nothing whatever to do with what I had in mind." Not a single statement in the report in Friday's paper had I either said or thought.

Miss Marks treated us less as members of a generation than as individuals. In my junior year I joined the playwriting class. I do not remember the required preliminary interview with Miss Marks, which is rather odd as it must have been something of an ordeal, but I have very vivid memories of the year that followed. We met in Attic Peace after walking self-consciously down the long driveway that led to the President's House, being admitted by a neatly uniformed maid, edging up the stairs with quick side glances into any rooms that had open doors, and scuttling into the security of Miss Marks' eyrie. There was a couch for us to sit on, but we were permitted to use the floor if we preferred, as we usually did. At some time during the afternoon light refreshments would appear: cocoa or lem-

onade with cookies. I remember gingersnaps and graham
crackers, but one of my contemporaries speaks of Petits
Beurres, so perhaps I am wrong. The tray must have been
prepared in the presidential kitchen, for I can't remember
Miss Marks fussing over preparations.

We exposed our plays for the consideration of Miss Marks
and our peers at every stage from idea through finished
performance, for the year ended with a public presentation
of the plays she considered best. By that time they had
taken on a strong coloring of her personality and taste. Her
style of teaching was very much like that of the great me-
dieval painters, and anything that came out of Attic Peace
might well have been labeled School of Jeannette Marks.

Frances Tatnall was writing a play about a French village
destroyed in the war and adopted by an American millionaire for its reconstruction. Her point was that the American
millionaire was destroying it even more effectively than the
German guns had done. We all knew that Joseph Skinner,
president of our board of trustees and owner of silk mills in
Holyoke, had adopted such a village, and we were aware,
without ever having to verbalize the knowledge, that Miss
Marks liked the play because she disliked Mr. Skinner. Her
approval in this case was the kiss of death. Frances was the
most deeply rooted individualist among us, a Philadelphia
Quaker on whom all my ideas of that breed have been
formed. She could not or would not remodel her play to
suit Miss Marks' ideas (the difference is not really important) and the result was that she never finished it.

My own *The Lady Bolshevik* was completed and acted
with myself in the leading role, rather like the plays we put
on in the garage in my childhood. During the early part of
my research for this book I thought I was afraid of coming
across a copy; eventually I recognized and admitted to myself that I was hoping to do so, but all I ever found was a
list of props in my own handwriting. The play owed something to Barrie, something to Shaw, and a great deal to Miss
Marks, but the central idea must have been essentially my
own. The scene was laid in a college dormitory into which

a burglar had intruded and been captured by a romantic and enthusiastic student of sociology with vague notions about the desirability of robbing the rich to give to the poor. She systematically covered the dormitory for the terrified burglar, and on turning the money over to him proposed that she go along with him and become his partner in crime. He protested that he already had a wife and six children, a line which brought down the house, as the burglar was played by the English Literature Department's Mr. King, not only a man but an Englishman. He made the burglar a Cockney.

Emma Patterson's *One Raisin Too Much* and Rezia Rowley's *The Man Who Spelled Backwards* were on the same program, with the authors similarly participating. Emma's was about a home-based still that exploded at the climax after an elaborate build-up, but since Rezia's had been written the previous year in a different class I find that I remember very little about it.

Maxine McBride of the class of 1924 has described a production of that year in an unpublished article.

The zero hour approached, with Professor Aunt Jen's watchful eyes on me as she sat in the wings of the stage, a shotgun on her lap, an ash-can beside her . . . Professor Aunt Jen Marks had plastered a man's moustache on my face. My role was to eat the beefsteak being served me in the play called Beefsteak and Browning *and announce "Delicious beefsteak!" But the beefsteak being served to me was tough and cold. To my horror my moustache tangled with the beefsteak. How could I say my lines! Only by swallowing my moustache. So I swallowed my moustache with the beefsteak and gulped: "Delicious beefsteak!" while the audience mostly of Mount Holyoke College students and faculty roared with laughter. Professor Aunt Jen Marks comforted me when I made my exit to the wings, her own face puckered with laughter.*

We had, I think, an uneasy feeling that this was all pretty silly and not really a contribution to our education. Partly this came from internalizing the views of the English Department, in which many of us were majors. Their low opinion of our plays was not disguised by their formal courtesy to Miss Marks. Nor did Miss Couch of the Speech Department approve more highly of our productions than the English faculty did of the plays. Dramatic Club plays were extracurricular activities, but they were supervised by the Speech Department, maintained a lofty intellectual standard, and required a lot of hard work. Miss Marks worked us hard enough, goodness knows; rehearsals went on late into the night, and often we missed dinner. She would supply in its place "a rich but frugal meal"; I remember that on one occasion it consisted of cheese sandwiches and chocolate bars.

I suppose Miss Marks' sense of humor must have been pretty childish, and this may have been what appealed to the childishness in us, although we were at a stage of development at which we felt we should have outgrown childishness and certainly ought not to share it with our elders.

During the year in Playshop we hardly ever saw Miss Woolley. Miss Marks always referred to her as "the president of Mount Holyoke College" with an inflection that supplied the quotation marks. This made us uncomfortable enough, but it was worse when the president appeared in person. She came to Attic Peace once during the year for some sort of festivity; we played a game of charades at which she wasn't very good, and Miss Marks went out of her way to make her appear stupid. We were all glad when the party was over.

Maxine McBride supplies another story of the relationship at about this period. When Maxine was several years out of college and married, she was invited back to help with the production of a play she had written and stayed at the President's House. Making conversation at dinner Ethel Barbara Dietrich asked, "Well, Maxine, have you learned to cook?"

"I can make gingerbread with whipped cream and a cherry on top," Maxine said.

"Oh, Maxine!" Miss Marks groaned.

"I *like* gingerbread with whipped cream and a cherry on top," Miss Woolley added, closing the exchange.

It was during my years as a Mount Holyoke student that Miss Marks published *Genius and Disaster, Studies in Drugs and Genius.* Reading the flattering reviews it received in the *New York Times*, the *Saturday Review of Literature*, and other periodicals, I am surprised to remember how little impression it made on us as students. The book is a study of the effect of drug addiction on the work of Poe, Swinburne, Coleridge, James Thomson, Francis Thompson, Elizabeth Barrett Browning, and others. Several chapters had appeared in earlier versions in the *Yale Review* and *North American Review*. Much of it was digested from the lectures in the nineteenth-century poetry course, so that the material was not new to us, but we should have been impressed by the reviews. Instead we would seem again to have internalized the views of the English Department. There was no gossip this time about Miss Marks' own possible involvement with drugs, or at least none that reached me; the general view seemed to be rather that her notion of a connection between drug addiction and creativity was far-fetched and idiosyncratic.

(It is not necessarily true that the judgment of posterity is any sounder than that of one's contemporaries, but it should be noted that *Genius and Disaster* was reissued in the seventies when Miss Marks was dead and public interest in the subject of drug addiction substantially greater than in the twenties.)

A year later, in 1925, Dr. Arthur Jacobson, a physician, published a somewhat similar book entitled *Genius: Some Revaluations*. He had been so much impressed by Miss Marks' book that he dedicated his to her.

Inscribed to Jeannette Marks, Professor of English Literature in Mount Holyoke College in admiration of her pioneer work as a liaison officer between a rationalized literary criticism and present-day medicine.

One chapter of his book is a summary of hers, and concludes:

This book trumpets the truth as authentically as did the ram's horn of Joshua's priests before the walls of Jericho.

There ensued a correspondence that continued for several years and in which Miss Marks sought information about homosexuality. She was fifty years old in 1925, and presumably the problems of sex were less urgent than they had been earlier, but that of sex identity still plagued her. She considered for a time the possibility of writing a book on homosexuality in literature; Dr. Jacobson encouraged the idea and suggested material for it. Michelangelo, Shakespeare, and Symonds were among the writers he thought she should include. The book was never written, but the correspondence continued for some time with suggestions on his part as to her reading. Her questions concerned insanity and suicide as well as homosexuality, and his replies recommended a variety of literary and scientific works and included some discussion of the ethical aspects of overt homosexuality, toward which his own attitude seems to have been extremely ambivalent.

Lay knowledge of the nature of homosexuality was extremely limited in the twenties. The famed liberation of speech in sexual matters was concerned with "normal" sex. *The Well of Loneliness* was not published until 1928, and the furor it caused is difficult for a reader in the seventies to understand or even believe. Perhaps the attitude of the times is best exemplified by the fact that Compton Mackenzie's *Extraordinary Women* was published in the same year without exciting any objection. The difference in the two fictional treatments of lesbianism was that Mackenzie presented it satirically as a deliberate and rather amusing perversion; Radclyffe Hall held that it was the result of a genetic variation over which the individual had no control, and pleaded for sympathy for its "victims." The only line in Hall's book that refers even obliquely to physical contact going beyond a kiss was on page 358: "and that night they were not divided."

The uneasiness Mount Holyoke continued to feel over the Marks-Woolley relationship did not need to rely on the word or the concept; there was plenty of fuel in the open aspects of their professional relationship. If, as seems highly probable, the two women had forbidden themselves any physical expression of their love for twenty years, the result of her self-control must have seemed to Jeannette Marks quite as bitter as the fictional Stephen's. Stephen is a woman, so named, as Jeannette had almost been, by a father who wanted a son. In *The Well of Loneliness* she pretends to have fallen in love with another woman, when her real object is to free her female partner for a "normal" marriage and children; her resultant lonely misery finds little consolation in the thought that her sacrifice has achieved its object. Jeannette Marks' therapies for an "unwise friendship" — confession, prayer, medical advice, a sense of humor — had left her at fifty still so ignorant of her own nature that she was forced to rely on books and doctors to explain to her what she did not know about herself.

Havelock Ellis' *Sexual Inversion*, published eventually as part of his *Studies in the Psychology of Sex*, had been available in English for more than twenty years, and Compton Mackenzie's novel indicated that gossip about the literary and artistic lesbian society in Europe was sufficiently widespread to ensure the understanding of a *roman à clef* in America, but what Ellis had said about the extreme ignorance and extreme reticence of women regarding any manifestation of their sexual life remained true.

As students we still talked of "crushes" and regarded them as a sign of immaturity; the really grown-up flapper was experimenting with the limits of petting and necking, using, of course, male partners. That a woman of fifty could have been almost as ignorant as we were ourselves seems at this distance of time difficult to believe but may have been entirely possible. Whatever Miss Marks learned from Dr. Jacobson, she did not carry out her idea of writing a

book about homosexuality. With her department chairmanship, the nineteenth-century poetry and playwriting
courses, and the Poetry Shop Talks, she was busy enough
to have justified giving up her own writing altogether.

The Shop Talks had become established as an important
feature of the literary life of the college. In 1924 we heard
Bliss Carman, Aline Kilmer, Richard Le Gallienne, and Margaret Widdemer, in 1925 Robert Hillyer, Edgar Lee Masters,
David Morton, and Genevieve Taggard. By that time a new
series was offering some competition and would eventually
outlive the Shop Talks.

If the student playwrights all worked with Miss Marks,
the student poets were generally attached to Professor Ada
Snell of the English Department. They all took her verse
forms course in sophomore year, and she was adept at spot-
ting and encouraging talent. Moreover, since she had no
literary ambitions of her own, or only long-buried ones, she
was able to find satisfaction in the work of her students
without trying to direct it. She was aware of undergraduate
contests and opportunities for publication, and managed to
secure recognition for several of her students. It was therefore natural that when Irene Glascock, a promising young
poet from the class of 1922, died the winter after her graduation, her parents should turn to Miss Snell for assistance
in setting up a suitable memorial. Miss Snell edited a small
volume of her poems for publication in 1923, and a year
later established the Kathryn Irene Glascock Memorial
Prize for students not only of Mount Holyoke but of neighboring colleges as well. The competitors came by invitation
to read their verse before an audience of Mount Holyoke
students and faculty and a panel of distinguished poets who
would act as judges. In 1924 the contestants were Martha
Keller of Vassar, William Troy of Yale, and Roberta Teale
Swartz of Mount Holyoke, the judges Fannie Stearns Davis,
Robert Frost, and John Livingston Lowes.

I think it is a tribute to the ladies of the Mount Holyoke
faculty that it did not occur to any of us as students that
this was a power play designed to undercut the Poetry Shop

Talks. Miss Marks had worked for almost ten years to establish them, handling the wearisome details of correspondence and publicity herself with often difficult and sometimes unreliable speakers. Her response to the competition of the Glascock readings was to enlarge the scope of the Shop Talks to include the drama; in 1926 the speakers for Play and Poetry Shop Talk included George Pierce Baker and Richard Boleslavsky.

We went happily to both series and enjoyed the opportunity to chat informally with twice as many celebrities as one of them would have furnished. The Glascock contest outlived its founder and recently celebrated its fiftieth anniversary; the Play and Poetry Shop Talks ended when Miss Marks retired.

That summer Miss Woolley was appointed to the executive committee of the Institute of Pacific Relations, which met for the first time in Honolulu. She was beginning to have something of a national reputation as a political liberal. The *New York Times* carried her statement of support for John W. Davis, the Democratic candidate in the 1924 presidential election.

We did not complete the work we began by going to war. By severing all relations with the outside world we have made it difficult for Europe to readjust itself. Our entry into the League of Nations is the direct way in which we could help to make another war impossible.

The Institute of Pacific Relations was an informal organization attempting in a smaller field to achieve the same objects as the League of Nations. Described by one reporter as "a completely unofficial and irresponsible . . . group of individuals from the various Pacific countries," it was nevertheless headed by Ray Lyman Wilbur of Stanford University and A. Lawrence Lowell of Harvard, who could scarcely more appropriately than Miss Woolley be described as irresponsible. The term referred to the fact that they were privately funded and had no government sponsorship. The institute had grown out of the Y.M.C.A. Pacific

Conference in 1920, and although it had expanded to include political, economic, and social as well as religious themes and representatives, it maintained a strong Christian coloring.

There were representatives from China, Japan, Korea, and the Philippines as well as from Canada, Australia, New Zealand, and the United States, but none from Russia or India. The object, at least on the part of the American delegation, was social and educational: to mingle on terms of equality with representatives of other races and to inform Americans as to their characters, their aims, and their grievances.

The conference had ample coverage in the liberal journals and was also noticed by magazines directed to the general reader. It had the reputation of being mildly left wing, not actually frowned upon by officialdom but unlikely to win its seal of approval. Miss Woolley's participation, like that of Presidents Lowell and Wilbur, on the one hand lent the enterprise dignity and solidity, on the other subjected them to the charge of being parlor pinks.

On the whole we as students were pleased at this. Most Mount Holyoke students in my day were the daughters of political conservatives, successful middle-class men in business and the professions. There were still a substantial number of missionary daughters and an unusually rich admixture of students from abroad, particularly from the Orient. Fumiko Mitani of my class became head of the Women's Christian College in Tokyo and was able, though not easily, to resume some of her American ties after World War II. For many of us Miss Woolley's brand of liberalism eased the process of growing up and learning to look objectively at our own families. Sinclair Lewis and H. L. Mencken told us that our fathers were stupid or villainous or both. This was heady wine, and yet we remained fond enough of our parents to want to bring them some of our new enlightenment. For this Miss Woolley was a splendid vehicle. Her dignity, her national reputation, her personal charm, made it impossible for them to dismiss her or disapprove of her as they would later of Miss Marks in her advocacy of Sacco and Vanzetti. Miss Woolley's ideals were nobly Christian; at worst she could be regarded as somewhat impractical and unworldly, and her eminent success in financing the college made this rather difficult.

During my senior year we heard a good deal about Honolulu as we earlier had of China. In June of 1926 I left Mount Holyoke for my adventure in the great world, and the camera froze again, leaving me with memories of Miss Marks and Miss Woolley that did not alter as they aged and changed.

One of my vivid memories of that year is of coming from Springfield to South Hadley in Mr. Buss' car with Miss Woolley and Miss Marks. There must have been one or two other students, but I don't remember who they were. Miss Marks had taken us to see the pre-Broadway tryout of Channing Pollock's *The Fool* and afterward backstage to meet him. We did not know until we set out for the return journey that we were to pick up Miss Woolley at the Springfield station. Her addition to the party put rather a damper on the conversation, but I was sitting on the front seat with Mr. Buss so that I didn't have much occasion to worry about keeping up my end. It was only as we neared my dormitory that I realized that her presence set an awkward dilemma for me. When we were out after hours we normally signed out and took a key, but by senior year we seldom bothered. Our friends did not go to bed early, and it was simple to toss some pebbles at a lighted window and get someone to come down and let us in. But not in front of Miss Woolley. I considered saying that I had lost the key and standing by while Mr. Buss went through the process of arousing the housemother and having me admitted, but it was not a pleasant prospect. I decided that Miss Woolley was unlikely to know the routine of dormitory life, and when Mr. Buss drew up at the only entrance to which automobiles had access I said good night and thank you, added "We go in the other side," and walked firmly around the end of the building out of sight. It worked perfectly, and Frances Tatnall let me in. Only now after all these years do I wonder whether Miss Woolley was really deceived. We had no muggers or sex deviates on the campus to worry about in those days; she could have felt comfortably sure that I would be safe, and perhaps she wanted no more than I did to wake up the housemother. I'll never know.

The next I heard of Miss Marks was in connection with Sacco and Vanzetti. By 1927 the murder in the course of a payroll robbery for which they had been tried and convicted seven years earlier was all but forgotten. They were acknowledged anarchists; their arrest had occurred at the time when Attorney General A. Mitchell Palmer was conducting a bitter and effective campaign against "Reds." As the temper of the times changed during the twenties, liberals came to accept without question that the two men were political prisoners suffering for their beliefs. I can't remember that I ever read an actual account of the crime; the names Sacco and Vanzetti came into my consciousness as those of martyrs to a cause at a time in my life when I was particularly susceptible to the romantic appeal of martyrdom.

One Mount Holyoke student who spent a summer at Fleur de Lys remembers that Miss Marks' advocacy of that cause provided her first realization that "grown thinking people could have ideas quite opposite from those held by my parents." This had happened to me somewhat earlier and I had quarreled with my father over Sacco and Vanzetti. It occurred to me that he was in some ways uncomfortably like Sinclair Lewis' Babbitt; it did not occur to me until much later that I might be like the Bryn Mawr daughter with the vague social consciousness. By 1927 Miss Marks was by no means alone in the Mount Holyoke faculty defense of the two prisoners. In the spring of that year Professor Ellen Bliss Talbot of the Philosophy Department spoke in chapel about the case, and "before noon the whole college had signed a petition to the governor," in the words of a somewhat critical reporter for the college *News*. Miss Marks' championship went beyond that of the others.

The two men were sentenced to death by Judge Webster Thayer on April 7, 1927, the execution set for July 10. Appeals to the governor for clemency and his appointment of a three-man commission to advise him delayed the execution date from July 10 to August 10. A few days before that date there was a final postponement to August 22. On the tenth Miss Marks left Fleur de Lys for Boston and remained there, working with the defense committee until after the execution, which took place actually on the twenty-third, a few moments after midnight. Miss Marks joined the funeral procession as she had joined the protest parade. I saw her picture in my hometown newspaper. On the final day of the reprieve Mary Woolley sent a telegram to Massachusetts Governor Fuller.

Have just returned from the Institute of Pacific Relations in Honolulu to learn of critical situation in Sacco-Vanzetti case. There are many thinking people who believe them innocent. There are many more who are not convinced they are guilty. Their execution while there is a shadow of a doubt as to their guilt would be a tragedy for Massachusetts and a blow to confidence in American justice. Urge such deliberation as will establish facts beyond a doubt.

As a piece of eleventh-hour advice this could not possibly have had much effect, since a commission appointed by the governor and including Miss Woolley's colleague at the Institute of Pacific Relations, A. Lawrence Lowell, had spent four months earlier in the year in reviewing the evidence and had advised the governor to allow the execution to proceed. In a newspaper headline it would, of course, be shortened to the assertion that Miss Woolley had joined the protest against the execution, and it must be regarded as the strongest concession Miss Marks was able to gain from her. It marked a turning point in their relationship. Up to that time Miss Marks had been criticized for the obvious favoritism Miss Woolley showed her in matters pertaining to her department; from that time on it began to be said that she exerted what was, in the opinion of many, an unfortunate influence on Miss Woolley's opinions. Miss Woolley was, however, in a position to face down opposition more easily and more effectively than she had in 1910. In 1927 she was elected president of the American Association of University Women, with which she had worked from its earliest days as the Association of Collegiate Alumnae. By 1927 it was a large, powerful, and influential organization, and its presidency added substantially to Miss Woolley's stature.

Miss Marks' book on the Sacco-Vanzetti case was called *Thirteen Days* and concerned itself only with the period between the final postponement and the execution. She did not argue the merits of the case, which had been discussed by Felix Frankfurter, Heywood Broun, Walter Lippmann, Max Eastman, John Dos Passos, H. G. Wells, Lincoln Steffens, Mary Heaton Vorse, John Reed, and many others. Her book was simply a straightforward account of working with the defense committee through those tense two weeks. It was frankly emotional and remarkably evocative of its period.

Toward the end of the decade the playwriting course developed into the Laboratory Theatre, which became the major interest of Miss Marks' last years at Mount Holyoke. Her godmother, Helen Frances Kimball, died in 1925 and left some money to the college. It was used to endow the Play and Poetry Shop Talks and to establish a new literary prize for the best critical essay in the field of poetry; it provided also the nucleus of a fund for the establishment of the new theater. The work of her Playshop course, which was officially an offering of the English Department, impinged also on the work of the Speech Department and the extracurricular Dramatic Club. Miss Marks was not willing to draw on either club members or Speech students to cast the plays written in her Playshop. They had to be acted by members of the same small group that had written them, and directed by Miss Marks herself. There was at the time no really suitable auditorium in the college for the performance of plays. The chapel served for religious services and some lectures, and the large all-purpose auditorium in Student-Alumnae Hall was pressed into service for almost everything: lectures, debates, Dramatic Club plays, the annual Junior Show and quadrennial Faculty Show, and many others. The Garret in Mary Lyon Hall was used for informal or experimental Speech Department and Dramatic Club performances. Miss Marks was not happy with any of them nor with the need to share facilities; she began to urge Miss Woolley, who had raised money successfully for so many other buildings, to raise some for a laboratory theater for the exclusive use of Miss Marks' own classes.

With the prosperity of the twenties the campus was burgeoning; there were two new and luxurious dormitories: Rockefeller, replacing an older one of the same name which had burned at Christmas of 1922, and Hillside, beyond Lower Lake at the slope of Prospect Hill. Each of them was divided into two separate units, north and south, with separate dining rooms, kitchens, and lounges, so that they were actually equivalent to four dormitories to house the still growing student population. There was also a handsome new science building for botany, zoology, and biology, named for Cornelia Clapp, and such a contrast to shabby old Shattuck Hall that the Chemistry and Physics departments began to push strenuously for a new building of their own. The basis of appeal for funds for a laboratory theater would no doubt have been wider had Miss Marks been willing to share it, but since she wasn't, she began her planning on a very modest scale. The building that the trustees eventually authorized for a temporary playshop laboratory was to be of frame construction and such a size that it could be moved and used as a garage when the college eventually achieved a full-scale laboratory theater. For even this small building no money was appointed; it would have to be raised by private solicitation. Along with the plans for the building, Miss Marks' concept of the playwriting course and the function of her department were expanding. The name of the department was changed to the Department of English Literature and Drama, and the title of the course became Playshop, which had been its unofficial designation for some time. The course description in the catalogue now read:

an experimental course in creative play-writing and in the production of one act plays. With public production of selected student plays, the course includes some training in putting on plays, as well as coaching in acting.

In neither of these fields did Miss Marks have any professional experience or even theoretical training. The rivalry with the English and Speech departments was thus exacerbated and the general resentment of Miss Woolley's favoritism intensified. After her elevation to the department chairmanship Miss Marks had been made a full professor and then named to one of the few endowed chairs on the faculty; she was now Kennedy Professor of English Literature and Drama. Resentment on the part of the faculty was no longer outspoken, but for that reason was probably all the stronger, and it was now directed almost exclusively at Miss Marks. In all her other dealings the faculty found Miss Woolley admirably just and eager for their advancement in salary and prestige; with habit it became increasingly easy to deify her and attribute any recognized faults in her to Miss Marks' influence. Miss Marks made it easier by the arrogance with which she used her privileges. Students were now beginning to be caught up in the intricacies of her feuds with the other departments. One English major failed all her courses in that department in her senior year, giving as her reason that she had no time for anything but Playshop. When the Dramatic Club proposed to offer a prize for the best original play written by a student in the college, Miss Marks refused to cooperate unless the competition were restricted to present and past students in her course. The Dramatic Club was not willing to limit itself in this way, and indeed it is quite possible that one of the competing departments had hoped in this way to show up Miss Marks. Whatever the reason, the prize was never of-

fered, and production in Miss Marks' little theater continued to be the highest honor available to an undergraduate
playwright.

In 1924, she had added a second young man to Leslie
Burgevin in the English Literature Department. Most departments by this time had one and were looking for more
— but to have two was unusual. Harold King, a recent
graduate of the University of Birmingham, England, was
immediately and wildly popular; his youth, his accent, and
his sex were all in his favor. Now the Playshop could have
a real man for male roles while the Dramatic Club still had
to make do with girls in plus fours or borrowed trousers.
His popularity waned only slightly when for his second year
he brought back a bride from England, Constance, a pretty
red-haired girl, who, according to the campus grapevine,
carried him a cup of tea in bed every morning. She was also
added to the teaching staff of the department, but the couple
did not get along with Miss Marks as well as the bachelor
had done. After a year or two of teaching the courses no
one else in the department wanted, Constance took Harold
back to England. Miss Marks had been sold on the idea of
a male henchman, however; she later employed two more
young men to help in the theater, contributing thus to a
steadily growing trend which she later was bitterly to
oppose.

Money for the little theater came in slowly in driblets,
amounts ranging from $2.50 to $50.00. Miss Marks' accounts covering these gifts were meticulous but not altogether accurate; her correspondence with the college comp-
troller on the subject became somewhat acrimonious. Miss
Woolley, accustomed as she was to fund-raising, solicited
and secured the largest gifts. By 1929 the little building,
which was eventually to cost $25,000, was becoming a
reality.

Throughout the year Miss Marks worked over it with the
delight of a child enjoying a doll's house. She supervised
every detail of construction and furnishing. The entrance,
the windows, the seats, the backstage arrangements, all

came under her keen and critical scrutiny, but her particular delight was the electrical equipment. The control board was as elaborate as that of the most modern professional theater, and she insisted on operating it herself. When students were being made up for their roles, each one had to come on stage individually to allow the effect to be tested under various lights.

The first performances were given before an invited audience in the spring of 1929: *Soup* by Constance Meadnis, *Die Keppel* by Katherine Patrick, and *Black Wing* by Bertha Gillespie. Miss Marks described herself on the program as "Director, Script Head and Electrician." Increasingly her greatest pleasure in the theater was to play with the spotlights, experimenting with color and pattern as her father had done in the great Philadelphia Exhibition of 1884.

Faith Stacy of my class was a graduate assistant that year and included in her personal diary some description of encounters with Miss Marks that offer an extraordinarily vivid picture of her at that period. At home in Attic Peace on January 3 Jeannette Marks was wearing:

a washed-out ripped smock, a khaki colored shirt, her usual green neck-tie, a new neutral wool sweater, her skirt, greyish stockings and new oxfords — brown . . . Her hair is very much alive — short . . . She hummed some tunes a little out of tune. She has lovely hair — it's aureal about her head.

On January 18

She wore a nice new wool suit, stockings to match, her new shoes, and a nice light-weight blue wool scarf — plaid, worn thrown over her shoulder. There is a blue in it that makes her eyes bright blue. She was wearing her cane and feeling jaunty. In the front hall of her house were dogs and dogs to fall over, but each one she greeted kindly and with considerable affection. We went to the Playshop, taking Turvey, an umbrella with which to strike off attacking dogs, and a search light.

On a formal occasion, however, when introducing a speaker, she wore:

her black, low-neck sleeveless velvet with a blue flower on the right hip. Also her glasses on a long silver chain. She looked very nice. Her hair was nicely cut and fluffy too.

With the success of her little theater thus assured, Miss Marks embarked on work on a new book which was to be her longest and most substantial. Her interest in Elizabeth Barrett Browning had centered, as the chapter in *Genius and Disaster* indicated, on the poet's addiction to morphia. Her work on the new book, however, began with a visit to the home of the Barrett family's Jamaican ancestors. In spite of her devotion to the cause of the underdog, Miss Marks was a good deal of a snob, and she greatly enjoyed being entertained on New Year's Eve of 1929 in the home of Brigadier General Alfred Moulton-Barrett at Albion, Jamaica. She was up at dawn on the first day of 1930 to record the events of the evening and to go out at earliest daylight to make notes from the tombstones in the Cinnamon Hill graveyard. The book on which she was starting work did not appear until after the middle of the decade, and when it did most of her critics, especially those at Mount Holyoke, thought that the emphasis on Elizabeth's Moulton-Barrett ancestors in Jamaica was disproportionate to their influence on her work or her life.

Back at the college Miss Woolley was entering on the decade that was to see her greatest triumph and her deepest disappointment. She had celebrated her sixty-fifth birthday in 1928. This was the mandatory retirement age for members of the Mount Holyoke faculty, and perhaps the trustees expected Miss Woolley to join them voluntarily. Florence Purington, who retired as dean a year later, afterward claimed that she and Miss Woolley had had a private understanding that they would retire at the same time. Nothing was said publicly, however, about Miss Woolley's plans. She was still vigorous and youthful in appearance, with an erect carriage and an unimpaired speaking voice and platform manner.

The question of why she chose to postpone retirement is an important one, as she could probably have had a much greater influence in the choice of her successor in 1928 than she was able to command in 1937. A good many people thought that she stayed on at the urging of Jeannette Marks, now firmly ensconced in Attic Peace and unwilling to leave it. Her tenure as a professor could not be affected by Miss Woolley's retirement, but her living arrangements and the substantial advantage to the Playshop of her position of favoritism would be upset.

This was undoubtedly a factor in Miss Woolley's decision to remain, but scarcely the only one. For a New England woman of her generation money was as private a matter as sex. Her salary in 1928 of $9000 plus house rent valued at $3000 was supplemented by $986 in lecture fees. Out of this she contributed generously to the upkeep of Fleur de Lys and to the needs of her younger brother Frank, who was consistently unfortunate in his business affairs. Although as she became better known, outside activities were taking more and more of her time, the remuneration they offered did not compare with her Mount Holyoke salary. Even in 1928 it must have been clear to her that she would need to work for some years longer in order to build up an adequate retirement income; the disaster of 1929 changed the necessity from urgent to imperative.

All of Miss Woolley's own investments were in the hands of her brother Erving Yale Woolley, an investment banker associated with Lee, Higginson and Company. In addition he handled most of Miss Marks' invested funds and some of the college's. Hindsight has labeled this injudicious nepotism on Miss Woolley's part, but it is at least arguable that the financial disaster of 1929 would have fallen with equal weight on the college wherever the money had been invested.

When things began to go badly even before the memorable day in October, she had no word of reproach for her brother.

"I want to substitute my securities, as far as they will go, for Jeannette's in the joint account," she wrote in October, and early in November, "When the time comes for selling, do clear up Jeannette's account first."

The Wall Street debacle found her very ill prepared to meet any emergency. In February of that year she had sent her younger brother Frank $400, the last, she said, that she possibly could. He had asked for $500 as the minimum amount with which he could get through the month, but he accepted the $400 and promised to depend on his own efforts thereafter. In May, when his situation was again critical, the best she could do was ask the older brother to try to get him a job. She promised to hold the position of head of one of the college houses open for his wife if it should become necessary for the family to break up.

In this, as in some of her conduct with Miss Marks, it is possible to raise a question as to whether Miss Woolley always recognized the point where public and private obligations conflicted. The question of Harriet Woolley's fitness for the job of housemother did not enter into the negotiations; to offer it to her was purely an act of charity. There are evident here some serious and important ambivalencies in Miss Woolley's view of the position of woman in society. The work of a housemother was the sort to which well-bred ladies descended in the nineteenth century when it became necessary for them to support themselves. Miss Woolley's position vis-à-vis her own family was still that of the nineteenth century. In the society in which she grew up she would have been expected to live in her brother's house after the death of her parents if she remained unmarried, and to serve in whatever family emergencies of illness, death, or loss might present themselves. When she became professionally and financially independent she contributed to the support of her father's household, paying the wages of her mother's maid of all work for several years. The attitude of both the successful and the unsuccessful brother was that her assistance was a matter of course, to be taken for granted. They had wives and families to support; she had only herself to consider. If they thought of Jeannette Marks at all, they could assume that she was financially independent.

By November of 1929 both Miss Marks and Miss Woolley were in serious financial difficulties. Miss Woolley did not think of turning to her brothers for relief; instead she borrowed money for current expenses from Joseph Skinner of the board of trustees. But help with current expenses could not go very far; at sixty-six she had to face the necessity of working longer to build a new competency for the remainder of her life.

Social Security was unheard of in 1930. In California the Townsend Plan to give every citizen over the age of sixty-five $50 a month was regarded not merely as socialism but as fiscal insanity. A middle-class man in business or a profession expected to save enough money to provide for his old age; if for any one of various reasons he failed to do so, the worst he had to fear was being a burden to his children. Fear of the "poorhouse" was to be expressed as a joke, perhaps concealing a nagging anxiety; in actual fact only the poor went to the poorhouse. His wife's fate in old age was, of course, bound up with that of the man; he expected to provide for her as well as for himself.

The class of professional women had not been in existence long enough to establish norms in this matter. With salaries comparable to those of men and rather fewer responsibilities during their most productive years, they no doubt were expected and expected themselves to match their brothers and fathers in thrift.

When at sixty-six Miss Woolley realized that she must again provide for her old age, New England pride, family pride, feminine pride, all fought against allowing anyone to suspect her motive. She simply refused to set a date for her retirement, talking vaguely of 1931, when she would have completed thirty years in the college, or of 1933, when she would be seventy years old.

Her conduct must have seemed to the New England businessmen of whom her board of trustees was largely composed peculiarly and irritatingly "feminine." She was a distinguished woman, her reputation bound up with that of the college; they wanted to honor her publicly, and they felt obliged as gentlemen to treat her as they would have treated their mothers in a similar situation — but they could not imagine their mothers in a similar situation, and Miss Woolley was not about to retire into a passive old-ladyhood.

X

The Disarmament Conference

THE TRANSITION from the twenties to the thirties was perhaps most aptly marked by an editorial in the college *News* in January 1930, requesting that Miss Woolley should conduct more of the chapel services than she had been doing. This must have seemed particularly sardonic, since she had yielded control of the chapel service to a student board in the late twenties after a long and petulant squabble about required chapel. She did as she was asked, but the students of the thirties do not remember her chapel appearances with the affectionate admiration that we of the twenties do.

In the same year *Good Housekeeping* magazine named her one of the twelve greatest living women in America. The other eleven were Jane Addams, Ernestine Schumann-Heink, Helen Keller, Grace Coolidge, Willa Cather, Carrie Chapman Catt, Minnie Maddern Fiske, Cecilia Beaux, Grace Abbott, Dr. Florence R. Sabin, and Martha Berry. In the 1970s the list serves chiefly to suggest the transitoriness of fame. In 1930 it irked Miss Marks. The intention must have been to include only one college president and one author, so that Miss Woolley had less competition in her field than Jeannette Marks in hers. She could hardly have hoped that, if Willa Cather had been passed over, she could herself have been included, but she was able by this time to recognize in herself and acknowledge the envy which had always been a component of her admiration and affection for Mary Woolley. Miss Woolley on her side had learned to deprecate her own achievement and extol her friend's in the way Jeannette found most comforting.

After its preliminary announcement in the summer of 1930, *Good Housekeeping* ran twelve individual laudatory articles about the twelve women. Mary Woolley's appeared in March 1931. She was in Boston presiding over the fiftieth anniversary celebration of the American Association of University Women. The Springfield *Republican* asked her to state when she intended to retire. She answered that she was not prepared to make any announcement on the subject. *Time* magazine said in June that she would retire in 1934 at the age of seventy.

At some time during the spring she notified the board of trustees that she had accepted an invitation to serve on the Layman's Foreign Missions Commission to the Orient, an appointment that would involve her absence from the college during the 1931–32 academic year. Accounts differ as to this plan and its eventual abandonment; Arthur Cole in his official history of the college's first hundred years says that she gave it up at the combined urging of trustees, alumnae, and students, because she was needed in South Hadley. She first cut down the time she planned to be away from two semesters to one, and in the end abandoned the plan when she received a much more attractive offer. This left the retirement date altogether up in the air.

There were certainly plenty of problems at the college to engage her full attention. An embarrassing contretemps forced her to yield on the issue of smoking. Her seventeen-year-old niece Eleanor was caught smoking in the spring of 1931. Miss Woolley, with Spartan rectitude, imposed the usual penalty, but the rules against smoking were thereafter relaxed. Miss Woolley gave as her reason her reluctance to force students into dishonesty. The repeal of the national Prohibition amendment was being urged at the time for the same reason.

The initial concession was to allow smoking off campus, but since this meant that motorists passing through South Hadley got their first glimpse of the college in the form of little knots of students gathered by the roadside or perched on the railings of the bridge puffing furiously, smoking rooms were introduced in the dormitories and other college buildings.

The aftermath of the stock market collapse of 1929 was still growing. It had not only cut drastically into the college's capital funds but had left many students without adequate resources to complete their college course. The board of trustees began to eye the day-to-day college expenses in a way they had previously found beneath their notice: the housekeeping, heating, supplies, food, and administrative expenses. Money and discipline were thus added to the normal load of problems facing the president of the college.

Joseph Skinner, Miss Woolley's old reliable friend on the board, resigned in 1931 after twenty-six years, possibly as a gentle hint to her that it was time for the old order to change, or possibly because he was unwilling to join in the pressure increasingly being exerted on her. He was succeeded as president by Henry Hyde, who apparently also disliked and attempted to evade the difficult and painful task of trying to persuade her to retire.

At the very end of the year an invitation arrived that quite threw into the shade the Commission to the Orient one. On December 23 President Hoover requested Miss Woolley to serve as the only woman member of the Conference for the Reduction and Limitation of Armaments to be opened in Geneva, Switzerland, early in 1932.

The appointment is said to have come as a surprise, although it is difficult to believe that Mount Holyoke could have been completely unaware of the political dickering behind it.

Dorothy Detzer of the Women's International League for Peace and Freedom gave her account of the proceedings to Jeannette Marks several years after Mary Woolley's death. The State Department had agreed to accept any woman on whom all the women's organizations could agree — a somewhat tongue-in-cheek male chauvinist offer. On the morning of December 23 Miss Detzer learned from Drew Pearson that President Hoover intended to announce his delegation that afternoon, and that it included no woman. Just what proof Miss Detzer had that all the women's organizations could agree on Miss Woolley she did not say. There had been some discussion of Miss Woolley's qualifications in earlier correspondence in which the reports had been favorable. She was on the D.A.R.'s blacklist because of her pacifist activities, but she had been a member for many years and the chance that they would oppose her strongly on short notice seemed very slight.

Miss Detzer went to James Grafton Rogers, an assistant secretary of state with whom she was acquainted, and reminded him "that women and elephants never forget." He went to see Secretary of State Stimson, and in the early afternoon called Miss Detzer back to say that the appointment was safely assured.

According to all South Hadley accounts, the first Miss Woolley knew of what was going on was a telephone call from Miss Detzer in the afternoon of the twenty-third. Shortly afterward, and while she still had no official notification, calls from the press began to come, then the newspapers with the news of her appointment, and at last Secretary of State Henry L. Stimson officially requesting that she serve.

She evidently did not consider any but an affirmative answer. She must have been aware to some extent that she was being used as a token woman and a token pacifist in a delegation overwhelmingly masculine and belligerent, but she could quite reasonably have believed also that she would find an opportunity to make some of her ideas effective.

By Christmas Eve South Hadley was full of reporters and photographers. Television was still in the future, but motion picture cameras invaded the reception room of the President's House, and, in Jeannette Marks' words, "the press from all parts of the country ... beat its way by telegram, telephone, and personal calls into Mary Woolley's office."

Miss Woolley had been accustomed to a limited public life for thirty years or more, but this was an introduction to a new world, the world of high-pressure public relations and politics. She stuck to her old rule, to say nothing startling. It worked well enough under these circumstances; she was news because she was the only woman delegate to the conference, and the reporters rather enjoyed inventing their stories. They invented a smoking room in the President's House, "where she lives with three other spinsters." This had to be a reporter's imagination. Miss Marks, Miss Newhall, and Miss Dietrich all smoked on occasion, but out of deference to Miss Woolley's well-known prejudice the younger women avoided intruding their indulgence on her attention. Miss Marks smoked at least partly to annoy her and undoubtedly did it in whatever part of the house suited her best. And certainly Miss Woolley had never made any effort to prevent her male guests from smoking in her official residence, although Miss Newhall or one of the secretaries may have tried to confine the smoking of photographers and reporters to a single room.

The slightly pejorative use of the word "spinster" was a sign of the times that should have carried a little flag of warning. Miss Dietrich was an economist of international reputation, Miss Newhall now the director of admissions for the college, and no one had ever before thought of calling Miss Marks a spinster. For the first time in perhaps forty years they were being regarded by young men simply as women who had failed to catch husbands.

The appointment was by no means universally popular. It was regarded, probably quite rightly, as a political move designed to capture the women's vote. There were those who opposed it because as a woman Miss Woolley would no doubt be ineffective; like Gilbert and Sullivan's model major general she didn't know what progress had been made in modern gunnery and knew no more of tactics than a novice in a nunnery. On the other hand, the American Legion opposed "with all the energy and strength at its command any attempt by long-haired men and short-haired women to reduce our defenses."

Miss Woolley had never bobbed her hair, but the combination of pacifism and college girls was enough to certify her guilt by association.

Whether the individual editor approved or disapproved, the appointment was news; all over the country it appeared on front pages and on editorial pages as a subject for comment. The students at home for Christmas vacation heard their fathers and mothers discussing it across the breakfast table, and even the least pacific of them were pleased to see Mount Holyoke so prominently and favorably mentioned. When Miss Woolley left for Washington during the first week in January the girls lined the driveway and the road as their elder sisters had done eleven years earlier to send her off with serenades and cheers.

Only two weeks were allowed for briefing to make up for all the ignorance about which the pundits worried. On January 5 Miss Woolley lunched with President Hoover, Secretary of State Stimson, General Charles Dawes, and Norman Davis. On January 19 she was guest of honor at a dinner in New York sponsored by so many organizations that it was scarcely possible to get all the names on the printed invitations: the American Association of University Women, the Mount Holyoke College Club, the Foreign Policy Association, the League of Nations Association, the Women's City Club, the Women's University Club, the New York League of Women Voters, the American Woman's Association, the Panhellenic, the National Board of the Young Women's Christian Associations, the National Federation of Business and Professional Women's Clubs, and the College Clubs of Wellesley, Vassar, Barnard, Radcliffe, Smith, Bryn Mawr, Cornell Women, Goucher, Wilson, Wells, Hunter, Mills, Elmira, and Adelphi. In between she studied bulky documents in the State Department.

On January 20 she sailed on the *President Harding* in the company of Senator and Mrs. Claude Swanson, Admiral and Mrs. Arthur Hepburn, and many other political and military celebrities.

When the ship had reached Quarantine, Ruth Nichols and Mabel Vernon, pioneer aviatrixes (to use the terminology of the decade) flew out in a hydroplane to board with a gift of flowers from Eleanor Roosevelt, then first lady of New York State. In newspaper photographs the bouquet of roses, jonquils, and iris almost concealed the recipient. Lillian D. Wald, representing the Women's International League for Peace and Freedom, informed her that sixteen trunks containing signed petitions for peace had been loaded aboard. They came from eleven national women's groups and included a number of individual signatures variously estimated at from 400,000 to 600,000.

The implication of all this was that the women of the world wanted peace, that war was a game for men. This view, which goes back in history at least as far as Aristophanes, was one of the tenets of the Women's International League for Peace and Freedom. For these pugnacious pacifists Miss Woolley represented her sex pitted against male chauvinism in its most treacherous and belligerent form. She saw herself rather differently. As she had entered the Brown University classroom forty years earlier, she entered now into the company of male colleagues whose intelligence and ability she respected, hoping to win their respect for hers. She opened the door tentatively, but she held it open for the women behind her. She wrote to Jeannette Marks:

You are right in thinking that there are difficulties even in being a woman: I must be effective but not aggressive; womanly but not womanish; equal to social obligations but always on hand for the business ones; informed, but unable to take my pipe and join the other "pipers" in the corridors during translations — et cetera, et cetera! However, all the males are good to me, and so are the females . . .

Here she returns to the tone in which she spoke of never having received anything but the utmost courtesy from Brown University male undergraduates, but she can do no more than hint at the gravest disability of her situation. The men could bring their wives to discharge the social obligations that were an important part of their work. Miss Woolley couldn't bring Miss Marks. Not that Miss Marks would have been of much help in discharging any social obligations, but the point remains that the social and professional advantages of the pairings that had taken place in the women's colleges were strictly limited to the campus. In the great world beyond its gates each woman was entirely on her own.

In addition to the male official delegates who were her colleagues, the ship carried a number of women as unofficial delegates, representatives of the women's peace organizations responsible for her appointment. Their major interest in the conference was to see that the petitions they were escorting should be presented in properly dramatic form, and this was the first task that devolved upon Miss Woolley after arrival in Geneva.

The ambivalence of her position was emphasized by the reception at Cherbourg, where she and Mrs. Swanson, the senator's wife, were presented bouquets of yellow mimosa and pink carnations. The reception committee included the mayor of Cherbourg and the president of the Chamber of Commerce; no wives were mentioned in her report of the occasion. After tea and a "polite conversation of mingled French and English" the mayor wished them godspeed in these words: "Good luck to you at the Conference. Disarm everybody — except France."

In the train to Paris the only woman delegate shared a compartment with Admiral Arthur Hepburn and Mrs. Hepburn and the latter's sister. At the Paris station they were met by another barrage of photographers, and then she and the Swansons were escorted to the American Embassy, where Ambassador Walter E. Edge and Mrs. Edge served them lemonade and sandwiches as a nightcap. (One wonders whether the lemonade was in deference to Miss Woolley's views or her sex, or whether American embassies abroad actually did not serve liquor during Prohibition — and also whether the senator and the ambassador may not have enjoyed a little nip quietly apart from the ladies.) Miss Woolley had the bedroom next to the one Lindbergh had occupied five years earlier. The next morning Ambassador Edge himself headed the delegation that accompanied her and the Swanson party to the Gare St. Lazare to take the train for Geneva. There were more photographers there and in Geneva, but when at last she was settled in a suite at the hotel Les Bergues she could begin to think about the real work for which she had been selected.

She was appointed immediately to a committee to consider the presentation of petitions, not only the sixteen trunkloads which had accompanied her from America, but similar collections from around the world. The total number of names signed was in the millions, the total number of organizations represented so large that all reporters could do was subdivide them into categories: churches, League of Nations associations, Socialist peace societies, student organizations, and women's groups from fifty-two countries.

Putting Miss Woolley on this committee clearly indicated her status as liaison officer between the unofficial and the official delegates to the conference. The unofficial ones wanted the petitions presented formally, dramatically, and with dignity; the official ones considered them a bore and a nuisance. As the only woman on the five-member committee on petitions, Miss Woolley won her point.

It was one of the times, I think, when it was fortunate to be a woman, for the chivalry of the French and Jugo-Slav and South American members could not bear to refuse a lady anything that her heart was "set on" as mine apparently was on the public presentation of petitions! ... We had our way by an unanimous vote, in spite of the danger involved!

The presentation took place on Saturday morning, February 6. Transportation of the documents required the use of a truck pulled by a tractor. Fifteen women carried the boxes and bundles of signatures into the great hall where four hundred more women, identified as to nationality by wide sashes across their chests and over their shoulders, carried them ceremonially to the podium. There were so many that basketfuls had to be removed from time to time in order to make room for more.

The practical utility of this ceremony may be doubted; it could even have worked in reverse. The *Journal* of the American Association of University Women quotes an unidentified male member of the delegation as having said:

Perhaps we can use her to pacify the peace organizations. Unless you survived the London Naval Conference you wouldn't believe how exigent they can be.

If that was the intention it worked fairly well. Miss Woolley proved to be good newspaper copy; the reporters who expected "a frail old lady, the faded voice of the scholar, the pedant's stoop" were pleasantly surprised to find her at almost seventy erect, rosy-cheeked, clear-eyed, and in full possession of her famous memory. Will Rogers featured her in one of his daily columns.

Well, we are all here ready for disarmament. The first laugh was when the Japanese delegation arrived. I don't know why, but it just struck everybody funny. They have a large bunch and everybody expects to see 'em take over the city and have it under martial law by morning. The younger members of their delegation that started out to the conference have been called back for military service.

Our female delegate, Miss Woolley, is the outstanding novelty. I had an hour-and-a-half chat with her this afternoon. Didn't know whether to call her Miss, Mrs., Professor, Doctor or what, so I just called her Doc, and Doc and I got along great. I had taken an interpreter but I didn't need him, but some of my stuff had to be repeated to her. She is very plain, likable, broad in mind and body, feet and plenty of 'em right on the ground. You would like her. She is not the type for a college president at all. Thirty million women of the world have hope and faith in her common sense versus diplomacy.

*It's no joking matter getting the world to disarm. Maybe
a woman can do it. It's a cinch men can't, so good luck to
you, "Doc."*

This was frequently quoted at Mount Holyoke, usually
with the references to the size of her body and feet de-
leted. There is here perhaps a suggestion of the intrusion
of gentility which was to become a serious problem in the
college during the decade.

Miss Woolley on her side found that "to a novice in the
diplomatic field, the attitudes and actions of trained diplo-
mats were incomprehensible." She did not fail to note that
all five woman delegates to the conference — she was the
only American, and American insularity frequently turned
this into the statement that she was the only woman, but
actually there was one each from Canada, Great Britain,
Poland, and Uruguay — were appointed to the newly formed
Moral Disarmament subcommission, "which," she commented, "was regarded, I suspect, as a somewhat unneces-
sary appendage to material disarmament."

She worked also on the Budgetary Control Committee,
where she fought valiantly, if, in the event, fruitlessly, to
limit armaments by limiting the amount of money to be
spent on them.

She attended committee and subcommission meetings
conscientiously, but complained privately about the infre-
quency of the meetings of the General Commission. Socially she was kept quite adequately busy; in her invitation
file for the first week in February were bids to lunch with
the Aga Khan and Begum, to tea with the University
Women of Geneva, and to a dinner at the Club International
for the Moral Disarmament Committee. The French she
had learned at Mrs. Davis's school for young ladies proved
inadequate to the demands now made upon it, but all sessions of the conference were doubled in length by the non-
simultaneous translation from one official language to the
other, and all the hotel servants, shopkeepers, and taxi driv-
ers in Geneva were able to communicate in English. She

attempted from time to time a further polite conversation of mingled French and English but did not allow herself to be unduly embarrassed or discouraged by her failures. She did, however, become increasingly disenchanted with the conference itself and with what she perceived as the discrepancy between its announced aims and the real intentions of most of the delegates. Like the mayor of Cherbourg they were all saying: "Disarm everybody — except us," but no one was saying it aloud. The chapter about the conference in her autobiography, much more fully fleshed out than any other, is entitled "The Doldrums." In July she wrote to Jeannette:

In re-reading my letter it sounds as if I were a man-hater. There are splendid men here, idealists, courageous, doing their best — but there are also men thinking only of their own nationalistic interests and blind as bats to what those "interests" really are.

Whatever else the conference may or may not have accomplished, it represented for Miss Woolley a respite from the grueling day-to-day economies forced on her at home. A grateful government provided first-class lodgings and meals for which she had no need to count the cost. The continuing national publicity also enhanced her reputation at home. She returned late in July in time for a month with Jeannette at Fleur de Lys before returning to the difficult problems that faced her in South Hadley.

XI

The Succession to the Presidency

ACCORDING TO MISS MARKS, Henry Hyde, president of
the board of trustees, told Miss Woolley unofficially in
September 1932 that the board wanted her to remain in
office until the centennial of the college in 1937. Both the
setting and the conversation as reported by Miss Marks are
exceedingly improbable, much more like a scene from one
of her plays than a report of a real conversation. She had
the colloquy take place in Buckland at Mary Lyon's birth-
place, whither Harriet Newhall, Mr. and Mrs. Hyde, and
Miss Woolley had repaired apparently for a sort of September picnic. All that remains of the house in which Mary
Lyon was born is a cellar hole, and to reach it requires a
stiff climb from the automobile road. A good many Mount
Holyoke women have made the climb at one time or another; the view from the top is reward enough for the un-
sentimental. Nevertheless it seems an odd place for a conference or even a picnic in the busy college month of
September.

Whether or not the colloquy took place as reported, Mr.
Hyde died the next year without ever having made it official. Miss Woolley, however, from that time on maintained
her intention to retire in 1937, in which year she would be
seventy-four years old. If the date chosen was unwelcome
to most of the trustees, it was at least firm and appropri-

ate. For Miss Woolley it meant five more years of work under very difficult circumstances; for the trustees it meant a chance to plan for the future and for her successor. If Miss Marks is to be believed, individual trustees continued privately during the next three years to attempt to persuade Miss Woolley to retire before the scheduled date. Officially, however, the board accepted her decision.

If Miss Woolley continued in office beyond the time she had originally planned because she needed the money, it is somewhat difficult to understand her conduct during those five years. They were hard years for the college as well as for her; she had been requested specifically, by students, faculty, and trustees, to lessen her outside commitments in order to devote more time to the college. Yet, having chosen to stay, she devoted less time to the college than ever in the thirty preceding years. Her engagements during April for one of these years, as listed in the subsequent *Alumnae Quarterly*, included the Philadelphia United Campaign, the Federation of Women's Church Societies in Worcester, Mass., the Harrisburg, Pa., Chapter of the A.A.U.W., the New Jersey College for Women, the State Normal School at Potsdam, N.Y., the A.A.U.W. at Canton, N.Y., St. Philip's Church in Easthampton, Mass., the Mount Holyoke College Club of Plainfield, N.J., the College and Fortnightly clubs of Summit, N.J., and the College Entrance Examination Board and A.A.U.W. Committee on International Relations in New York City. Correspondence files suggest that she accepted speaking engagements as requests came in, refusing only those for which the date was already engaged.

How is this to be explained? From 1932 on, rumors circulated that her health had deteriorated to an extent that affected her mind. Knowing this, she may have deliberately chosen to court exposure wherever she was asked to speak in public. She still spoke well, and the number of the requests proved that she was still in demand. She may also have enjoyed her associations with alumnae and admiring outsiders more than the demanding ones with a new generation of students and an unprecedented set of problems at the college. She never condescended to explain.

In her photographs taken during these years she looks old and ill, but she did not publicly complain of her health.

The college meanwhile struggled through the five difficult years with very little guidance from her. Applications for admission fell alarmingly. Mount Holyoke had been accustomed for years to have several applications for every vacancy. One year during the thirties, according to Miss Newhall, it was necessary to accept everyone who applied. "Mount Holyoke in Hartford" was a Depression-born inspiration offering Mount Holyoke freshman courses to girls living at home. Their brothers could go as commuters to Trinity College, but it did not admit girls. The Y.W.C.A. of Hartford offered classrooms, and a library was assembled by borrowing from Mount Holyoke, the Hartford Public Library, and Trinity. Instructors traveled from South Hadley two or three times a week. Twenty-two girls started in the fall of 1933, of whom nine entered Mount Holyoke the next year. Miss Woolley's only contact with the experiment was to conduct a Christmas vesper service.

In 1932 and again in 1933 the college ended the year in the black by a very narrow margin, $1300 in '32 and $12,000 in '33. These balances were obtained by some miracles of management. Lottie Bishop reported for the board of trustees that lower food prices were overbalanced by the fact that the dining halls served more food — the girls were buying fewer meals at restaurants and tea rooms. In spite of all such economies, however, 1934–35 ended a whopping $50,000 in the red. Staff and faculty cuts were avoided, but the faculty took a voluntary 10 percent salary cut — voluntary, that is, for everyone except Miss Marks, who made it clear for the rest of her life that she had objected vigorously and fruitlessly. The cut was restored after a single year, and even without the money immediately in hand the trustees ventured to install a sorely needed new heating plant in 1934 and to authorize renovation and redecoration of the older dormitories in time for the centennial celebration.

Miss Marks, twelve years younger than her friend, was at the apogee of her Mount Holyoke career. Her title as chairman of the Department of English Literature had been expanded to include the Drama; the English Literature Department now offered a major in Theater Arts, combining twenty-one semester hours of historical reading courses with eighteen in "practical theater." The one-year playwriting course had been expanded to two and its emphasis shifted from writing to production.

Miss Marks' share of the writing was now acknowledged. Maxine McBride's *Three Wise Men and a Star* was published in a collection of Laboratory Theater plays in 1932 as by Maxine McBride and Jeannette Marks. Later plays were class creations without individual authorship; an idea would be discussed in class, tentatively cast, and worked out through lines invented spontaneously onstage. It was still possible to write a full-length play under Miss Marks' tuition, but few students were encouraged to do so. In addition to two six-hour Laboratory Theater courses a Master Plays course provided for the producing and acting of classics of the theater.

As the Laboratory Theater waxed, the Dramatic Club waned. In 1935 it looked as if it might have to be dissolved. It was at this point that in a desperate last-ditch effort at resuscitation the club ventured to offer a prize for the best original one-act play and was refused permission.

Miss Marks' popularity with her faculty colleagues was at an all-time low. At this late date the idea that there might be something unwholesome in an entirely feminine community was coming to the fore. Probably the first time the word "homosexual" appeared in the Mount Holyoke *Alumnae Quarterly* was in 1932 when Mary Wentworth McConaughy of the Education Department wrote on mental hygiene at the college. She presented the idea of homosexuality as a bugaboo from fear of which some girls suffered as a result of reading books like *The Well of Loneliness*. Her attitude toward such girls was bluffly reassuring, and nothing in her article suggests that such a thing ever actually existed at Mount Holyoke. There were those, however, who deprecated Miss Marks' intense and usually brief friendships with her students. She was, or appeared to be, entirely indifferent to such criticism.

The Play and Poetry Shop Talks with increasing prestige brought increasingly important people to the campus: the Abbey Players of Dublin, Witter Bynner, Robert Edmond Jones, Alan Lomax, Edna St. Vincent Millay, Allardyce Nicoll, Gertrude Stein, and Mary Wigman among others. The little theater itself continued in active use, and Jeannette Marks' work on the book that eventually became *The Family of the Barrett* was progressing satisfactorily.

But perhaps most satisfying of all was the opportunity for the first time in her life to engage in a full-scale battle with MEN. If Miss Woolley had enjoyed studying, working, and conferring with men, Miss Marks had never been able to establish any relationship other than that of inferior or superior. In her youthful illnesses she had clung to her male doctors with a childlike dependence last exemplified in the relationship with Dr. Jacobson in the twenties; her mature relationships with men were always in the role of boss — property owner or department chairman — in which she suffered only passive men or those who could offer a good imitation of passivity. Now with the aging and tired Mary Woolley as her tool, she could come to grips with Mount Holyoke's trustees. The quarrel eventually involved her with the women on the board as well as the men, but she was easily able to dismiss women who didn't agree with her as traitors to their sex.

For a year or two the battle was simply for survival, to keep Miss Woolley in the presidency as long as possible.

Anna Jane Mill, a young Scotswoman who joined the English Literature Department in 1932, with a St. Andrews Ph.D., reported many years later on her first impressions of the college and the department at that time. She quoted from memory a bit of doggerel popular that year.

This is the town of South Hadley,
The place where the faculty pray,

Where Chuckie speaks only to Jeannette
And Jeannette speaks only to May.

Opening faculty meetings with prayer had already become an anachronism in the twenties, but Miss Woolley continued it to the end of her regime. Chuckie Chuckles was one of the family of collies.

Young Professor Mill, perhaps because she *was* young and foreign, saw Miss Woolley and Miss Marks with clarity but with a tolerance that was not usual. She tells the story of Miss Marks' having arranged for Portia, the black maid in the President's House, to bring a jug of hot milk to all department teas for Miss Mill's benefit. Miss Mill did not ordinarily drink her tea with hot milk, but at department teas she submitted to doing so. On more important matters she stuck to her guns when necessary.

"Miss Marks had a sense of humor," she reported, "but you could not count on this. I think that in some ways she has been maligned . . . but I know that she was a difficult person."

After Henry Hyde's death in 1933 Alva Morrison was elected president of the board of trustees. He had been chairman of the finance committee, and as such was all but openly impatient with Miss Woolley's handling of the financial affairs of the college. He was an investment banker in Boston and, ably seconded by Howell Cheney, of a Connecticut silk manufacturing family, and Harry P. Kendall, son of the then oldest living graduate of Mount Holyoke, headed the opposition to Miss Woolley and a good deal of what she stood for. In summing up the situation in 1937 the Boston *Globe* said:

In degrees varying with their temperaments, these men of affairs had experienced masculine impatience with the ways of spinster management.

"Spinster" again! There was no hint of disapproval of the emotional attachment between Miss Woolley and Miss Marks, although some may have been expressed in private conversations. The point of attack here was precisely that they had no sexual experience and consequently no "real" knowledge of life. This was a criticism that applied equally to all the learned ladies who had formed their social lives around one another like the professors in *The Princess*. Their by no means insubstantial intellectual achievements were airily dismissed because, as another trustee — a woman this time — wrote to a friend:

a man with a nice wife would give social tone which the faculty has lacked.

A Committee on the Succession to the Presidency was appointed from the board of trustees as early as 1932. In 1934, Mr. Morrison appointed a new committee of three men and two women. He himself served on it along with Howell Cheney and Harry Kendall and two alumnae, Mary Hume Maguire and Rowena Keith Keyes. Mrs. Maguire, a tutor in history at Radcliffe, called on Miss Woolley in the spring of 1935 in her capacity as secretary of the committee. Miss Woolley may have seen the request for suggestions as to her successor as merely another step in the campaign to force her to retire; she did send a suggested list of names of women to the trustees individually, but not until after the end of the 1934–35 academic year.

It was at this time apparently that Mary Woolley first realized, or certainly that she first recognized, the possibility that her successor might not be of her own sex. On July 1 — the first day of the new academic year, so that the possibility of her retirement in '35 was now ended — she wrote to each of the trustees a strongly worded letter in support of the choice of a woman — any woman — to succeed her. Earlier that year an alumnae group had stated its requirements for a new president:

1. *The President must make Mount Holyoke her major interest.*

2. *The President should . . . guide the educational policies of the college and . . . consult with the faculty.*

3. *The President inspires, understands, and sympathizes with the undergraduates.*
4. *The President must be able to apportion funds wisely . . .*
5. *The President must be able to impress the public with her own and Mount Holyoke's significance.*

The implications here are, first, that this alumnae group was taking it for granted the new president would be a woman (the pronouns used throughout are feminine) and, second, that Miss Woolley's failures and weaknesses were being stressed in comparison with the strengths required in her successor.

In the fall of 1935 Miss Woolley's brother Erving, on whom she had depended heavily for financial advice and guidance as well as for supportive affection, died quite suddenly of spinal meningitis. Miss Woolley's grief was generously and sympathetically shared by the college, but it was impossible to ignore the fact that it left her even less able than before to deal with the manifold problems confronting her.

By January of 1936 no decision had yet been made as to Mount Holyoke's next president. The search was continuing vigorously and swinging more and more strongly toward a male candidate. There was nevertheless strong sentiment on the board for choosing a woman. Frances Perkins, '02, wrote to Rowena Keyes on January 23 that she thought it desirable that a candidate should have the opportunity of marriage and children of her own.

It is very difficult to secure the full attendance and service from a young woman who is in the midst of her years of child-bearing and rearing. A woman who has reached forty or fifty has that behind her.

Miss Perkins was here speaking from her own painful personal and professional experience, but she was also adumbrating a problem of which women were to become increasingly aware over the next forty years. At the time of Miss Woolley's appointment in 1901 the choice of a married woman, particularly one with children, would have been quite literally inconceivable. By 1935 her suggested list of candidates included three married women with enviable professional records: Mrs. Anna Brinton of Mills College, Mrs. Millicent Carey McIntosh, head of the Brearley School in New York and mother of several children, who was a niece of M. Carey Thomas, and Mrs. Mary Ely Lyman of Vassar and Union Theological Seminary. Miss Woolley's suggestions as to how to deal with the husbands of these three are interesting; a place might be found, she thought, for Professor Brinton in the Mount Holyoke Philosophy Department; Dr. Lyman, older than his wife, was about ready to retire and presumably could enjoy his retirement in South Hadley. Dr. McIntosh was a physician, "and the possibilities in that case I do not know." Whether she thought a male physician inappropriate for Mount Holyoke girls or did not believe that a New York one would find such an offer attractive she does not say.

By February the choice was beginning to crystallize, and early in the spring of 1936 the position was offered to Professor Roswell Gray Ham, a member of the English Department of Yale University, and a husband and father. A widower with two sons, he had recently remarried; his wife was an attractive young woman, member of a distinguished and well-to-do New Haven family. The trustees agreed that she would be a charming hostess, and in this role no one could possibly fail to agree that she would far outperform Jeannette Marks.

Dr. Ham had made a respectable military record as a Marine captain during what was then known simply as the World War. This alone, entirely apart from his sex, was enough to disturb many alumnae whose pacifist views Miss Woolley had helped to shape, and conversely it had helped to recommend him to trustees who deplored those views and their influence on the young. The fact that his service had been with the Marines now gave the more militant alumnae opposed to his appointment a convenient tag line.

Miss Woolley was notified of the appointment on May 18 and promptly protested it in a dignified letter reiterating the points she had made on July 1, 1935. The actual election was held at a meeting of the trustees on June 6. Miss Woolley, at her own request, made two appearances before the board that day, pleading that the election might be postponed so that more time could be given to the consideration of alternative female candidates. Several representatives of the Conference Committee of the college faculty also appeared with the same request. It was denied, and after Professor Ham was elected it became clear that advance publicity on the election had been given to the press as much as two weeks earlier.

The trustees undoubtedly hoped that, faced with a *fait accompli*, Miss Woolley would capitulate gracefully, but they reckoned without Miss Marks. With more enthusiasm than skill Miss Marks flung herself into a campaign to cancel the appointment or force Dr. Ham to retire from the field.*

The opposition to the appointment was masterminded throughout by Miss Marks, although she seldom allowed her name to appear except in private letters, judging quite rightly that her motives would be highly suspect.

Officially and to a considerable extent actually the campaign was spearheaded by two feminist alumnae, Amy Rowland and Carolyn Smiley. Miss Rowland had been an alumna trustee. She was associated with the Cleveland Clinic, and overenthusiastic supporters sometimes awarded her the title of doctor. Miss Smiley was a teacher and editor who had worked for ten years in India and was currently living in California. Miss Rowland was listed as chairman and Miss Smiley as secretary of the Alumnae Committee for Investigation. Miss Smiley was throughout the more aggressive and militant of the two.

*During that spring she had been deeply involved in a campaign to repeal the law requiring a loyalty oath of Massachusetts teachers. More than seven hundred Mount Holyoke students signed a petition for repeal. Miss Marks complained privately to Bertha Putnam of the History Department that Miss Woolley would not help, but the president of the college was nevertheless attacked as responsible for the student showing. The American Legion and its women's auxiliary argued for the retention of the oath and assailed Miss Woolley as communistic and utterly unfit to head a college.

The campaign started mildly enough. Miss Woolley proposed to publish in the summer *Alumnae Quarterly* a statement of her own position in relation to Dr. Ham's appointment. The issue was to be devoted to that subject, and Miss Woolley's statement would be not merely a sour note but a serious embarrassment to the editors, as she must have realized. Nevertheless, she expressed herself as being surprised when the editor and assistant editor said they didn't think they could print it. Such a thing had never happened to the president of the college in the nineteen-year history of the *Quarterly* — and Miss Woolley was still the president of the college. In the end her protest was published in fine print on the last page of the *Quarterly* with a prefatory statement that it had been done at her request — this in a *Quarterly* with a photograph of President-elect Ham on the cover and laudatory articles about him filling most of the thirty pages. From a public relations standpoint the effect could hardly have been worse.

The protest was mild and ladylike, as were all Miss Woolley's statements. She may have been stubborn, but she was never militant. The issue was simple: Mount Holyoke had been founded and had worked for one hundred years to educate women for positions of responsible leadership; if in its centennial year it could not find a woman capable of carrying on the work, the work had been a failure.

With this as a basis the alumnae committee went to work on three fronts: (1) to arouse enough alumnae to make an effective protest, (2) to find legal technicalities in the election procedures and the by-laws of the college that might invalidate the choice, and (3) to enlist women's organizations that would support the alumnae in their fight.

Miss Woolley was a disappointment from the beginning. Two weeks after the unhappy June 6 meeting she presided again at a meeting of the board of trustees and reported to Jeannette in Westport that all "went smoothly . . . with no reference to the succession and all recommendations approved." A few weeks later she wrote: "I am trying to give no opportunity for the charge that my position is due to 'personal pique,' and it is not altogether easy."

The alumnae to whom appeals were sent proved for the most part apathetic. By the fall of 1936 the weight of the Depression years was lifting, but most Mount Holyoke alumnae, like most American citizens, were more concerned with their personal economic problems than with the status of women. Those who felt most strongly that Miss Woolley's wishes should be respected were motivated rather by personal loyalty to her than by adherence to any principle. There were many who agreed with the trustees that Mount Holyoke needed an infusion of the male viewpoint.

Frances Perkins and one other alumna trustee were working to reopen the question on the board. (Miss Perkins' advocacy in 1936 could not be of much help. Mount Holyoke alumnae were proud that the first woman cabinet member had come from their ranks, but her social and political views were antipathetic to many of them as they were to the majority of her colleagues on the board.) Almost 1200 names had been secured on petitions to reconsider by the time of the November board meeting. The trustees consented to accept the petitions and to hear Miss Woolley for a second time on the subject, but they pointed out that many of the names on the petitions were those of husbands or friends rather than alumnae, and they refused to alter their decision.

The A.A.U.W., under the direction of Kathryn McHale, who had succeeded Miss Woolley as president, entered a dignified and well-reasoned protest to which no one paid much attention. In private correspondence with Miss Marks, Miss McHale expressed her concern for Miss Woolley's health and need of a financial competence as rather more important concerns than the affront that had been offered to women scholars and administrators.

The National Woman's Party, a much more militant organization, proposed a much more militant protest. They wanted, among other things, to chain some of their members to the gates of Mount Holyoke as suffragettes had chained themselves to the fence of the White House a dozen years earlier.

Miss Woolley vetoed this plan, though it is hard to see why she should have been allowed to do so. Her official position in relation to the Alumnae Committee of Investigation, now more quotably renamed the Committee of 100, was that she had no control over what it might say or do. Actually she was in close touch with it through Jeannette Marks, and approved most of its actions. A really independent committee expressing its protest without reference to her ideas of propriety might have been more effective and would certainly have been more newsworthy. Miss Marks spoke strongly in favor of "fighting and scratching," but she continued to try to get Miss Woolley to do it and to avoid the public use of her own name.

Carrie Chapman Catt, an old woman in whom the fighting spirit was still very much alive, replied to an appeal with the observation that what had happened served Mount Holyoke right for having allowed itself to be dominated by an all or predominantly male board of trustees during the hundred years of its existence.

The November meeting of the board had closed the door on any further hope of appeal in that direction. In January of 1937 the Committee of 100 made a spectacular final effort through a flier sent to all alumnae and to many newspapers. Headed *The Case of Mount Holyoke Versus the Committee of Nine* (the presidential search committee had been enlarged by four members in its last months), it contained a dozen brief items: "President Woolley's Protest," "Yale in South Hadley," "Quarterly Bans Miss Woolley," "Wills Being Changed," "Is It Too Late to Act?" President-elect Ham's academic and military careers were summarized in unflattering terms, and one of his letters of recommendation, quoted out of context, appeared to suggest that Yale was happy to be rid of him. There were several suggestions that disaffected alumnae might withhold funds. "Is It Too Late To Act?" which provided its own negative answer in a subhead, proposed that alumnae should request the resignation of trustees who had served on the search committee and should, as individuals and as clubs, withhold Centennial funds unless Dr. Ham would withdraw.

The only names signed to the document were Amy Rowland and Carolyn Smiley, but Miss Woolley had seen it and
had written Miss Smiley: "to the extent of my knowledge
the statements on the fliers are accurate." Miss Smiley
released this letter to the press along with the fliers, and the
newspaper headlines featured Miss Woolley: PRESIDENT
WOOLLEY RAPS TRUSTEES, MOUNT HOLYOKE SHIFT ALARMS DR.
WOOLLEY, MARY WOOLLEY BACKS PROTEST AT MOUNT
HOLYOKE.

Miss Woolley was in Boston lecturing on Dwight L.
Moody when the storm broke. True to her old rule "I never
say anything startling," she assured the Boston *Transcript*
that the Mount Holyoke College administration could have
nothing to do with "the strife among the alumnae . . . It
really is a question which rests with the alumnae body. I
can see it in no other way."

She prepared a general statement for the press, released
on February 4.

*Recent reports in the public press concerning the presidency
of Mount Holyoke College have attributed remarks to me
which I have not made.*

*I have consistently maintained the position of favoring
a woman, culminating in my statement to the trustees
under date of June 6, 1936, but I have made no statements
to the public and, with the exception of a single interview
concerning the principle involved in changing the presidency from a woman to a man, I have given no interview.*

Then for one of the few times in her life she took to her
bed. Dr. Pattie Groves, the college physician, is responsible
for the statement that she had suffered an acute dilatation
of the heart. Specialists were called in, but in spite of their
advice she refused to remain bedridden for more than a few
days. The Centennial was only three months away, with
Commencement to follow, and there was work to do.

The final effect of the flier was directly opposite to its
sponsors' intentions. Alumnae who received it or read
about it in their newspapers were angry or embarrassed.
The Alumnae Council meeting in March called in represen-

tatives of the Committee of 100 to confer on the issue; a "statesmanlike" speech by one of the alumnae swung the dissidents in favor of harmony for the good of the college, and the committee representatives signed a statement saying that they were in agreement with the council. Carolyn Smiley had not attended the meeting; in Miss Marks' words, she was "on duty elsewhere." She and Miss Marks and, most important, Miss Woolley remained irreconcilable.

Officially the alumnae had accepted the action of the trustees and pledged their support to the new president for the good of the college. Almost everyone believed that there was nothing more to be done except to bind up the wounds of the injured; like the college in Tennyson's *Princess*, Mount Holyoke was to be turned into a hospital at the dawn of its new era.

The original plan had been to celebrate the Centennial in the fall on the actual anniversary of Mary Lyon's opening the seminary doors, but Miss Woolley's friends had suggested to the trustees that it would be kinder to her and easier for everyone concerned to hold the celebration in the spring while she was still president of the college.

In return for this concession the trustees hoped that she would consent to award an honorary degree to Dr. Ham or at least to accept him as a delegate to the celebration. She quietly but firmly refused even the smallest concession, although she did privately invite Mrs. Ham to look over the President's House at her convenience.

The Centennial was held almost exactly thirty-six years after the inauguration in May of 1901. The "sprightly middle-aged matrons" of Miss Woolley's 1912 letter were much in evidence, but she herself was very far from her imagined old lady spectator to be helped to the platform. With what can only be described as her remarkable talent for showmanship, she rose to the occasion, looking rested, in command of herself, and generally in better physical health than at any time in the previous five years.

The plans had been worked out carefully and thoroughly after the pattern set by the successful seventy-fifth anniversary celebration. The most important difference was that the weather, which had cooperated in both 1901 and 1912, chose this time to turn symbolic. The campus was at its springtime best with tulips and apple blossoms, but over and over again in the two days guests were sent scurrying indoors to escape the rain, and during many of the outdoor ceremonies their attention was deflected by threatening thunder showers. At the garden party on Friday afternoon Miss Woolley appeared with a Court of Honor representing each of the last ten decades. A procession of students symbolizing the future Mount Holyoke came down the hill, its queen kneeling before Miss Woolley to be crowned with flowers. At that precise moment a thunderstorm broke, with lightning and a downpour. Everyone ran for shelter without waiting for the singing of the Alma Mater. It might almost have seemed that Jeannette Marks had achieved the most spectacular of her stage effects.

In view of the number of times Miss Woolley had addressed an audience, both trustees and alumnae must have feared that she would make some public reference to her unhappiness over the choice of her successor, but at eleven o'clock Saturday evening, May 8, at the end of the postponed canoe pageant on Lower Lake, they could draw a long breath of relief; she had behaved throughout with her traditional dignity and had not mentioned Mount Holyoke's new president.

The Laboratory Theatre Centennial Production was dedicated to President Mary Emma Woolley in honor of her distinguished service in the education of women and in the cause of world peace. It featured a play written by Eleanore Price of the class of '32, *The Vest Pocket Standby*, a pacifist fantasy representing militarists as dolls to be wound up and set into action by their child owner.

After the Centennial Miss Woolley had still to preside at Commencement for the class of 1937 before her term of office reached its end. Technically, June 30 was her last day, precisely thirty-six and one half years from that memorable New Year's Day of 1901. Jeannette Marks left for Fleur de Lys early in June as usual, but Mary Woolley attended meticulously to business in her office throughout the month. It was ten o'clock on the night of the thirtieth when she left it for the last time.

Dr. Ham was in South Hadley for most of June, and with Jeannette out of the way several of Miss Woolley's friends tried to arrange a social meeting. She was adamant in her refusal, and, what must have created rather more difficulty, she did not invite him into her office to discuss with him any of the matters which would shortly be his responsibility. Olive Copeland, who was her secretary through June 30 and became his on July 1, had to carry the whole burden of the transition.

Miss Woolley was less meticulous about turning over the President's House for occupancy. Jeannette Marks and the two younger women living in the house had bought another one, called the Gables, where they planned to live and Miss Woolley to visit. Through the July heat Miss Woolley worked at sorting and packing china, silver, curtains, books, and papers for this house and Fleur de Lys. She bought new stair carpet and window-seat cushions for the Gables and wrote Jeannette about what was to go in her own room.

Jeannette meanwhile was busily engaged in getting Fleur de Lys ready for May, as she took pains to tell all her correspondents. Although they had shared the house and the expenses of running and improving it for more than twenty years, Miss Marks from this time on invariably spoke as if Miss Woolley had been evicted from her home by an ungrateful college and offered a refuge by a faithful friend.

Finally, on July 27, Miss Woolley left the President's House in a college car with Earl Buss as driver, followed by a small truck loaded with boxes and barrels and driven by Harold Rhoads. No cheering students lined the driveway; the farewell party that gathered at the car included only secretaries and house servants. Miss Woolley had said her permanent good-bys to office and home, but she had no idea when the car passed the village limits of South Hadley that she was never to see them again.

XII

Retirement

THE TWO HUNDRED MILES between South Hadley and Westport were for Mary Woolley a Rubicon extraordinarily wide and deep. She had no intention of regarding her life as finished or of retiring into a contemplation of its meaning. She still belonged to a very large number of organizations and in many of them she still held office. Her schedule of speaking engagements for the year ahead was at least as full as for the year just past. Except for the pickup truck following with its load of household and personal possessions, the trip was like those she had made every summer for more than twenty years. Yet everything in her life had changed, irrevocably and irreversibly. It was a change like the shaking of a kaleidoscope; all of the same elements remained present, but their relationships were altered beyond the point of no return.

The time had come when she could be at home with Jeannette, what both of them had longed for. But now Jeannette occupied the dominant position. The house they would share was hers; the active connection with the college was hers; the larger of their two incomes was hers. The half-conscious resentment Miss Marks had always felt about her friend's greater fame could now be expressed in action without ever becoming fully conscious.

The house was a large one; downstairs were a book-lined living room, a library, a large dining room, what would today be described as an "eat-in" kitchen, plus two pantries, a bath, and a small room used at various times as music room or guest bedroom. The porch, which ran around three sides of the house, was the summer sitting room. Upstairs were five bedrooms and another bath. All three of the main rooms downstairs had large open fireplaces, as did several of the bedrooms, and a furnace had now been installed in the solid stone-walled basement.

With only two residents in the house it should have been a simple matter to choose a comfortable and appropriate room for Miss Woolley's study. What Miss Marks did, however, was to have one of the small outbuildings fitted up with bookshelves, a desk, and filing cabinets, and order all Miss Woolley's books and papers delivered there. It was heated only by a wood stove. Miss Marks herself had always enjoyed working in a cabin of this sort; in her letters she frequently spoke of rising early in order to write from dawn to noon in some isolated spot. Miss Woolley's tastes and the demands of her work were quite different, but she offered no objection to her assignment to Cutwind.

A much more serious problem was Miss Marks' determination to make her friend a martyr to the cause of feminism. This was not an easy thing to do. Miss Woolley had retired at a ripe age and received every honor the college could offer her. Her objections to the sex of her successor had been attended to respectfully and answered courteously. She might hope that time would prove her right, but she had no intention of doing anything to hamper President Ham in his work.

Miss Marks, however, was still determined to rid the college of him. On June 30, while Miss Woolley was spending her last day in her office, Miss Marks was writing Kathryn McHale, president of A.A.U.W., trying to enlist her help in prolonging the fight and inducing Mary Woolley to help. In September, after her return to college, Miss Marks undertook with a small remnant of the Committee of 100 to investigate the possibility of a lawsuit to oust the new president on the grounds that his election had violated the charter of the college.

To anyone but Jeannette Marks it would have seemed not merely a losing fight but a lost one. Dr. Ham was immediately popular with students. Their reaction to him suggested that they really had suffered from the want of a father image; he was warm, friendly, permissive, and they took him to their hearts. In addition to his two sons by his first marriage, he and Mrs. Ham had a baby boy, so that there was indeed a nuclear family in the President's House, and this also the girls enjoyed.

The faculty may have been somewhat less enthusiastic than the students, but even those who had been most strongly supportive of Miss Woolley's position were embarrassed at the publicity the quarrel had produced and anxious to smooth things over. Miss Marks' general unpopularity may have contributed to easing the initiation for the Hams; many faculty members who might otherwise have been against the new president found a certain amount of pleasure in seeing Jeannette Marks get her comeuppance. She tried to ignore Dr. Ham's existence. Her attendance at faculty meetings had never been frequent; now she stopped going altogether, relying on Leslie Burgevin and Charlotte D'Evelyn to represent the department.

President Ham had certainly been forewarned of her hostility and the problems it might present, and in the event he outgeneraled her. Their first meeting was in his office in January 1938. To Jeannette Marks it would always be Mary Woolley's office, but she had not often entered it. When she and Miss Woolley had discussed college business it had been the older woman who climbed the stairs to talk in Attic Peace. Now her conference with President Ham concerned a plan of the English and Speech departments to conduct a special summer school in conjunction with Amherst the following summer. Miss Snell of the English Department was to head it, Professor Isabelle Couch of the Speech Department to teach, and Curtis Canfield, Amherst

'25 and University of London '35, director of play production at Amherst, to direct the plays. They would be working in an excellently equipped air-conditioned theater in Amherst, with which the Mount Holyoke Laboratory Theatre could bear no comparison.

Miss Marks objected predictably and strongly. Dr. Ham inquired whether she would cooperate with the English and Speech departments in presenting such a course as Mount Holyoke's own offering supposing the plan of cooperation with Amherst were dropped. Miss Marks replied with a decided no.

The Amherst–Mount Holyoke summer school was never held; perhaps it had never been seriously contemplated. But Jeannette Marks had been forced to bring her protest to the new president of the college and to state unequivocally her unwillingness to cooperate with her own colleagues. Moreover it had been made clear that her quarrel was with two women, long-time members of the Mount Holyoke faculty, and that the male president functioned as referee and peacemaker.

A month later she had to make an even more painful and public capitulation. George Lyman Kittredge came to lecture at the college under the auspices of the English Literature Department. As chairman of the department Miss Marks had the privilege and obligation of entertaining him. But before her plans for dinner in a private dining room in one of the college dormitories could be completed, she learned that Mrs. Ham was inquiring about Mr. Kittredge's schedule preparatory to offering her own party for him. There could be no doubt that if he were invited to the President's House he would accept; the only way Miss Marks could protect her own position as hostess and department head was to invite the Hams to her dinner. They came as her guests to a sit-down dinner for eighteen. It could not have been a very pleasant occasion for anyone concerned, but it marked an important victory for the kind of "feminine" social tact the trustees had relied on Mrs. Ham to provide.

A well planned and well fought out "war" between men and women would be far less bloody and far more effective than munitions.

Jeannette wrote to May in March.

. . . Kid gloves and good manners will not help . . . If I live some day I am going to write a satire called "Genteel," showing women in one great crisis after another, being polite, being "unselfish," being "womanly" and always losing the struggle for the things that really matter: peace, education, good government, the happiness of homes . . . What a mess men have made of the world with their deceit, their politics, and their destructiveness . . .

But in a sense she had already written the satire, and it had misfired badly. If Miss Woolley's "genteel" methods had failed, so had the biting and scratching. There was no one left even to offer her sympathy.

Vida Scudder, now seventy-eight years old, wrote Miss Marks pacifically from Wellesley:

I do hope you are reconciled by now to your new President. He really can't help his sex, and one hears that he is a nice person. I never cared a bit about "sex" anyway.

The only weapon that remained was Mary Woolley, and for all her gentility she could be made an effective one.

She was not staying at Fleur de Lys to assume the long-delayed old lady role. Almost as soon as Miss Marks went back to college, Miss Woolley embarked on a year-long lecture and committee tour. In New York she conferred with James Putnam of the Macmillan Company about her autobiography. He expressed interest, but to Miss Marks' annoyance May did not seem to grasp the fact that much of its salability would depend on public recollection of the fight that had preceded her retirement. In spite of the encouragement from Macmillan she continued lecturing to alumnae clubs, A.A.U.W. branches, and college audiences instead of settling down to writing.

In October she proposed making her first visit to the Gables after a speech in Northampton. Miss Marks dissuaded her; a visit at that time would embarrass her in her relations with President Ham. Throughout that academic year she offered temporary and immediate reasons for opposing each proposed visit; it was not until the fall of 1938, when President Ham had weathered his first difficult year and was presumably in the saddle for a long term, that she wrote: "DO NOT COME as long as that man is here."

In the summer of 1938 Miss Woolley attended a meeting of the International Federation of University Women in England, traveling without Miss Marks, who had never returned to Europe after the disastrous visit to Wales in 1910. It was to be Miss Woolley's own last trip abroad. As chairman of the People's Mandate to Governments to End War, referred to by Miss Marks as the People's Mandate for Peace, she hoped to go the following year to South America, where representatives of the organization would call on the head of state in each country visited. She was unable to go because her own resources were inadequate, and she was not willing to ask Mount Holyoke alumnae for contributions, as Jeannette wanted her to do. The issue of money was becoming a difficult one between them. Miss Marks had been accustomed for many years to generous subsidies from Miss Woolley's larger income; now that their positions had been reversed she continued to try to think of ways in which Miss Woolley could earn more or get more. She was apparently unable to understand why Miss Woolley, who had begged so successfully for Mount Holyoke for so many years, was unwilling to beg for herself. The representatives of the People's Mandate went to South America without her.

The Family of the Barrett, on which Miss Marks had been working for nine years, was published in 1938 to moderately good reviews. It followed the Barrett family meticulously through four generations in Jamaica almost entirely unconcerned with literature, and in its last quarter concentrated on Elizabeth Barrett as the more important poet in the Barrett-Browning coalition. Miss Marks did not believe that Elizabeth's relation with her father was abnormal or her childhood unhappy. She paid a good deal of attention to her subject's morphia addiction and efforts to control it. On page 534, after briefly describing the discovery of morphia, Miss Marks says: ". . . and in this discovery is found the course of the 'Lesbian' problem of Elizabeth Barrett's life." The word Lesbian is enclosed in quotation marks. Neither in the text nor the notes is there any explanation of what she means. The reader is free to assume that she sees a connection between drug addiction and lesbianism, but what evidence of the latter she found in Elizabeth Barrett's life is never explained.

The other Browning scholars on the Mount Holyoke faculty were not enthusiastic about the book, and Miss Woolley was not in a position to push it as successfully as she had some of the earlier ones.

The year 1938–39 was an even more difficult one for Miss Marks at Mount Holyoke than 1937–38 had been. Considering his provocation, President Ham was on the whole conciliatory, not to say generous, but he moved now to make some long-overdue reforms. The English and English Literature departments were combined, though still with separate chairmen. Charlotte D'Evelyn headed the English Literature section and Helen Griffith, later succeeded by Margaret Ball, the English one. There were those who thought Ada Snell, the former chairman, as difficult a character as Jeannette Marks herself. Miss Marks was left in charge of the Laboratory Theatre and listed in the catalogue as its director, with her full staff remaining. The fact that it included two men she had chosen may have had something to do with that decision; President Ham was reputed to be moving in the direction of a 50–50 faculty, and the Laboratory Theatre was one of the few departments in the college that already maintained that ratio. He also undertook himself to teach a course in the English Literature

Department. Kathleen Lynch had a sabbatical leave in 1939–40, and President Ham took over her course, English Drama from 1660 to 1900. He proved a popular teacher, drawing a larger registration for the second semester than for the first. Miss Marks never forgave Miss Lynch.

The notification of all these changes precipitated an illness that kept Miss Marks away from the college for almost three months in 1938–39. She spent that time not at Fleur de Lys, which even with central heating was not overly comfortable in the dead of winter, but in the camp belonging to her sister and brother-in-law, Bacon's by the Sea, in Florida. She did not, however, take an early retirement as President Ham must have hoped she would. After the publication of *The Family of the Barrett* she embarked on a course of lectures, which added to her income and took her frequently away from the college. Her brochure offered a choice of five lectures: "The Treasure Island of the Brownings," "Happy Children," "Edward Moulton Barrett on Trial," "Robert Browning and the Tar Brush," and "Adventures in Discrimination." Her advertised fees were $75 for one lecture, $100 for two, $175 for three, or all five for $300, the prices for multiple lectures being based on scheduling that would allow them to be delivered within one two-to-five-day period. Charlotte D'Evelyn, her successor as chairman of the English Literature section in the joint department and a faithful and tactful friend, was forced at one time to protest the neglect of her teaching involved in the very ambitious program of traveling and lecturing, and to suggest that she might take a leave of absence for a semester. Presumably this would have been an unpaid leave of absence. Miss Marks did not take the hint, but altered her schedule sufficiently to disarm criticism.

Miss Woolley continued her own strenuous schedule of travel and lectures. It was not until the summer of 1939 that she started work on the projected autobiography. She began writing in longhand, first on plain white paper and then on an assortment of out-of-date letterheads. She had retired from the presidency of the A.A.U.W. in 1933, but there remained some stationery with her name listed as president and some on which she figured as chairman of the Committee for the Western Hemisphere and the Far East. She also used the stationery of the People's Mandate to Governments to End War, which carried her own name and that of Carrie Chapman Catt in its list of officers. She wrote on the back of these sheets in her large, flowing hand, beginning with her ancestry and her earliest childhood memories in proper chronological fashion but making very slow progress. She resumed work in each succeeding summer through 1943, each time noting on the covering folder the date when she made a fresh start. From internal evidence in the work itself and Miss Marks' later comments, it seems probable that she was responding to prodding from her companion rather than spontaneously undertaking work that might give her pleasure.

Jeannette also pointed out at about this time that it would be possible for Miss Woolley to earn substantially more money by signing up with a lecture bureau that would book her at prices commensurate with the demand. Miss Woolley objected because such a bureau would not allow her to continue free lectures in support of causes that couldn't pay the contractual fee. Nevertheless she eventually yielded and signed a contract in February 1940. At the beginning of March she was away from home for eight days, during which time she delivered seven speeches. Miss Marks had said that an agency could schedule her engagements in such a way as to cut down travel time as well as expense, but the cost in energy was not included in the computation.

Westport is a whistle stop on the main line of the New York Central Railroad from New York to Montreal, and trains were then numerous and comfortable enough to provide adequate transportation, but the house is a mile or more from the railroad station, which was served by no public transportation. Miss Woolley still did not drive and in Miss Marks' absence there was no car belonging to the household.

Miss Woolley belonged to the College Club in Boston and

the prestigious Cosmopolitan Club in New York. A residence in either city might have seemed more appropriate to her needs and interests after 1937 than the isolation of Westport. However, she apparently never considered any other arrangement than sharing the house that meant so much to Jeannette. She served also as a sort of unpaid caretaker from 1937 to 1941. There are numerous letters from Miss Marks giving orders about care of the house and grounds for Miss Woolley to relay to the workmen.

Miss Marks once wrote from South Hadley identical letters to the half-dozen tradesmen whose back lots abutted on her property, pointing out that she had spent a great deal of money on improvements since inheriting the estate and that their untidy back yards constituted an eyesore. She ended by threatening to remove her trade if conditions were not improved, and sent copies of the letter, without comment, to Miss Woolley. Since several of the tradesmen held a monopoly in that area of the services they offered, the job of soothing their ruffled feelings would be essential to the continued smooth functioning of the Fleur de Lys household. Miss Woolley must have managed it satisfactorily, for no further correspondence on the subject remains.

Miss Woolley was popular in Westport as she had been in South Hadley; she sent flowers and food to sick neighbors and regularly attended the village church. She might have been known in the village merely as Miss Marks' friend rather than as the former president of Mount Holyoke College and current president, trustee, chairman, or adviser to countless worthy organizations, but as such she was well and favorably known, a worthy daughter of the parsonage.

Miss Marks not only prevented Miss Woolley's return to the campus but resolutely refused to give any college news except an account of her own misfortunes. Harriet Newhall, however, continued to provide a liaison and a steady if fruitless pressure toward reconciliation. There were also many visitors from the college, all of whom attested to the warm hospitality offered at Fleur de Lys. Anna Jane Mill of the English Literature Department reported that she stopped en route from Nova Scotia to college, intending an afternoon call, and found herself staying for a week. There was a daily procession to the lake with all of the dogs. Miss Marks, Harriet Newhall, and the dogs all swam; Miss Woolley, in an "old-fashioned" bathing suit of black or navy blue, waded out waist deep and ducked.

There were formal invitations to return to the college, for the dedication of the new chapel and for a Commencement address, among others. They were all refused individually in a courteous formula, although a ratias not offered until several years later.

Miss Marks' sixty-fifth birthday came in the summer of 1940, but since it was in July, after the beginning of the academic year, she was able under the tenure rules to remain at Mount Holyoke for a year beyond it. The question of her own successor could not be such a *cause célèbre* as that of Mary Woolley's had been, but she expressed the view that it ought to be a woman trained in the Mount Holyoke Laboratory Theatre. Since very few of these had gone on to work in the professional or academic theater, and of those few none had yet made a distinguished career, this offered a very limited choice. She did not propose promoting either Dean Currie or Lawrence Wallis, who had worked with her for almost a decade. In February of 1941 she heard that the chosen successor was of their sex.

May dearest [*she wrote*],
    These are hard days for you as well as for me, and I am reluctant to add to the burden of dreary thought you must carry. But it is best for you to hear, while you are away, that a man has been appointed Director of the Laboratory Theatre ... This kind of thing will be done to women, is being done to them every day, until the 1000 laws and more which stand in the books against the possibility of a woman having rights equal to a man's are cancelled by the amendment which would give women Constitutional Equality ... It would be a comfort to me now, and I should hear fewer hours of the night strike, if you who no longer believe in special legislation for women as a substi-

*tute for Constitutional Equality would come out definitely
for the amendment. You could do so much and some of us
can do so little.*

*Your loving
Jeannette*

The logic here is what a male chauvinist would call "feminine." It is difficult to see how the Equal Rights Amendment could have affected either that particular appointment or President Ham's. But it showed a shrewd grasp of the probable reaction of the person addressed. As president of A.A.U.W. Miss Woolley had shared the organization's view that the amendment would deprive working women of certain important safeguards. She did not turn about face on receipt of this letter, but, in Jeannette Marks' words, she "began to think about the relationship between opportunities for women and equality before the law." A year later she wrote to a friend: "I think many women like myself are thinking through the whole subject and are likely to come out on the side of a Constitutional Amendment." Before the end of 1942 Mary Woolley formally endorsed the Equal Rights Amendment, joined the National Woman's Party, and founded Women in World Affairs.

Jeannette Marks' own retirement was uneventful. The difficult and probably thankless task of writing the tribute that should appear in the *Alumnae Quarterly* on her retirement was entrusted to Professor Leslie Burgevin, who had served with her in the department for twenty years. He accomplished it magnificently.

*The results of the impact of a personality upon a college
community, especially with such a person as Professor
Jeannette Marks, are quite impractical of measurement.
The seed idea thrown out to germinate in another's mind,
the illumination from a brilliant mind which enables others to see the dream of excellence that draws other minds
to it —nothing of all this can ever be suggested by the bare
record.*

He then summarized the record, which did indeed sound impressive reduced to such brief scope, and continued:

As an executive she showed energy, drive, initiative, persistence, capacity for framing the large design, and attention to detail. She would never admit defeat, and was not easily turned aside from her purpose ... The fight for freedom for women is but one phase of a millennia-old struggle for freedom of all mankind — freedom from ignorance, superstition, and bondage. She believes profoundly in the values of this freedom for women ... Not ... many perhaps ever came to know the warm friendliness of a temperament not to be understood by everyone ... She supported all good causes and would give her assent or influence to nothing ignoble.

Her retirement, of course, meant a further change in the design for living at Fleur de Lys. Now both ladies were in residence permanently with forays out for meetings, lectures, and conferences. Like Miss Woolley, Jeannette Marks refused to return to the college and meet her successor, but unlike Mary Woolley she was offered no invitations to change her mind. At long last Jeannette had the wish she had expressed almost forty years earlier in her letter of May 9, 1902: "Dearest, can't we have a home?" But in a curious way the fears she had expressed in those years had also been realized.

Dearest, if I say I will come next summer, will you take care of me and help give me a chance to do the work I long to do? ... If I give all to you and give up the idea that I must protect myself from you, will you really care for my work as well as loving me? ... I cannot be happy away from you, yet supposing I should be worthless because I have given in to you ...

If her return to the college in 1913 had indeed been "giving in" it would seem to have been amply rewarded. Her twenty years as chairman of the English Literature Depart-

ment had been active and fruitful ones; the establishment
of the Laboratory Theatre was the work for which she preferred to be remembered. Now, however, when she had
leisure and means to return to the writing which had been
her earliest ambition, she seemed no longer to care for it.
She chose rather to live her active life almost entirely
through her influence on Mary Woolley. It would seem,
moreover, as if Jeannette now insisted on the separation
which had for so many years been imposed by circumstances. The two breakfasted separately and spent the
morning in their respective offices; they met for the first
time each day at lunch. They shared the services of a secretary who worked for each of them on alternate days.

The war brought troubles — rising expenses, difficult
travel, a shortage of servants — but offered no such ideo-
logical problems as had the First World War. Even before
Pearl Harbor Miss Woolley signed a petition of protest to
Secretary of State Cordell Hull against the shipment of food
to the Vichy government in France and spoke against a new
trade agreement with Japan on the grounds that it was "no
time for appeasement."

This proved also true in her relations with the college.
By the time Miss Marks retired in 1941 she had successfully
staved off Miss Woolley's visits to the campus for four
years. Now it was time to present a rationale for the refusal. On February 6, 1942, Miss Woolley wrote her cousin
Belle Ferris:

*The policy that I am following in not going back to Mount
Holyoke is my protest against what was done. You know
me well enough to realize that I never say a word against
the present administration. The question is something big-
ger than the personal ... Two or three days ago the* New
York Times *listed eight new appointments at Mount Holyoke College, four men and four women. The posts given
to the men were of professorial rank; the posts given to the
women were of instructors rank ... I could say much
more; perhaps, however, it is sufficient to convince you
that I cannot give up my protest.*

The protest thus formulated became the central focus of the remaining years of her life. The rationale was not altogether adequate. Miss Woolley had worked harmoniously with male presidents of women's colleges throughout most of her active years without ever suggesting that she thought their positions untenable. The fact that Mount Holyoke, like Wellesley, had been headed by women for its first hundred years made a difference, perhaps, but there was by this time most obviously nothing to be accomplished by a continued protest except frustration for Miss Woolley herself. President Ham had now functioned successfully through four difficult years; the opportunities Mount Holyoke had opened to women remained open and were being steadily enlarged. The introduction of more male professors gave Mount Holyoke students in their formative years precisely what Miss Woolley had wanted for herself fifty years earlier, contact wth male minds. The increasing number of positions for women in the coeducational universities and even in those bastions of conservatism, the men's colleges, more than balanced the increased number of men at Mount Holyoke.

The continued refusal to return to the college could do nothing except cut Miss Woolley off from any opportunity to enjoy the fruition of her life's work. Through the alumnae and her continuing work with A.A.U.W. and women's peace organizations, she maintained many of her old friendships. Fleur de Lys was always hospitably open to anyone who cared to visit — but Jeannette was the hostess. No longer could she retreat to a supper tray in Attic Peace when May's guests bored or irritated her. The inevitable result was that the only guests who came were those who liked Miss Marks as well as Miss Woolley, a distressingly small proportion of the Mount Holyoke faculty and alumnae. The two old ladies could live now as had the Ladies of Llangollen, entirely for each other and openly acknowledging the depth of their mutual affection.

The fact that Miss Woolley's letter of explanation was addressed to a cousin rather than a professional colleague suggests that her family may have been exerting some pressure to counteract Jeannette's influence. "You know me well enough to realize that I never say a word against the present administration" is an obvious evasion; her refusal to return to the campus was a more telling criticism of the new administration than anything she could have said. "I cannot give up my protest" is perhaps her final capitulation to Jeannette.

Alumnae admirers and faculty friends alike continued to hope that she could be reconciled. Most of them correctly attributed her refusal to Miss Marks' influence but believed, or wanted to believe, that she retained enough independence to make her own decision in this matter. Harriet Newhall, now an important executive officer in the college working harmoniously with the new administration, showed a more than filial devotion to the two old ladies. She spent all her vacations with them and used all her influence to persuade Miss Woolley at least to accept some of the many courtesies the college offered her. Her efforts were as vain, however, as those of Miss Woolley's other friends and her family. What she had threatened in 1910 and 1919 she had now done — left the college and all it meant to her for the sake of Jeannette. She seems to have found whatever sacrifice was involved entirely worthwhile.

In the summer of 1944 Miss Woolley failed for the first time to resume work on the autobiography. Her eighty-first birthday was passed without particular note. On the thirtieth of September, back in Westport after a strenuous visit to New York, she suffered a crippling stroke. The local doctor did not expect her to survive for more than a few hours, but actually she lived for three more years, years that again profoundly altered her relationship with Jeannette Marks and gravely affected her permanent reputation.

Although Fleur de Lys was in many ways ill designed for the care of an invalid — remote from nurses and doctors, difficult to heat evenly, served by a single bathroom on each floor, with kitchen facilities a flight of stairs below the bedrooms — apparently no consideration was ever given to moving Miss Woolley elsewhere. For the first few days she remained in a small downstairs bedroom Miss Marks had been using as a study; then she was moved upstairs to her own bedroom where somewhat later a hospital bed, the gift of Harriet Newhall, was installed. A nurse was hired, not without difficulty, and the new secretary served as assistant nurse.

During the next three years Jeannette Marks tended her friend with an admirable solicitude, tainted, nevertheless, by an unpleasant ghoulishness of which it is impossible for any reader of her book *The Life and Letters of Mary Woolley* to remain unaware. Whether or not Miss Marks herself ever realized it, she was enjoying the helpless dependence of the person who had been the most powerful force in her life for almost fifty years.

Miss Woolley's right arm was paralyzed and her speech gravely impaired. When she signed her will in January of 1946 it was with a shaky X attested to by three nurses as witnesses. And yet over her signature there appeared a number of clear and cogent statements as to her views on the rights of women and the current situation at Mount Holyoke. In June of 1946 one such letter went to the field secretary of the college.

The naming of Mary E. Woolley Hall brought me genuine pleasure, for in several ways the Mary E. Woolley Hall was part of my work at Mount Holyoke College — work on which I shared with others some claim.

The announcement of the Mary E. Woolley Visiting Professorship, however, troubles me for several reasons. The use of my name in this connection and under these auspices might suggest that I am in some way reconciled to the broken tradition of women as leaders of Mount Holyoke College. Since my position on this matter is so well known, it seems to me best that my name should not be used for this Visiting Professorship. When Mount Holyoke College again appoints a woman as President I shall be glad to have my name used for the Mary E. Woolley Visiting Professorship.

My conviction remains that the successful leadership of women for over one hundred years at Mount Holyoke has entitled and continues to entitle women to that leadership. With time this conviction has deepened, not lessened, and the protest which I made of this action while in college will continue to the end of my life.

According to Miss Marks' own account, Miss Woolley had been barely able to compose and dictate a telegram of acceptance a month earlier when she received notification of the renaming of Student-Alumnae Hall in her honor, and had since suffered a relapse. But in that same June the New York *Herald Tribune* carried a letter over her signature.

As I understand it the [American Civil Liberties] Union's objection to the Equal Rights Amendment is, really, based upon the abolition of protective laws. My first answer to that is that protective laws in the coming day should be made for human beings, men as well as women. My second answer is that the privileges accorded to women by our present laws are not commensurate with the lack of rights embodied in the thousand and one discriminatory laws still on the statute books of various states of the United States . . . I do wish again and again to stress the truth that it is only as human relations are shaped by women — as well as by men — with the thinking of both directed by the good heart, that we shall ever achieve the better world for which we are hoping and for which some of us are working.

These two letters cannot possibly have been written by Miss Woolley, and it is scarcely possible that she dictated them verbatim. Even the internal evidence of their style attests to Jeannette Marks' authorship. Jeannette evidently felt that she and her friend were now so completely one that she could legitimately speak for both.

There were many visitors during the first months of the three years, not so many as there would have been in a hospital or nursing home in any of the large centers where

Mary Woolley had been active but a goodly number. As the months stretched on, Jeannette Marks, under the guise of "protection," shunted many of them away. Harriet Newhall continued to provide the only reliable contact with the college. Christine Everts Green, president of the Alumnae Association, received copies of the "confidential report" Miss Marks prepared for members of the Woolley family and the Ferris cousins. These were consistently gloomy in tone and consistently blamed the illness on the action of the Mount Holyoke trustees almost ten years earlier.

The years from 1944 to 1947 were not easy ones in which to secure the services of nurses and housekeepers. Miss Marks was never reduced to doing the heavy and unpleasant work herself, but she had to struggle with the task of finding and hiring nurses and kitchen help and keeping them reasonably well satisfied.

Mary Woolley died on September 5, 1947. A small Quaker funeral service was held in the library at Fleur de Lys. Obituaries appeared in the *New York Times* and *Herald Tribune*, and there was some talk of a large public memorial service in New York, but nothing came of it. In a swiftly moving America the three years of illness had obscured Miss Woolley's national prominence, and her recent relations with Mount Holyoke made it very difficult for the college to participate in such a plan. A memorial service was held at the college in November, and that was all.

Jeannette Marks at seventy-two happily could not have known that she faced seventeen years of loneliness. Of the two women, May had always suffered more from any separation than Jeannette. In 1901 she had written:

But my work is one thing. I am interested in it; I intend to put myself into it, but it is not myself. You are that . . .

Over the years the identification had developed in a curiously twisted way. For the three final ones Miss Woolley had been Miss Marks' whole life; her physical care and the expression of her presumed views had occupied all of the younger woman's attention and energy. Now that she was gone, it was almost as if Miss Marks' reason for living were gone with her.

She plunged at once into the only work that could have provided her any comfort or satisfaction in her bereavement, her life of Mary Woolley. It should have been a memorable book as well as a personal satisfaction, but its writing confronted Miss Marks with problems she found herself unable to solve. She had inherited all of Mary Woolley's papers, both personal and professional.

I give and bequeath to Jeannette Marks and to Harriet Newhall, or the survivor of them, all of my papers and manuscripts, with the hope that they may make such use of them as they deem best.

Probably her first step in preparation for the work was to reread all the letters that had passed between her and her friend since 1895. Both of them had carefully preserved every one in its original envelope. The letters to Jeannette were both more numerous and more voluminous than those from her. Reading them, sorting them, and deciding what use to make of them provided a real working through of the first stages of grief. At that point in her planning she intended to write a book that should tell the whole story of the fifty-two-year friendship and what it had meant to both women. On many of the most revealing of the letters she wrote, "Use this," but she did not, in the end, use any except the relatively impersonal ones from China and Geneva. She left no record of why or how she reached this decision. Harriet Newhall continued to spend her vacations from college at Fleur de Lys and offered substantial secretarial help; whether she also ventured on editorial advice must be a matter of conjecture. Harriet had attempted up to the time of Miss Woolley's stroke to reconcile her with the college; now she may have hoped that Miss Marks' book would heal all remaining wounds.

The college wanted a biography of Mary Woolley that would commemorate her fame, already beginning to fade, and Jeannette Marks was in many ways the obvious person to write it. Her reputation as an author had never stood high within the college, but she was a published one and she unquestionably knew more about Miss Woolley than anyone else living. The college hoped, and Harriet Newhall worked through eight long years to help Jeannette Marks produce a book that would do justice to Mary Wooley's memory.

The abortive autobiography did not give much help. Miss Marks had not been permitted to see it during Miss Woolley's lifetime, although she may well have taken a look during the three years' regency. The book had been discussed between them primarily as a moneymaking project, and when she saw what had been completed Miss Marks was annoyed first at the late date at which it had been undertaken and then at the scantiness of the result. It provided very little material she could use.

Her indignation at the male succession to the Mount Holyoke presidency had become an obsession. Now, with Miss Woolley unable to object, she could make it the central fact of the life — a tragedy that had not only destroyed Miss Woolley's life, ten years after the event, but had cast its shadow before into her earliest girlhood experiences and the frustrations of her father's life. In the finished work President Ham was never mentioned by name; he figured simply as "a man."

On matters of ancestry Jeannette worked as she had worked on *The Family of the Barrett*, with enormous effort and erudition turning up little known facts which also had little relevance to her subject. Her greatest difficulty, however, came from the fact that she had never been much interested in Mary Woolley's work until the question of the succession arose. In their early years at Mount Holyoke she had expressed her indifference frankly; after she became chairman of the English Literature Department the indifference had changed to hostility against anything in the college that siphoned off funds or privileges from her own work. Nor had she left friends on the faculty who could or would be of very much help to her in this area. After one publisher had rejected the work, pointing out, among other things, that the editor "never learned . . . precisely what Mary Woolley contributed to education at Mount Holyoke, what new courses she instituted, what deepening plan of education she had for women, how it differed from other feminine schools of the time," Miss Marks wrote Emma Carr and Mary Sherrill of the Chemistry Department inquiring about Miss Woolley's work with scientists.

One of the questions which has been hurled at me ran this way: "By what means did Miss Woolley convert an anemic college of seminary status into one of the greatest colleges for women in the United States?"

The phrasing of the query was enough to ensure an unsatisfactory answer. Professor Carr had been a student at Mount Holyoke when Miss Woolley came in 1901, had caught her interest in science from Henrietta Hooker and Cornelia Clapp, who were then teaching it, and traced Mount Holyoke's distinguished work in science back from them through Lydia Shattuck to Mary Lyon herself. Her article, "One Hundred Years of Science at Mount Holyoke" in the *Alumnae Quarterly* for November 1936, did not even mention Miss Woolley, as Miss Marks could easily have discovered for herself. In Miss Carr's view Mount Holyoke's tradition in science was already remarkable when Miss Woolley came, far above the level of "an anemic college of seminary status," and Miss Woolley's contribution, important enough in an executive, was simply to recognize that excellence and fund it adequately so that it could continue and expand. Whatever Miss Carr may have answered, Miss Marks' finished book contained nothing about the sciences at Mount Holyoke. Miss Carr figures in it merely as the chairman of the Faculty Conference Committee that tried in vain to delay the appointment of Dr. Ham in June 1936, in order to allow time for further consideration.

The keen if somewhat cruel observation that had gone

into "The New Trustee" was no longer functioning, and there was not even a pretence of objectivity. Mary Woolley was the heroine of this book, and nothing was admitted to its pages which did not fit with a portrait modeled on Little Eva, Elsie Dinsmore, and Pollyanna.

Miss Marks made a conscientious effort to leave herself out of the book and make it a generous tribute to her friend's greatness. The effort was self-defeating. The intimacy had not given her a unique insight into Miss Woolley's character; it had merely joined the two personalities with such complexity that by the end of their lives neither one could have said with any accuracy what each had contributed to the other. Fanny Ratchford, after reading the manuscript, wrote from the University of Texas:

I hate prominence so much myself that I am instinctively suspicious of eminent persons as empty-headed conscienceless self-seekers . . . I had a . . . suspicion that you were the conscience and strength behind her, and that she reaped the acclaim that belonged to you . . . you steal the show.

No one, I think, could have accused Miss Marks of intending this effect, but the secret envy that had erupted in stories like "The New Trustee" and "Mrs. Llewellyn Jones' Sister" was all the more apparent for being unacknowledged. The suppression of the narrator as a character left the point of view confused and confusing. Only in the final section did "J.M." appear as a character, patient, wise, generous, and indulgent to her sometimes troublesome and demanding invalid. It was clearly an idealized version, containing a good deal of wishful thinking and perhaps even of regret or remorse, but it had a substantial basis of truth. Elsewhere in the book Jeannette Marks figured only tangentially, as an admiring student, as a guest in the Woolleys' home, as the recipient of letters from China and Geneva, as a consultant in the quarrels over the succession to the presidency, and finally as hostess and chatelaine. There is no hint of the passionate attachment of the Wellesley years, the polite feud with Miss Woolley's mother, the quarrels and reconciliations of the early years at Mount Holyoke, the desperate effort to break away and stand on her own feet, the adjustment to life as a satellite in the President's House.

The greatest weakness of the book from Mount Holyoke's point of view, however, was that about a quarter of it was devoted to a lengthy and detailed recapitulation of the quarrel over the appointment of Miss Woolley's successor. To have done this without ever mentioning Roswell Ham's name was something of a feat, but not one that Mount Holyoke could admire. Along with Miss Woolley's letters Miss Marks had kept all the papers relating to the events of 1936–37, and as she retold them now her indignation burned as hotly as it had fifteen years earlier. Most Mount Holyoke alumnae, faculty, and friends felt that Miss Woolley's conduct in the quarrel and afterward had been uncharacteristic, perhaps even unworthy of her. They wanted to see her recreated as she had been in the days of her glory and to forget that the end of her career had not been its crown. Miss Marks' recapitulation tended to stress the unsavory details of the political maneuvering involved rather than the principle to which she insisted Miss Woolley had adhered throughout. Jeannette Marks' own name never appears and her own part in the quarrel is not acknowledged, but it is clear to anyone familiar with the situation that criticism of her influence was open and unpleasant in those years. The choice of a man as Miss Woolley's successor could be seen as a criticism of her private life style rather than of her public accomplishment. That Miss Marks should have resented this is, of course, entirely understandable, but her failure to make the personal basis of her resentment explicit weakens her book for the reader who comes to it uninformed and spoils it for the one with preformed prejudices.

During the eight long years devoted to writing and revising, the book provided a *raison d'être* for its aging author. It involved correspondence with the college library and publicity office as well as with old friends and potential publishers. Harriet Newhall continued her faithful assistance although it must have been obvious to her in the later years that the book could only cause new offense at the college. She typed much of the correspondence and prepared the index; to what extent she may have been responsible for the omissions can only be conjectured.

The book was published in 1955 by the Public Affairs Press in Washington, D.C. Miss Marks was eighty years old in that year, and Roswell Ham had been a successful and popular president of Mount Holyoke for eighteen years. The book put finis to any hope that Miss Marks might ever again enjoy her associations there. The growth of the Little Theater from the beginning she had provided apparently offered her no satisfaction, nor did she take any part in the burgeoning Little Theater movement across the nation. Her bitter resentment against Mount Holyoke crowded out every other interest in her life. President Ham had taken the place of her father in her emotional existence. Harriet Newhall had great difficulty in persuading Miss Marks to send to the college the mementoes Miss Woolley had left in her will.

About her own papers and books Miss Marks was indecisive. She gave those connected with the Brownings to the Wellesley College Library, along with manuscripts of several versions of her book about Miss Woolley and copies of some of their letters. As to what should eventually go to Mount Holyoke she kept changing her mind; the instructions she gave Harriet were confused and contradictory.

After Miss Newhall's retirement in 1958 she joined Miss Marks as a permanent resident of Fleur de Lys. They cultivated the vegetable garden, cared for the dogs, who provided the greatest emotional satisfaction of Miss Marks' life in its final years, and worked together on the last book, destined never to be published. Having completed the biography of her friend, Miss Marks now allowed herself the indulgence of an autobiography, but the same reticences that had hampered her in the earlier one were still operating, and her powers were clearly failing. *The Family of the Wild Pigeon Steam Mill*, a title chosen from a property that had belonged to her paternal grandfather, is rambling and disjointed, although there are vividly sketched brief scenes that display the skill of the professional writer.

The opening sentence — "Probably it is all too true that the first question asked about a family in America is, 'Were they rich?'" — states one of the major themes of the book. The never-resolved conflicts about wealth and power recur, along with confused memories of an unhappy childhood, unrelieved by any insight or adult comprehension. There is nothing about the achievements that transcended that unhappiness, and very little about the fifty years with Mary Woolley. Only one rather ambiguous passage glances at the nature of the friendship.

A friendship which was better than life itself came to my rescue and Mary Woolley and I became close friends. I do not remember that the time ever came when we were identifiable solely as close friends. But at this length of distance of time it really doesn't matter particularly one way or the other which way you put it.

Her intensely ambivalent feelings about her father are expressed in numerous ways, perhaps best summed up in this passage.

When he went galloping by on one of his great thoroughbred stallions it was as if someone had come up out of the past and, as predestined, rode into the future.

There is nothing whatever about the Mount Holyoke years. On the whole it is a depressing book for the reader, although there are indications that it may have given the writer much pleasure and release during her last years of lonely illness.

In 1960, when she was alone in the house with her dogs, she suffered a fall that fractured her hip. She lay on the floor all night with only the collies for company; when she was found the next day she was promptly moved to a hospital, and she was never able to return to Fleur de Lys to live. When she was well enough to leave the hospital she went to the Elizabethtown home of one of the nurses, Mrs.

Elizabeth Cross, who cared for her and the dogs during the remaining years of her life.

Miss Marks blamed Harriet Newhall's absence for the accident and never quite forgave her. She made a new will leaving everything she possessed to Mrs. Cross. This eventually left the ownership of Mary Woolley's papers a moot question; did they belong to Jeannette Marks' heirs or to Harriet Newhall's? At the time they were stowed away in the attic at Fleur de Lys and no one seems to have given the matter any thought.

Friends who visited Miss Marks in Mrs. Cross' large Victorian brick house at the center of Elizabethtown tell of a hospital bed set up in a front room, where with books, papers, dogs, flowers, and a good view of village life she passed her days not unhappily. Shortly before she died in the spring of 1964 she wrote:

It is wonderful really to see how flexible a book is and how it adapts itself to such phrases as, what obviously is not so, "the end of a book." Some books refuse to end . . . What is the use of ending? Why should I end this book? . . . when I am not satisfied or convinced that I have ever begun it?

Books by Jeannette Marks

1901 *A Brief Outline of Books and Topics for the Study of American Literature.* Pawtucket, Rhode Island, John W. Little and Co., Printers.

1902 *A Brief Historical Outline of English Literature from the Origins to the Close of the Eighteenth Century.* Pawtucket, Little and Co.

1906 *The Cheerful Cricket and others.* New York, Small, Maynard and Company.

1908 *English Pastoral Drama.* London, Methuen and Co.

1909 *Little Busybodies: The Life of Crickets, Ants, Bees, Beetles and other Busybodies,* with Julia Moody. New York, Harper Story-told Science Series.

1909 *Through Welsh Doorways.* Boston, Houghton Mifflin Co.

1910 *Holiday with the Birds: Their Plumage, Their Song, Nesting and Daily Habits,* with Julia Moody. New York, Harper Story-told Science Series.

1911 *The End of a Song.* Boston, Houghton Mifflin Co.

1911 *A Girl's Student Days and After.* New York, Fleming H. Revell Co.

1912 *Gallant Little Wales: Sketches of Its People, Places, and and Customs.* Boston, Houghton Mifflin Co.

1913 *Leviathan: The Record of a Struggle and a Triumph.* New York, George H. Doran Co.

1917 *Three Welsh Plays.* Boston, Little, Brown and Co.

1919 *Courage Today and Tomorrow.* New York, Woman's Press.

1921 *Willow Pollen.* Boston, The Four Seas Co.

1922 *The Sun Chaser, a Play in Four Acts.* Cincinnati, Steward Kidd Company.

1925 *Genius and Disaster, Studies in Drugs and Genius.* New York, Adelphi Co.

1929 *Thirteen Days.* New York, Albert and Charles Boni.

1938 *The Family of the Barrett: A Colonial Romance.* New York, Macmillan Co.

1955 *Life and Letters of Mary Emma Woolley.* Washington, D.C., Public Affairs Press.

1964 "Family of the Wild Pigeon Steam Mills." Westport, N.Y., unpublished.